Consulting Editors

Michael Barton
Associate Professor of American Studies and History
Pennsylvania State University at Harrisburg, Capital College

Nancy A. Walker
Professor of English
Vanderbilt University

This unique series consists of carefully assembled volumes of seminal writings on topics central to the study of American culture. Each anthology begins with a comprehensive overview of the subject at hand, written by a noted scholar in the field, followed by a combination of selected articles, original essays, and case studies.

By bringing together in each collection many important commentaries on such themes as humor, material culture, architecture, the environment, literature, politics, theater, film, and spirituality, American Visions provides a varied and rich library of resources for the scholar, student, and general reader. Annotated bibliographies facilitate further study and research.

Volumes Published

Nancy A. Walker, editor
What's So Funny? Humor in American Culture (1998).
Cloth ISBN 0-8420-2687-8   Paper ISBN 0-8420-2688-6

Robert J. Bresler
Us vs. Them: American Political and Cultural Conflict from WW II to Watergate (2000).
Cloth ISBN 0-8420-2689-4   Paper ISBN 0-8420-2690-8

US vs. THEM

US
VS.
THEM

AMERICAN POLITICAL and CULTURAL CONFLICT
from WW II to WATERGATE

by
ROBERT J. BRESLER
with Documents and Readings

American Visions ▪ Readings in American Culture
▪
Number 2
▪
A Scholarly Resources Inc. Imprint ▪ Wilmington, Delaware

SR
BOOKS

© 2000 by Scholarly Resources Inc.
All rights reserved
First published 2000
Printed and bound in the United States of America

Scholarly Resources Inc.
104 Greenhill Avenue
Wilmington, DE 19805-1897
www.scholarly.com

Library of Congress Cataloging-in-Publication Data

Bresler, Robert J., 1937–
    Us vs. them : American political and cultural conflict from WW II
to Watergate / by Robert J. Bresler ; with documents and readings.
        p.   cm. — (American visions ; no. 2)
    Includes bibliographical references (p.   ).
    ISBN 0-8420-2689-4 (alk. paper). —ISBN 0-8420-2690-8 (pbk. :
alk. paper)
        1. United States—Politics and government—1945–1989 Sources.
2. Culture conflict—United States—History—20th century Sources.
3. United States—Social conditions—1945–   Sources.   4. Politics
and culture—United States—History—20th century Sources.
I. Title.   II. Title: Us versus them.   III.   Series: American visions
(Wilmington, Del.) ; no. 2.
E743.B735   1999
306'.0973—dc21   99-36066
                                                                    CIP

∞ The paper used in this publication meets the minimum requirements of
the American National Standard for permanence of paper for printed library
materials, Z39.48, 1984.

For my grandson, Jacob

ABOUT THE AUTHOR

ROBERT J. BRESLER is professor of public policy at the School of Public Affairs, Pennsylvania State University at Harrisburg. He received his undergraduate degree from Earlham College in Richmond, Indiana, and his M.A. and Ph.D. in politics from Princeton University. Prior to joining Penn State, Dr. Bresler served on the faculty at the University of Wisconsin at Green Bay and the University of Delaware. He has been a visiting professor at Franklin and Marshall College in Lancaster, Pennsylvania, and the U.S. Army War College at Carlisle Barracks, Pennsylvania. In 1998 he was a Senior Fulbright Fellow at the American Studies Centre, National University of Singapore.

He is the author and coauthor of several books including *American Government* (1988, 1992, 1994) and *Contemporary Controversies* (1993). His articles and reviews on American politics and American foreign policy have appeared in such varied journals as *Political Science Quarterly*, *International Journal of Public Administration*, *Inquiry*, *Telos*, *Arms Control*, *Bulletin of Atomic Scientists*, *The Nation*, *Commonweal*, and *Journal of Politics*. Dr. Bresler is also national affairs editor for *USA Today: The Magazine of the American Scene*, where he writes a regular column on American politics.

ACKNOWLEDGMENTS

A number of people helped to bring this book to fruition. My two graduate assistants, Andrew Witten and Matthew Cowan, diligently culled through mountains of material before we settled on these readings and documents. While I was a Fulbright Fellow at the American Studies Centre-National University of Singapore, Professors Scot Guenter and Malcolm Murfett read my manuscript with great care and made valuable suggestions. Barton Bernstein, Michael Barton, and Nancy Walker also reviewed the manuscript and provided encouragement and a number of essential ideas. My editors at Scholarly Resources—Matthew R. Hershey, Linda Pote Musumeci, and Carolyn Travers—gave me assistance throughout the project, representing the highest standards of their craft.

My wife, Lin, librarian and helpmate of charm and intelligence, enabled me to uncover a number of valuable sources and overlooked the accumulated clutter of my office and the inevitable distractions of my mind. My daughter Jessica, son-in-law Carl, and the boys, Jordan and Greg, have shown great tolerance over the years for my incurable nostalgia for the midcentury America of my youth. My grandson, Jacob, to whom this book is dedicated, was born while I was finishing the first draft. I hope that that will be a good omen for him and for the book. Finally, I want to extend my gratitude and affection to all my beloved family, friends, and colleagues with whom I have shared and discussed these extraordinary times through which we have passed. In many ways this book is a product of our long, sometimes contentious, but always rewarding, conversations.

CONTENTS

I

ROBERT J. BRESLER

The Rise and Fall of the American Consensus

The nineteenth-century American poet and essayist James Russell Lowell once wrote, "Things
always look fairer when we look back at them, and it is out of the inaccessible tower of the past that Longing leans and beckons."[1] Time
can produce a comfortable haze through which we view the past, making it a safe repository of dreams and illusions: what we wish to be,
we imagine we once were.

Some consider the American midcentury, 1945–1965, as the Golden
Years. Nostalgia for that time has become a part of contemporary life.
We peer into it incessantly—through classic movie channels, recreated
fashions, trivia games, the inveterate collecting of baseball cards and
other memorabilia, "oldies" radio stations, and a constant parade of
popular history books. Such things make the America of midcentury
appear easily accessible.

Yet in another sense the era is curiously remote. Profound changes
in American political and cultural life give that time the look of
another country with proper and severe standards of public behavior.
The unspoken assumptions that once underscored much of daily life
no longer have the same force or validity. Cultural norms have been
altered beyond recognition: Victorian standards of sexual behavior have
lost what grip they may have had on many young people; gender roles
no longer bind as many women to particular careers (as schoolteachers,

nurses, secretaries) or family responsibilities; racial barriers have lost their legal support; subjects once taboo (incest, homosexuality, abortion) are constant topics of public discussion; and the popular music that once rippled with themes of love and romance now competes with hard rock and rap.

The political changes are no less profound. The Cold War that dominated international politics has ended, and Soviet communism lies in ruins. Groups frequently muffled and frustrated in the debates of midcentury America (African Americans, gays, feminists, environmentalists, and religious conservatives) are now major participants in the political arena. The private lives of politicians, once shielded from public view by a circumspect press, have become fair game for aggressive reporters. Young, media-savvy political consultants are the new shakers and movers of electoral politics, replacing middle-aged, cigar-smoking political bosses. Presidential candidates are selected in open primaries and caucuses, weakening the role of the party leaders. The Democratic and Republican Parties that harbored liberal and conservative factions have become more ideologically distinct, with conservatives dominating the Republican Party and liberals the Democratic. The federal courts, which carefully exercised the power of judicial review after President Franklin D. Roosevelt's attempt in 1937 to pack them, have taken a major role in attempting to resolve explosive political disputes such as gay rights, abortion, political term limits, single-sex education, and racial preferences. From the perspective today of a more open and unwieldy culture, the politics and culture of midcentury America may seem stable to the point of petrifaction.

As the twentieth century ends, Americans find these far-reaching social and cultural changes difficult to comprehend, but the efforts of many ideologues to appropriate the past for their own purposes make a clear comprehension easier. Conservatives may idealize the 1940s and 1950s as an era marked by social stability, an established social code, a secure moral order, and a sense of national unity and purpose. Liberals, on the other hand, may view it as a period of deadening conformity, racial and gender discrimination, cultural sterility, and excessive militarism. In fact, it fits neither caricature. Like any period, it was messy and complex. Nonetheless, it had its own flavor, and much of our contemporary politics and culture have sprung from it.

The Impact of World War II: Political and Economic Transformation

Whatever one concludes about the midcentury period, no one can understand it without an appreciation of the impact of World War II. Despite the tragic losses in blood and treasure, America emerged from the ashes of the war as a nation transformed—the world's dominant industrial, commercial, and financial power. The war that had ravaged the nations of Europe and Asia left America virtually unscarred. On the surface, it was an exhilarating moment for Americans on the home front, a unique time of national unity and common purpose.

The war had brought prosperity and removed many of the ugly remnants of the Great Depression. The gross national product (GNP) practically doubled. Thousands of Americans were lifted out of poverty and deprivation to the brink of middle-class status. Unemployment, as high as 14.6 percent in 1940, had shrunk to only 1.9 percent by the end of the war. With few big-ticket consumer goods produced during the war and jobs plentiful, personal savings had increased an astounding six times, from $6 billion in 1940 to $37 billion in 1945, and provided much of the capital for the postwar boom. Unlike our contemporary economy, the wartime prosperity was distributed across income groups. From 1941 to 1945 family income for the poorest one-fifth of the population gained 68 percent, compared with 20 percent for the wealthiest one-fifth. The lowest three-fifths of American families saw their share of the national income increase from 27 percent in 1936 to 32 percent in 1944.[2] Average weekly earnings doubled. Much of personal saving was in accounts of less than $5,000. A Federal Reserve Board study showed that 84 percent of New Yorkers owned war bonds.[3]

The profound legacy of the Great Depression served to emphasize the impact of the war boom. The depression had created among other things a health-care crisis. The quality of people's diets diminished. Close to 50 percent of the men who reported for the draft in 1941 were rejected, mostly for poor eyesight and bad teeth usually attributed to malnourishment. Making matters worse, hard times had resulted in a declining number of medical graduates: there were fewer doctors and dentists per capita by 1939 than there had been in 1929.

Ironically, the war elevated the quality of health care. Over sixteen million armed services personnel and their dependents became the beneficiaries of government-provided medical care. Industries, concerned to maintain a healthy workforce, began to extend health insurance to their workers and employees, and the increase in women workers brought a greater concern for sanitary conditions and safety rules. In boomtowns, fueled by war spending, the U.S. Public Health Service established community health centers offering supervised immunization programs. Typhoid fever, scarlet fever, and diphtheria dropped to historically low levels. Children's diseases such as measles and whooping cough also declined. Despite painfully high war casualties, life expectancy—which had not altered during the depression—increased three years from 1939 to 1945, and the death rate for infants was reduced by one-third.[4]

The industrial performance of the United States during the war astounded even the most optimistic observers, and the war economy spawned new industries. Radar gave new impetus to the electronics industry. Out of the Manhattan Project and code-breaking efforts came the computer revolution. The thousands of pilots, shippers, and managers who served in the Air Transport Command became leaders in the generation that built the modern airline industry.[5]

Americans appeared united in a common cause. Millions volunteered for military service. War bond drives raised billions of dollars. People accepted price controls and wage controls with relative equanimity. Food and gasoline rationing, though it caused much grumbling, did not stir substantial discontent. Unlike the Vietnam years, when draft avoidance was common, during World War II many men were embarrassed to be classified 4-F or even as essential civilian workers.

A political consensus was easing the contentiousness of American politics. During the 1930s and early 1940s there had been profound and divisive debates over the role of government at home and abroad. The Great Depression raised doubts about the legitimacy of the free enterprise system and spawned radical movements led by rabble-rousing populists such as Huey Long and Father Charles Coughlin. Many in the business community feared that President Roosevelt's New Deal would be the first step toward a government-dominated command economy. The rising specter of war in Europe and Asia, especially in the period 1939–1941, aroused a strong isolationist movement eager to keep America out of the hostilities and the political struggles of those regions. The war changed the terms of all such debates. Pearl Harbor weakened if not destroyed the isolationist illusion that the Atlantic and Pacific stood as two moats forever protecting a fortified America. Wartime prosperity restored much of the people's confidence in the economic system. In addition, the cooperation that developed between the business community and the Roosevelt administration muted the former's fears that a strong government was a natural enemy.

Before the war was actually over, broad bipartisan congressional support for the G.I. Bill of Rights signaled a shift in the debate about the proper role of government in assisting individuals. Unlike bonus bills for Civil War and World War I veterans, the G.I. Bill was a major social entitlement initiative and a conscious piece of social engineering. Veterans of World War II were to be handed not money but rather vouchers (although the term had not yet worked into the political vocabulary) for education and vocational training; subsidized loans for small business, farms, or homes; and, for the disabled, medical care and rehabilitation. Introduced by the Roosevelt administration in 1944, the G.I. Bill passed a Congress dominated by a coalition of conservative Republicans and Southern Democrats. Its effect was to elevate millions of American men into the managerial and professional classes. Between 1945 and 1950, 2.3 million veterans were attending colleges and universities. According to an Educational Testing Service survey, 35 percent of those veterans over twenty-two years of age would not have done so but for the G.I. Bill.[6] The passage of the bill did not mean that a major expansion of the welfare state would follow after the war (that was to come in the 1960s), but it did signal that even a conservative Congress was not averse to using the powers of the government for those considered deserving of support and with the political clout to attain it.

The war had affected people's attitude toward the state in subtle ways. People were still suspicious of government. They feared that a growing bureaucracy could limit their freedom and autonomy, yet they were growing more comfortable with a limited welfare state. They had little faith in government's ability to command the economy or redistribute the wealth. As the historian Alan Brinkley explains it, "The war, in short, was a significant moment in the shift of American liberalism from a preoccupation with 'reform' (with a set of essentially class-based issues . . . confronting the problem of monopoly and economic disorder) and toward a preoccupation with 'rights' (a commitment to the liberties and entitlements of individuals and the liberation of oppressed people and groups)."[7] Yet although the old radicalism of the planned economy and the redistribution of wealth was dying, the new rights-based (or entitlements-based) welfare liberalism was slow to emerge. The G.I. Bill, with its generous education, training, and housing assistance, was not to be a model for all Americans. Such entitlements were only for those with particular clout and, as Brinkley puts it, "a special claim on public generosity."[8]

The war and the New Deal exhausted the public's desire for fundamental change. Asked in the waning months of the hostilities whether they would like to see changes or reforms or have the country remain much the way it was before the war, 52 percent said "stay the same"; only 39 percent wanted change.[9] The federal government did acquire a broader role and a new legitimacy, however. Although there was little popular support in 1945 for an expansion of the welfare state, the New Deal reforms were becoming a permanent part of the political landscape. More important, none of Roosevelt's major initiatives (Social Security, subsidies to agriculture, the Tennessee Valley Authority, a minimum wage) were challenged in Congress in the years following World War II.

As the war progressed toward what seemed inevitable victory, the debate over the appropriateness of America's role as a leader of the international community was also reaching a plateau. In 1943 the former Republican candidate for president, Wendell Willkie, published a best-selling book that passionately argued for a new international organization, led by the United States, to preserve the peace in the postwar world. The success of *One World* indicated public receptivity to the idea. Soon after its publication the leaders of the Republican Party, which still harbored a strong isolationist wing, issued a statement endorsing American membership in a United Nations Organization— an essential postwar strategic goal of the Roosevelt administration. In the summer of 1945, the U.S. Senate overwhelmingly ratified the UN Treaty.

The issue was no longer whether the United States would be a world leader but rather how it was to exercise that role. The American people's willingness to see themselves as international leaders was indicated by their enormous confidence in the armed forces throughout the war, even in the early and darkest years. The historian Allan Nevins claimed, "Never had the American high command, in a long, arduous, and costly war, been less criticized."[10] Consequently, military leaders were held in the highest esteem: Gen. George C. Marshall, Gen. Dwight D. Eisenhower, Gen. Douglas MacArthur, Gen. Omar Bradley, Adm. Chester Nimitz, Gen. George C. Patton were all household names, as were highly decorated combat heroes such as Charles E. "Commando" Kelly and

Audie Murphy. According to the Gallup Poll, Americans ranked Eisenhower and MacArthur among the top two or three most admired men in the world, a status they retained for years.[11]

Beneath the economic prosperity were the seeds of profound changes in social mores, demography, and cultural expectations that would not be manifest for another two decades. The divorce rate between 1940 and 1944 almost doubled, and families were separated.[12] At the beginning of the war, draft boards had granted deferments to fathers, and in mid-1943 eight million men held such deferments. But this privilege did not last long: by the end of 1944 the number had dwindled to eighty thousand.[13] Women moved into the workforce in unprecedented numbers, increasing by 50 percent between 1940 and 1944. Previously dominated by young, single women, the female workforce now largely comprised older, married, or divorced women. Manufacturing, historically a male domain, saw a huge influx of women workers. In the auto factories alone they constituted 26 percent of the labor force during 1943. In most industries women suffered wage discrimination, and there was little provision for badly needed child care, yet given the spirit of the time and the decline of the feminist movement, there were few signs of protest.

The effect of the war on families was profound. By the end of the war almost 60 percent of the fathers between the ages of eighteen and twenty-five were on active duty. When fathers and older brothers went off to war and mothers to defense work, younger brothers and sisters had to assume more household responsibilities. Younger siblings also took on part-time and full-time jobs as soda jerks and grocery clerks. The attraction of jobs for younger teenagers was so great during the war that high school enrollments declined by 1.2 million from 1941 to 1944.[14]

With jobs in industry beckoning and millions being drafted, the war witnessed the most extensive migration of people in this century—some twenty-seven million people moved from their original county of residence. During the decade of the 1940s, 1.6 million blacks moved from the rural South to the industrial North to find factory and defense jobs; for example, Chicago's black population increased by 77 percent. These changes brought tensions. White-dominated unions and industries resisted hiring blacks and did so only as a result of government pressure and labor shortages. Race riots plagued Detroit in 1943, and white workers struck the Philadelphia Transit Company to protest the upgrading of Negro porters to drivers.[15]

The Impact of World War II: The Culture of Social and Political Cohesion

If the war unleashed some disunifying forces in American life, the popular culture served to fortify the themes of social cohesion and national unity. The sex and drug scandals of the late 1920s and early 1930s had brought about the restrictive Motion Picture Production Code, which set forth standards of good taste to which the studios slavishly adhered. The code insisted that films respect moral, religious, racial, and ethnic sensibilities. It included such regulations as "Revenge in modern times shall not be justified" (it should have added "except in times of war"); "Illegal drug traffic must never be presented"; "Seduction and rape should never be more than suggested. . . . They are never the proper subject for comedy"; "Ministers of religion . . . should not be used as comic characters or as villains. . . . Profanity, obscenity, smut and vulgarity are forbidden, even when likely to be understood by part of the audience. . . . Illicit sex relations are not treated as commendable. . . . Respect is maintained for the sanctity of marriage and the value of the home. Divorce is not treated casually nor justified as a solution for marital problems."[16] The undertone of popular songs, films, novels, plays, and radio idolized a stable world of secure families, loving parents, and children who were sometimes mischievous but eventually dutiful.

The themes of national unity pervaded the culture. Many popular songs were unabashedly patriotic ("He Wears a Pair of Silver Wings," "Praise the Lord and Pass the Ammunition," "There'll Be a Hot Time in the Town of Berlin When the Yanks Go Marchin' In"); some spoke of romantic longing and nostalgia ("I'll Be Seeing You," "You'd Be So Nice to Come Home To," "I Left My Heart at the Stage Door Canteen," "A Boy In Khaki—A Girl in Lace"); some were comic ("This Is the Army, Mr. Jones," "Der Fuehrer's Face"); and some were openly chauvinistic and even racist ("When Those Little Yellow Bellies Meet the Cohens and the Kellys").

World War II enveloped the lives of children as well. For those whose fathers were too old for military service and whose lives were not disrupted, it was exhilarating. This fact may seem somewhat ghastly in retrospect, but given the innocence of children, it is understandable. They saw an enemy so villainous that they had no doubt of the country's righteousness and the heroism of its fighting men. The movies, the comic books, the funny papers, and the radio programs so loved by children all reinforced these images.

The movies played a pivotal role in that reassurance, encouraged by the newly created Office of War Information (OWI), which was responsible for war propaganda. Its Washington office supervised the production of short government films; its Hollywood office, under the direction of newsman Nelson Poynter, played a subtler role. Poynter encouraged the studio heads to work war propaganda themes into their films. He and his staff produced a "Government Information Manual for the Motion Picture Industry," which promoted a vision shared by then vice president Henry A. Wallace, who hoped that the war would be a revolutionary struggle for human rights and result in what he called "the Century of the Common Man." The manual, stressing the democratic nature of the struggle and the need for a united America, urged that movies show workers and management setting aside their differences to sacrifice for the war. Combat films, it suggested, should have multi-ethnic fighting units to emphasize a liberal internationalist perspective. All the allied nations were to be portrayed favorably. Nationalist China was transformed into a liberal nation and the Soviet Union treated as a heroic ally. The manual was careful to state, "Yes, we Americans reject communism, but we do not reject our Russian ally."[17]

Although Poynter would eventually run into opposition in Hollywood and find his office closed by 1944, studio heads generally shared his vision. Many major producers were Jewish—Louis B. Mayer, Jack Warner, Adolph Zukor—and many writers were European émigrés, refugees from Nazism. Appalled and frightened by Hitler, they were more than willing to lend their support to the war. In the process, Hollywood produced an idealized picture of American life. As Neil Gablers puts it in *An Empire of Their Own: How the Jews Invented Hollywood*, "They would create [America's] values and myths, its traditions and archetypes. It would be an America where fathers were strong, families stable, people attractive, resilient, resourceful, and decent. . . . [They] created a powerful cluster of images and ideas—so powerful, in a sense, they colonized the American imagination."[18]

Movies romanticized the ghastly reality of war. Death usually happened without pain, and the gauze of self-censorship filtered what people saw in the newsreels. *Bataan*, a prototypical war movie produced in 1943, was the story of thirteen doomed American defenders on that Philippine peninsula. Most of the men in the unit were not professional soldiers, and they represented both economically and ethnically a cross section of America. They included a soda jerk, a salesman, a farmer, and a teacher. For ethnic diversity there was an Italian, a Jew, a Hispanic, a WASP, a Pole, an Irishman, and in this picture a black man—totally fictionalized, since blacks had not yet been integrated into combat units at that time. Producer Dore Schary, an outspoken Hollywood liberal, explained bluntly, "I just put one in, that's all. I said, 'to hell with it, we are going to have one Black.' We got a lot of letters complaining."[19] Despite the letters, the film was successful and well received. Many vividly remember Robert Taylor, the last survivor of the patrol, shouting in defiance behind his machine gun and firing away as Japanese soldiers swarmed toward his position. Of course, the Japanese were dehumanized in this film, but that was not what stuck with the audience; rather it was the image of our country symbolized by those doomed men. Metro-Goldwyn-Mayer (MGM), the studio that made *Bataan*, had submitted the script to Poynter's office, which was delighted with it. The OWI reviewer was pleased that the film illustrated "a people's army, fighting a people's war."[20]

Other movies were equally compelling: *Thirty Seconds over Tokyo*, about the Doolittle air strikes on Japan; *Objective Burma*, in which Errol Flynn drives the Japanese out of Burma with barely a mention of the British, who were doing most of the fighting on that front. Everybody got into the act. Bob Hope's comedies involved Nazi gangsters; in ordinary cops-and-robbers movies the villains were saboteurs; and in *Tarzan Triumphs* even Johnny Weissmuller chased Nazis through Africa, where they had parachuted into the jungle to occupy a fortress and exploit oil and tin. As one commentator noted, "The Germans are so despicable even the animals turn against them."[21]

The home front was rendered in its idealized form in David O. Selznick's *Since You Went Away* (1943). The film opens with the caption, "This is a story of the Unconquerable Fortress: The American Home." Claudette Colbert plays the mother, Anne Hilton, who remains doggedly loyal to her missing husband despite the temptation presented in the person of family friend Joseph Cotton. Everyone makes sacrifices. The family rents out a room to a crotchety elderly boarder; after hearing that her fiancé has been killed in action, the older daughter forgoes college to work in a veterans' hospital; the younger daughter, played by an adolescent Shirley Temple, worries that she can do only such kid stuff as rolling bandages and selling war stamps; Anne eventually goes to work in a factory as a welder. The villainess is a selfish society matron who complains about rationing and thinks that war work is beneath her. The film, which may seem overly long and sentimental to viewers today, captured for its wartime audience the vision that middle-class Americans had of themselves. One critic noted that it was "the definitive home-front movie . . . until a realist comes along to show us what life was really like in America during World War II."[22]

No matter how sentimental and cliché ridden these movies seem in retrospect, they earned their place in American culture. Were they an accurate picture of war or of the home front? Undoubtedly, it was all far messier and complex than Hollywood's portrayal of it. Nonetheless, many believed that the images presented in those films were what America strove to be—a country of regular folks fighting the world's bullyboys. Idealized as this vision was, these movies helped create the appearance of a unified and coherent common culture and offered a perception of reality that reassured many Americans.

By the end of World War II, America had clutched Hollywood and its stars to its bosom. The studios exercised iron-fisted control over their stars and the press, which depended upon movie advertising. Public scandals, mild though titillating, were largely about marriage and divorce. Those stars (and we now know there were quite a few) affected by alcoholism, homosexuality, or drug addiction were shielded from exposure by studio agents. The selfless patriotism of actors such as Clark Gable and Jimmy Stewart, who actually served in combat, and of many others who contributed their time to bond rallies, USO canteens, and entertainment for the troops in the theaters of war had the effect of binding them closer to the American people.[23] Hollywood's image was wholesome and patriotic.

The Postwar Boom and the Political Consensus

Wartime prosperity evolved into a postwar boom, also broadly shared, that continued for several decades, interrupted by only a few minor recessions. Per capita worker productivity increased 200 percent between 1947 and 1956; per capita income rose 35 percent in constant dollars between 1945 and 1960; home ownership increased 50 percent in the decade of the 1940s and again in the 1950s. The standard of living for the average American family was on a steady incline. From 1929 until 1953 the absolute number of families classified as poor dropped from 15.6 million to 11.7 million. Manufacturing wages doubled in the two decades following the war. A substantial number of workers in the 1940s and 1950s called themselves middle class, and such self-description was not simply wishful thinking. Increased wages allowed many families to purchase modestly priced homes in the suburbs, buy second cars, and enjoy family vacations. Within fifteen years after the war, 75 percent of the homes had automatic washing machines, and 87 percent had television sets. A country in which the majority had been working class and poor, even in the years prior to the depression, was now over 60 percent middle class.[24]

This unprecedented prosperity brought permanent changes in the nature of the workforce. New industries such as electronics, aerospace, and chemicals created a demand for highly trained professionals. By 1964 the number of professional and technical workers had doubled since 1940. Although the total of factory workers fell by 4 percent from 1947 to 1957, white-collar clerical workers grew by 23 percent. The increase in scientists was ninefold and engineers almost fourfold since the Great Depression years.[25]

Class conflicts had diminished with widening prosperity, and a more professional workforce had little enthusiasm for any program of radical change. The industrial labor movement (automobiles, steel, coal, rubber), which had emerged in the late 1930s as a powerful voice for social change under the protection of New Deal labor laws, had to reduce its hopes. During the war, union leaders had expectations for a second, postwar New Deal, more radical and far reaching than the first. The Congress of Industrial Organizations (CIO) had promulgated a postwar vision of a planned economy with guaranteed full employment, price controls, and wage guidelines. A strong ally of the CIO, President Roosevelt had given the labor unions some reason to believe that he shared their vision of postwar America. In his 1944 state-of-the-union address, he called for an economic bill of rights that would include the right to a useful job, to adequate earnings for food and housing, to medical care, and to a decent education.

These ambitious plans were for naught. There was no consensus for long-term social planning, more government regulation, an expanded welfare state, or even an aggressive antitrust policy. Polls showed that two-thirds of Americans opposed anything resembling the British Labour government's program for the nationalization of major industries.[26] The success of American labor unions in securing attractive wage increases had reduced the appetite even of their members for more government programs. In 1948, Walter Reuther, the head of the United Auto Workers, had negotiated the first cost-of-living adjustment in a labor contract that was to become a model for many union contracts. Reuther, long a voice on labor's left, had himself lost his appetite for a government superstate. Fearing what would happen if conservatives were to control such a state, he claimed, "I would rather bargain with GM [General Motors] than with the government. . . . GM has no army."[27]

Labor's vision was shrinking along with its ability to broaden its worker base. The wave of strikes in 1946 affecting the auto, rubber, oil, textile, and electronics industries (almost five thousand work stoppages by 4.6 million workers) soured the general public on the union movement.[28] At the end of the war more than 50 percent of Americans favored restrictions on unions, putting labor on the political defensive.[29] Reflecting this mood, the Republican Congress elected in 1946 passed— over President Harry S. Truman's veto and labor's bitter opposition— the Taft-Hartley Labor Act. The law required union leaders to sign anti-Communist affidavits, outlawed secondary boycotts, and allowed states to pass right-to-work laws, prohibiting the closed shop (mandatory unionism).

Union leaders' predictions that the law would destroy industrial unionism proved to be unfounded, but Taft-Hartley did cripple their effort, known as Operation Dixie, to organize in the South; the anti-Communist provision destroyed many of the South's Communist-led integrated unions. That failure cannot be blamed entirely on Taft-Hartley, however. Racial divisions, increasing farm mechanization, and growing prosperity in the cotton and tobacco regions also frustrated Operation Dixie.[30] Blacks, farmworkers, and white nonunion workers, groups likely to support radical economic policies, seemed beyond the reach of organized labor. Consequently, union leaders were left with a more conservative constituency that had little desire to rattle the status quo. Labor leaders had to be reconciled to a modest welfare state.

For other reasons, so did business leaders. Burgeoning prosperity under the two Democratic presidents, Roosevelt and Truman, reduced much of their resistance to the welfare and regulatory state. According to the economic historian Herbert Stein, "Business had learned to live with and accept most of the regulations it had strenuously opposed in the New Deal—the SEC [Securities and Exchange Commission], the minimum wage, the hours legislation, the FPC [Federal Power Commission], CAB [Civil Aeronautics Board], FCC [Federal Communications Commission], etc."[31] Nonetheless, the business community's acceptance of this New Deal legacy had limits. The National

Association of Manufacturers and the Chamber of Commerce were not afraid to use their influence to prevent its expansion. They were successful in opposing the continuation of wartime wage and price controls and the federal government's expansion into the fields of health, education, and housing. They also won a major victory with the passage of the Taft-Hartley Labor Act.

The public's acceptance of the New Deal reforms and its willingness and ability to pay for them matched the business community's acceptance. The New Deal and the war expenditures had reduced general fears of government. Federal spending as a percentage of GNP had grown from 5.5 percent in 1932 to 13.2 percent by 1947 and would never return to pre–New Deal levels. To pay for such increases, the level of taxation on incomes during and after the war years was without precedent in American history. The practice of withholding taxes, introduced during World War II, made the money disappear before earners even saw it. In 1939, income taxes took only 1.2 percent of personal income, and only about four million people had to pay them. When Americans were asked in 1944 whether they regarded the amount of income taxes they paid as fair, an astounding 85 percent responded "yes."[32] By 1945 such taxes were taking 11.2 percent of personal income and forty million Americans were filing income tax returns. The receipts had grown from 9.9 percent of GNP in 1940 to 16.2 percent in 1949.[33] The public did see some reduction in taxes from wartime levels, but they never fell to the prewar rates that had chiefly affected the upper-income brackets. As historian James Patterson describes it, "The nation went from a system of class taxation to one of mass taxation during the war."[34]

Having taken this leap in accepting a larger role for government, however, the public now wanted a pause. The pause set the stage for an economic truce among business, labor, and the general public. Liberals joined conservatives in proclaiming their faith in capitalism. Leon Keyserling, chairman of President Truman's Council of Economic Advisers, consistently argued that a vigorous private sector would provide the tax base for current and future welfare programs.[35] No major political group was waging a war on capitalism. The debate over economic policy continued, but it focused upon marginal changes in the role of government. The Cold War only served to reinforce the need for a strong central government. So long as the Soviet Union remained a threat, government was unlikely to shrink, for national defense expenditures could never return to pre–World War II levels.

The Cold War also skewed the political debate. In World War II our enemies were on the right (German nazism, Italian fascism, and Japanese militarism), and our allies included the Soviet Union. As long as the United States and the Soviet Union were allied, the American Communist Party spouted a patriotic line and even refused to run its own candidate for president in 1944, endorsing the reelection of President Roosevelt. But during the Cold War the new enemy, Soviet communism, was on the left. Public opinion was such that the Communists, allies of the democratic left during World War II, were now read out of any respectable left coalition. This deradicalization of the American left was symbolized by the formation of the Americans for Democratic Action (ADA). Founded in 1947 by anti-Communist liberal Democrats (including Hubert Humphrey, Eleanor Roosevelt, and Franklin D. Roosevelt, Jr.), the ADA was designed to remove any Communist taint from social reform and became the leading voice of postwar liberalism. Arthur Schlesinger, Jr., another founding member of the ADA, described this "vital center liberalism" as "a belief in the integrity of the individual, in the limited state, due process of law, in empiricism, and gradualism."[36]

Vital center liberalism declared fascism and communism to be twin evils. (In reality, any such discussion of "twin" evils was rhetorical: international fascism had been destroyed in World War II, whereas the threat of international communism was manifest and clearly defined.) There remained, nevertheless, a small remnant of the left that eschewed anticommunism and desired a political accommodation with the Soviet Union. During the 1948 presidential election its members rallied around the third-party candidacy of the former vice president, Henry Wallace. Wallace found his idealistic vision of a century of the common man incompatible with the hard realities of the Cold War, which required that the United States tolerate the colonialism of its European allies. He challenged President Truman's foreign policy of containing Soviet influence and even opposed the Marshall Plan for the economic reconstruction of Europe. His timing could not have been worse. In early 1948 the Soviets engineered a Communist coup d'état in Czechoslovakia and blockaded Berlin. After these events most of the public needed little convincing about the seriousness of the Soviet threat. Consequently, the presidential election was a disaster for Wallace and his accommodationist form of liberalism. Cast as an appeaser, especially by President Truman, he gained a mere 2.5 percent of the popular vote. Truman, who had garnered considerable public support because of the Marshall Plan and his dramatic airlift to counter the Berlin blockade, won an unexpected victory over a bland and uninspiring Republican opponent, New York's governor, Thomas E. Dewey.

Truman's victory also brought a Democratic Congress back to Washington and with it an opportunity to move the liberal agenda forward. True to those expectations, President Truman introduced an ambitious agenda in his 1949 state-of-the-union address. Dubbed the Fair Deal, the program included federal aid to education, a more progressive income tax, the repeal of Taft-Hartley, government health insurance, expanded public housing, and civil rights. Many liberals hoped the Fair Deal would continue the work done by Franklin Roosevelt's New Deal and promised by the late president in 1944.

They were to be disappointed. The election victory did not bring another round of reform and served only to emphasize the limits of vital center liberalism. The Fair Deal faced serious opposition in the nominally Democratic Eighty-first Congress, which was controlled by a coalition of conservative Republicans and Southern Democrats. During the presidential campaign, Truman had created a farmer-labor coalition that allowed him to carry the major industrial states of Ohio and Illinois along with Iowa, Minnesota, and Wisconsin. Like many other electoral coalitions, however, this one could not be translated into a governing one. Congress did produce a few reforms (an increase in the minimum wage from forty to seventy-five cents an hour, extended social security benefits, modest expansion of public housing, and higher price supports for farmers), but its record fell far short of liberal expectations. Labor pushed for repeal of Taft-Hartley but never succeeded. Federal aid to education was generally popular but fell victim to a dispute over aid to parochial schools. Public support for national health insurance was too weak to overcome the resistance of the American Medical Association. Truman's proposals to eliminate racial discrimination in employment also had little backing and faced ferocious opposition from Southern Democrats in the Senate.

It was the anticommunism of the vital center that carried the day, not domestic liberalism. Henry Wallace's repudiation at the polls sent a message that any national politician advocating an accommodation with the Soviet Union would be sent into oblivion. A series of unsettling events following Truman's 1948 victory deepened the anti-Communist consensus. In the spring of 1949, Alger Hiss, a former high-level State Department official, was tried and later convicted of spying for the

Soviets. The Hiss indictment followed revelations of an extensive Soviet espionage ring that had penetrated the government in the late 1930s and 1940s. In January 1950, Klaus Fuchs, a German-born British scientist who had worked on the Manhattan Project, was arrested by the British and confessed to spying for the Soviet Union.

In the fall of 1949 the "twin shocks" of Communist revolution in China and Soviet detonation of an atomic device caused public insecurity over the Communist threat to verge on paranoia and hysteria. Seizing the moment, Sen. Joseph R. McCarthy (R-WI) charged in February 1950 that Secretary of State Dean Acheson and others in the Truman administration knew the State Department was infested with Communists and refused to do anything about it. Although McCarthy failed to prove this charge and others that he would make, he touched a nerve. Many Americans, bewildered by the country's apparent loss of power and influence so soon after the triumph of World War II, were willing to believe McCarthy's essential message: it was treason in high places that accounted for the Communist victory in China and the Soviet possession of an atomic bomb.

When Communist North Korea invaded South Korea in June 1950 and President Truman immediately ordered in American troops, the anti-Communist sentiment hardened. At first, the UN-backed "police action" seemed to be coming to a successful early conclusion. As Thanksgiving approached, theater commander Gen. Douglas MacArthur, having pushed the invaders back across the thirty-eighth parallel, which divided the two Koreas, announced a "home by Christmas" offensive. But soon after MacArthur's hasty prediction some 300,000 Chinese troops crossed the Yalu River into North Korea and drove the UN forces back into South Korea. What had looked like a quick victory became a protracted three-year war that involved as many as 250,000 American troops. The introduction of Chinese forces was a painful reminder of the consequences of the 1949 Communist takeover in China. As the war progressed without resolution, McCarthy's charges had an even greater impact. Now he could claim that Communist treachery and the Truman administration's naïveté were responsible for our troops' fighting and dying in Korea.

During the Korean War anticommunism became an American crusade, and foreign policy took on a strong military cast. The defense budget tripled, and the nuclear weapons program was accelerated. Both the United States and the Soviet Union were building a new hydrogen bomb (H-bomb) with one thousand times the destructive power of the bombs dropped on Hiroshima and Nagasaki. Any prospect of a diplomatic settlement with the Communist states was remote at best. The Cold War, punctuated by limited hot wars such as Korea, became a fixture of the international landscape and would shape American politics and culture for a generation.

As a result of the twin shocks of 1949, the Hiss case, the Fuchs confession, the Korean War, and Sen. McCarthy's charges, anticommunism became the dominant issue of the early 1950s, pushing liberal reform to the sidelines for over a decade. Public opinion polls showed overwhelming support for legislation to restrict and even outlaw the Communist Party. Two-thirds of the public wanted Communists to register with the Justice Department, and 90 percent wanted them removed from defense jobs.[37] Following this mood, the Eighty-first Congress passed the Internal Security Act of 1950 over President Truman's veto. This law went beyond existing antisedition legislation, the Smith Act, under which the top leadership of the Communist Party and almost one hundred other members had already been tried and convicted.[38] One of the most restrictive antisubversive laws in American history, the Internal Security Act required Communists to register with the attorney general, banned them from government and defense jobs, and denied them the right to a passport. It even established legal authority for the government, should the president declare a national emergency, to hold anyone suspected of subversion in detention. Although the Supreme Court later declared much of this bill unconstitutional, at the time it sent a clear message of the risk to anyone associated with communism or Communist causes. Fear of communism often meant fear of radicalism in all things political and cultural.

Stephen J. Whitfield has argued that "the Cold War also narrowed and altered American culture. This form of politicization arose because super-patriots themselves adopted the methods of their Communist enemies, and because the axis of partisan politics shifted so dramatically to the right."[39] Numerous other historians have seen McCarthy and McCarthyism as representing the true spirit of anticommunism. On the other hand, Richard Gid Powers argues that "the history of anticommunism is not the same as the story of anticommunist extremism, any more than the history of malpractice is the history of medicine. The victims of anticommunism were not persecuted simply because of their political views and associations, but because they defended (though sometimes unwittingly) a political ideology at war with human freedom."[40]

The Cold War
and the Cultural Consensus

The Cold War did not immediately affect Hollywood. The films of the early postwar era focused on domestic problems left unattended during the war. In 1946, before the Cold War dominated the environment, Hollywood was at its peak of influence, popularity, and profit. One of its most memorable films of that year, *The Best Years of Our Lives*, reflected postwar expectations. The film expresses these hopes in the lives of three combat veterans returning to a fictional middle-American city: a middle-aged banker who had become an army sergeant; a soda jerk who was an air corps captain; and a high school football hero who had lost both hands when a torpedo hit his ship. As a *New York Times* reviewer wrote, "This film is cut from the heart-wood of contemporary America." None of their problems—the banker trying to relate to his stuffy elitist profession; the airman finding his old job and his faithless wife not what they had been; and the handicapped sailor struggling against self-pity and fear of dependence—is resolved. Nevertheless, their stories were told in compelling terms, vesting these ordinary people with such humanity that audiences left the theater optimistic about the future. The message was not complicated: Americans had fought a war for a more tolerant and humane world, and perhaps we may have one. Both artistically and commercially the film was a major success, winning seven Oscars and attracting the biggest box office since *Gone with the Wind*. It obviously resonated with millions of Americans.

The Best Years of Our Lives marked a new seriousness in the movies, an effort to get away from costume dramas, melodramas, and glossy musicals. Some attribute this shift to the influence of the Italian neorealist school—motion pictures made in the streets of postwar Italy such as Vittoria de Sica's *Shoeshine* (1946) and *The Bicycle Thief* (1948); Roberto Rossellini's *Open City* (1945) and *Paisan* (1946). In any case, American filmmakers were starting to tackle real social problems, often controversial ones. In *Home of the Brave* (1949) director Stanley Kramer confronted racial prejudice in an army combat unit. In *Gentleman's Agreement* (1947) director Elia Kazan and producer Darryl F. Zanuck dramatized the issue of anti-Semitism, as did producer Adrian Scott and director Edward Dmytryk in *Crossfire* (1947). In *Pinky* (1948) Jeanne Crain (a white actress) portrayed a young Negro nurse who passes for white in the North; in *Lost Boundaries* (1949) Mel Ferrer headed a black family passing for white. In *The Snake*

Pit (1948) Olivia de Haviland played a woman confronting the brutal treatment of the mentally ill. In *The Men* (1950), Marlon Brando's first film, producer Stanley Kramer presented an unsentimental treatment of paraplegic war veterans. The commercial success of these productions also marked a new sophistication of the American audience. A survey taken in 1946 showed that moviegoers increasingly were drawn from the upper-income, educated strata of society.

The Cold War and McCarthyism soon had a chilling effect on the daring and creativity of moviemaking, however, and realism and social controversy would become dangerous subjects. Yet the storm developed slowly. In the fall of 1947 the House Un-American Activities Committee (HUAC) had begun an investigation into Communist influence in Hollywood. Ten eminent film directors and writers refused with defiance and belligerence to answer the committee's questions about their past or present membership in the Communist Party. Called the Hollywood Ten, they became the focal point of controversy.

At first, the Hollywood liberal community came to their defense. Directors William Wyler and John Huston and such stars as Humphrey Bogart, Lauren Bacall, Judy Garland, Danny Kaye, and Frank Sinatra formed the Committee for the First Amendment. When the Hollywood Ten were cited for contempt of Congress and subsequently jailed, however, the film community began to pull in its wings. Many members of the Committee for the First Amendment claimed they had been betrayed by the Hollywood Ten, once they discovered all had been (or still were) Communists. Whatever the motivations, it was becoming clear to people in Hollywood that association with causes considered sympathetic to communism would be fatal to their careers.

In November 1947, meeting at the Waldorf-Astoria Hotel in New York City, some fifty film executives representing Paramount, Columbia, MGM, RKO, and Twentieth Century-Fox issued a statement that "nothing subversive or un-American has appeared on the screen." They agreed to fire five of the Hollywood Ten still in their employ and anyone else who was known to be a Communist or who refused to answer HUAC's questions. Although the studio heads insisted that they were not to be "swamped by hysteria or intimidated from any source," the mood was altered almost overnight. For example, RKO fired two of the Hollywood Ten, Adrian Scott and Edward Dmytryk, a few months after they had just completed the highly successful *Crossfire*.

In 1951 the House Un-American Activities Committee resumed its hearings into Communist influence in Hollywood. This time they found little opposition in the industry and, more important, countless witnesses lining up to testify—former Communists who wanted to prove publicly that they had broken with the Party, including those who had invoked the Fifth Amendment's protection against self-incrimination. Anyone admitting to past membership was also required to "name names": that is, to testify under oath about others in or sympathetic to the Party. Those who would not cooperate found themselves unemployable or blacklisted. A few paid the price, but more went along with the committee. Among those who did "name names" were some of Hollywood's biggest names, including Lee J. Cobb, Sterling Hayden, and Elia Kazan.

The entire industry became obsessed with removing any taint of Communist influence. In 1953 the Screen Actors Guild (SAG) under the leadership of its president, Ronald Reagan, introduced a loyalty oath for new members and required that its officials sign non-Communist affidavits. The same year the membership of SAG voted 3,769 to 162 to ban Communists from membership. In 1954 the Screen Writers Guild voted 325 to 12 to do the same.[41] Among the most creative talents driven out of the industry—some for years, others for a lifetime—were writer-director Carl Foreman (*Home of the Brave* and *The Men*), Hollywood Ten writer Dalton Trumbo (*Thirty Seconds over Tokyo*), and the Academy Award-winning actresses Anne Revere and Gale Sondergaard. The industry consciously pulled away from controversy and put its resources into wide-screen spectaculars, biblical epics, routine Westerns, innocuous romances, and low-budget science fiction films. According to one study, whereas almost 30 percent of the films produced in 1947 had a serious social bent, by 1953 the figure was down to 9 percent.[42] And most of the so-called social pictures were blatant anti-Communist propaganda. Between 1948 and 1954 Hollywood produced more than forty such films, mostly spy thrillers about the infiltration of Reds into unions, government, and defense plants. Communists were portrayed as sinister hypocrites operating from penthouses and planning the workers' revolution. The pictures included such titles as *The Red Menace* (1949), *I Married a Communist* (1950), *I Was a Communist for the FBI* (1951), and *My Son John* (1952). On the whole, they were forgettable.

The atmosphere that affected Hollywood also intruded upon the private lives and sexual morality of its stars. People understood and often snickered at the high divorce rate among Hollywood people, but they were expected not to flaunt unconventional habits in public. For example, Spencer Tracy and Katharine Hepburn lived together for decades, despite Tracy's refusal to seek a divorce from his wife, Louise. Understanding the rules of the game, Tracy and Hepburn were discreet, and their press agents kept the media at bay. For major stars who openly defied social conventions, however, the judgments could be harsh.

Particular venom was directed at Ingrid Bergman, a Swedish-born actress who had captivated American audiences in the mid-1940s in such films as *Gaslight*, *For Whom the Bell Tolls*, *Casablanca*, *Spellbound*, and *Notorious*. By the early 1950s she was a virtual pariah, unwelcome in America. She had left her husband to live openly in Rome with Italian director Roberto Rossellini. When she and Rossellini conceived a child out of wedlock, the scandal took on monumental proportions. They were roundly criticized in the press, and even Congress took notice. Sen. Edwin Johnson (D-CO) denounced her from the Senate floor on March 14, 1950, declaring that her "unconventional free-love conduct must be regarded for what it is—an assault upon the institution of marriage"; he called her " a powerful influence for evil." Johnson even introduced a bill to have the Department of Commerce license actors, directors, producers, and films. Under this scheme, individuals could lose their licenses for acts of moral turpitude, and films could not encourage contempt of law, or public or private immorality.[43] (An indication of how attitudes can change, however, occurred in 1972, when Sen. Charles Percy (R-IL) declaimed on the Senate floor that "Miss Bergman is not only welcome in America; we are deeply honored by her visits here.")[44]

The blacklist, the Bergman affair, and the McCarthy witch-hunts showed a dark side of the political and cultural consensus. Still, it was an underside and not entirely emblematic of the time. These were the intolerant excesses of a society whose desire for stability could drift into a demand for conformity. Decades of depression and war had made stability seem attractive. In addition, Americans had seen utopian hopes betrayed in Europe and had helped to pay the price. Hitler, with his perverted promise of an Aryan paradise, had plunged the world into war and racial genocide, and now Stalin was converting the vision of a classless society into the reality of a gulag. In the late 1940s there were daily reports of religious and political repression behind the Iron Curtain. The stories were vivid and gripping. One of the most dramatic was Hungary's trial and imprisonment in 1948 of Joseph Cardinal Mindszenty, a leading prelate of the Catholic church. New York archbishop

Francis Spellman proclaimed February 9, 1949, as a day of prayer for Mindszenty's release from "Christ-hating Communists."[45]

That same year, British writer George Orwell's classic anti-utopian novel, *1984*, was published and sold over 350,000 copies in the United States in its first year. Lionel Trilling, one of America's leading literary critics, called the book "momentous."[46] Orwell had struck a responsive chord with both the general public and intellectuals. Whether or not it was his intention, his best-seller reassured many that America, devoid of extremist politics and nestled in a vital center, stood as the most realistic alternative to the false dreams of twentieth-century European totalitarianism.

This belief became a theme of many of America's leading intellectuals. Capitalism was not fulfilling the Marxist prediction that it would sow the seeds of its own destruction by impoverishing the many and rewarding the few. Intellectuals looked at unparalleled prosperity, moderate labor unions, and corporate leaders willing to tolerate a welfare state and saw in them the death of Marxism. Arthur Schlesinger, Jr., proclaimed, "Let us by all means discard Marx."[47] Sociologist Daniel Bell went so far as to proclaim "the end of ideology. . . . Ideology, which once was a road to action, has become a dead end."[48] From his perspective the class war was over, and there were no more mass movements to romanticize.

An even grander proclamation appeared in a 1952 symposium published by the *Partisan Review*. Titled "Our Country and Our Culture," the symposium included contributions from such leading intellectuals as Norman Mailer, David Reisman, Sidney Hook, Max Lerner, and Reinhold Niebuhr. Most echoed the tone of the editor's introduction: "Politically there is recognition that the kind of democracy which exists in America has an intrinsic and positive value: it is not merely a capitalist myth but a reality which must be defended against Russian totalitarianism. . . . Most writers no longer accept alienation as the artist's fate in America, on the contrary, they want very much to be a part of American life. More and more writers have ceased to think of themselves as rebels and exiles."[49]

Content in moderate and prosperous America, many of these intellectuals found their talents supported and nurtured by universities, foundations, and the government. They were no longer outsiders. Those who had championed radical politics during the 1930s were now fearful of popular movements. It became intellectually stylish to associate populist politics with the extremes of fascism, communism, and McCarthyism (deemed a hysterical and resentful form of anti-communism). As Arthur Schlesinger, Jr., wrote in *The Vital Center*: "The Soviet experience on top of the rise of fascism reminded my generation rather forcibly that man was, indeed imperfect, and that the corruption of power could unleash great evil in the world."[50] A healthy political system and self-confident culture were the best antidotes against the passions of utopian fanatics. These mainstream intellectuals, believing that the American system worked to discourage mass-based ideological politics, were willing to settle for a society marked by modest progress and respect for individual rights. Many embraced the concept of pluralism as the logical alternative to radical utopianism. Pluralist politics stressed bargaining among a multiplicity of interest groups (business, unions, farmers, veterans, minorities), each of which would pursue its own self-interest, check the excessive influence of the others, and create a society of balance and harmony.

The intellectual celebration of pragmatism and gradualism was reflected in the political environment. The two major political parties under the control of their moderate wings had little to fear from insurgent movements. The 1948 presidential challenges of States' Rights candidate Strom Thurmond and Progressive Party candidate Henry Wallace had been so weak that their parties virtually disappeared. By no surprise, in 1952 the major parties produced as candidates two men of the center, Gen. Dwight D. Eisenhower for the Republicans and Gov. Adlai Stevenson of Illinois for the Democrats. Eisenhower had defeated Sen. Robert A. Taft (R-OH), who represented the last hope of the isolationist, anti–New Deal wing of the party. Stevenson was drafted at the convention through the behind-the-scenes maneuvering of President Truman and a group of party bosses. These leaders feared the insurgent candidacy of Sen. Estes Kefauver (D-TN), who had risen to fame in his televised hearings investigating organized crime and political corruption. Kefauver was the first politician to gain national prominence through television, a medium with which politicians of Truman's generation did not feel comfortable. They came from a school that believed presidential nominations should be trusted to party leaders and kept away from rabble-rousing opportunists.

Notwithstanding the circumstances of his nomination, Stevenson was anything but a party hack. He was a witty and urbane Illinois aristocrat whose grandfather had served as vice president under President Grover Cleveland. His elegant and understated speeches endeared him to the intelligentsia, who considered Stevenson one of their own. His style suited a spirit of moderation and contained no ideological fervor. Like Eisenhower, he was an avowed internationalist who believed that world leadership required Americans to cool the passion of their politics and behave with a degree of political maturity. He had little regard for conspiracy theorists and those enamored of McCarthy's paranoia. In his Godkin Lectures at Harvard in 1954, Stevenson repeated this argument: "Unaccustomed as we are to moderate speech, our petulance, temper or partisanship can have its effect on us as well as the foreigner, especially when it is cloaked in the garments of righteousness and impatience with any solutions that do not promise quick returns."[51]

Eisenhower, who defeated Stevenson in the general election, lacked his opponent's eloquence and did not gain the same admiration of the intelligentsia. Nonetheless, Ike was every bit a man of the center, and his election did much to solidify the general consensus. His nomination victory over Robert Taft and subsequent election placed the Republican Party solidly in the mainstream of American politics. As the first Republican president since the New Deal, Eisenhower understood the central political reality of his time: that far from fearing government, Americans had developed an appetite for it. True to this understanding, the Eisenhower administration developed a consolidationist approach to the welfare state that made the New Deal a permanent part of the political landscape, off limits to any serious conservative attack. In 1954, the president wrote his brother Edgar, who had been critical of his domestic policies, "Should any political party attempt to abolish Social Security, unemployment insurance, and eliminate labor laws and farm programs, you would not hear again of that party in our political history."[52]

Eisenhower also understood that the Cold War could be an effective rationale for any expansion of the federal government into new areas of domestic life. Fanciful as it may seem today, his administration made the argument that new roads built under the Interstate Highway Act of 1956 would facilitate evacuation from the cities in the event of a Soviet nuclear attack. The National Defense Education Act of 1958, which funded new graduate programs, was a direct response to the Soviet Union's successful launch of Sputnik and to the perception, at the time, that the United States was losing its technological edge. Even the modest Civil Rights Acts of 1957 and 1960, designed to facilitate black voting registration in the South, had a Cold War rationale: supporters claimed that such laws could enhance American influence in postcolonial Africa.

These programs and their accommodation to an expansion of the state were at the heart of what Eisenhower called Modern Republicanism. During the 1950s a growing economy, a reduced post–Korean War defense budget, and the modest cost of his domestic programs allowed Eisenhower to balance the budget and maintain a Republican allegiance to fiscal conservatism. Nonetheless, what resulted was a smorgasbord of liberalism and conservatism without any sharp edges or clear definition. A later critic concluded that, "Modern Republicanism was not so much a philosophy as a balancing act."[53]

Whatever his ideological ambiguities and lack of excitement, President Eisenhower's moderation and reassuring leadership seemed to fit the times. In foreign policy he skillfully avoided the pitfalls of extended wars in Asia by negotiating the end of the Korean conflict and keeping the United States out of another war in Indo-China. When Soviet dictator Joseph Stalin died in 1953, Eisenhower renewed a diplomatic dialogue with the USSR. In the summer of 1955 he participated in the first summit conference of the Cold War, in which both the Soviet and Western leaders pledged to work to avoid a nuclear war. This was a strategy consciously designed to reduce tensions. And because Ike was the first Republican president in twenty years and a war hero, his party dared not charge him with appeasement.

The historian Paul Johnson gives Eisenhower major credit for the downfall of Joe McCarthy, who had done as much as any man to raise the temperature of American politics to a fever. Johnson claims that the Korean War had added to the public anxiety that made McCarthyism possible; once Eisenhower engineered a settlement, "the Senator could be reduced to size."[54] With the Korean War over, Eisenhower worked behind the scenes to engineer McCarthy's political demise. McCarthy had clumsily attempted to win favors for staffer G. David Schine, who had been drafted. When this maneuver was publicly disclosed, the senator foolishly responded that Schine was being held hostage to prevent an investigation into Communist influence in the army. A special Senate investigation was authorized to look into these charges. The Army-McCarthy hearings, as they were known, were nationally televised, and McCarthy was made to look like a reckless buffoon. By the end of 1954 his behavior had so annoyed his Senate colleagues that they voted overwhelmingly to censure him. From then on he frightened no one, and his crusade lost much of its zeal. McCarthy died in 1957 from the consequences of chronic alcoholism.

With the Cold War stabilizing, the Korean War settled, and McCarthy in disgrace, the political environment began to mellow. The country seemed to want a respite from the abrasive and jolting events of the previous decades. Although Eisenhower's Modern Republicanism had no passionate adherents, it had few zealous opponents. When the Democrats regained the Congress in the 1954 elections, Eisenhower found willing partners in Speaker of the House Sam Rayburn (D-TX) and Democratic Senate leader Lyndon B. Johnson (D-TX). Together they passed moderate voting rights bills in 1957 and 1960, expansion of Social Security, statehood for Hawaii and Alaska, and aid to higher education.

Easily reelected in 1956, once again defeating Adlai Stevenson, Eisenhower conserved political capital. He viewed his popularity as a source of American unity and consciously avoided, when possible, investing it in controversial and contentious causes. Despite the Supreme Court decision in *Brown v. Board of Education of Topeka* (1954), calling school segregation unconstitutional, Eisenhower took no public stand on the issue and introduced no legislation to hasten enforcement of integration. Nor was he under real pressure to do so, since he almost carried the black vote in 1956 without taking much action on desegregation. The liberal Democrats in Congress, fearful of alienating their southern colleagues, were similarly cautious. The civil rights movement—with the exception of the Montgomery, Alabama, bus boycott of 1955—had yet to take to the streets. The strategy designed by the cautious leaders of the National Association for the Advancement of Colored People (NAACP) was largely focused on the courts.

The Culture of the Personal
The 1950s witnessed the coming of age of those born in the 1930s, a unique though relatively small generation. Although they were born during the Great Depression, their early life experiences gave them numerous reasons for optimism. The first memories of many were of wartime victories. As adolescents in the 1940s and college-age students in the 1950s, they were the first young American generation to experience mass prosperity. They had seen their country come out of the depression, emerge victorious in World War II, and stand down Stalin in the early years of the Cold War.

In comparison with those who came before and after, they were a small population cohort. In 1950 there were fewer fifteen-year-olds than there had been in 1940.[55] Thus, they had better chances for acceptance to elite colleges, good jobs, homes, and promotions. They married earlier and had children earlier than previous (and later) generations. Pilloried by their professors as hopeless conformists who yearned for comfort and security rather than adventure and risk, they brought no passion for social change and radical politics to their college experience. Labeled the "silent generation," they were suited to the Eisenhower era.

The silent generation came of age when politics seemed without passion. Both politics and culture were moving away from mass movements, broad social themes, and radical critiques. Anticommunism, the glue that held much of the political and cultural center, was largely a rejection of utopian ideas. The end-of-ideologists emphasized only the limits of political action. Personal problems did not have a public dimension. Problems that were once considered political now were defined as psychological, sociological and cultural.

Avant-garde cultural forms such as cool jazz and abstract art manifested a detached, self-conscious intellectualism. The most notable contemporary fiction had little explicit political content. The novels of Saul Bellow (*The Adventures of Augie March*), John Updike (*Rabbit, Run*), and Philip Roth (*Goodbye Columbus*) concerned outsiders who sought to create their own values and fulfill their own desires. Those works that had a political dimension were generally written by conservative novelists such as Herman Wouk (*The Caine Mutiny*), James Gould Cozzens (*Guard of Honor*), and Allen Drury (*Advise and Consent*). In them the main characters defended traditional institutions against seedy characters who would undermine them.

This cultural embrace of the personal included a large dose of skepticism. To some extent the voguish philosophy of existentialism took the place that radical politics held for intellectuals of the 1930s (and again in the 1960s). A mode of thinking rather than a systematic approach, existentialism stressed disillusionment with traditional sources of authority, including religion and science. One literary and philosophic figure who gained an almost cultlike following was Albert Camus, an Algerian-born citizen of France, who had broken with the left and denounced utopianism. Camus was neither a Christian nor a Communist. His most notable novels (*The Stranger*, *The Plague*, and

The Fall) and essays (*The Myth of Sisyphus* and *The Rebel*) struck the theme of the isolated individual in a world he can barely comprehend, let alone control. In these works, meaning could be found only in maintaining one's revolt against injustice and in asserting one's will against the benign indifference of the universe.

Camus's approach to life found fertile ground in the skepticism of the 1950s. If, as he implied, salvation was personal, so was damnation. Americans who were reentering private life in the postwar era were prepared for such themes. Hollywood too had begun to show a darker side of human nature in a genre that was to be one of its lasting legacies—film noir. This term was not in vogue when most of these pictures were made; it would have been considered pretentious and not understood in those less sophisticated days. Rather, such films were referred to as either gangster movies, murder mysteries, or psychological dramas. It was the French critics in the 1950s who adapted the phrase from *roman noir,* the black novel, a term used to describe the nineteenth-century British Gothic novel. These films showed a darker America, one inhabited by gangsters, hustlers, and other assorted losers—people trapped in their own paranoia and fear. The enemy was never defined as society or the system or the government; it was more obscure, maybe deeper. It was the evil that lurked in us all. These were shadowy, somber pictures that the critic Robert Sklar describes as "explorations of an interior landscape of mind and emotion quite novel in the extroverted American cinema." The heroes were cynical loners or disillusioned war veterans inextricably bound to the past and unsure about the future, unable to distinguish good from evil, not knowing whom to trust, frequently susceptible to villains who were seemingly attractive and sympathetic.

These films marked a shift of screen drama from an outer world to an inner one. They showed a country more complex and ambiguous than the motion picture industry had become accustomed to portraying, a far cry from the idealized America that Hollywood had depicted during World War II. "In Depression movies, horrible threats came from alien sources, from vampires and jungle beasts," Sklar has pointed out. "By the 1940s, horror lay close to home, in the veiled malevolence of trusted intimates, in one's own inner thoughts."[56]

Few critics considered these films to be social statements. No matter how cynical the characters, it was cynicism about life or their own condition, not about the country. The films challenged writers to suggest adultery or promiscuity but never to display, mention, or condone them. As Rita Hayworth, who plays a woman of dubious reputation, tells her former lover, played by Glenn Ford, in *Gilda* (1946), "If I'd been a ranch, they would have named me the Bar Nothing."

Many of these films came from the novels of such notable mystery writers as James M. Cain and Raymond Chandler. They starred such actors as Humphrey Bogart in *The Big Sleep* (1946), Kirk Douglas and Robert Mitchum in *Out of the Past* (1949), John Garfield in *Nobody Lives Forever* (1946), and Burt Lancaster in *The Killers* (1946). They also represented major directorial achievements: Billy Wilder's *Double Indemnity* (1944) and *Lost Weekend* (1945); Otto Preminger's *Laura* (1944); and Fritz Lang's *The Women in the Window* (1944), *Scarlet Street* (1945), and *The Big Heat* (1953). The list is long and memorable.

The exploration of interior life in films and novels particularly affected the young and sparked the emerging glimmer of a youth culture. It began in innocence. The teenager was a concept unique to the twentieth century and perhaps invented by America, the product of compulsory education and child labor laws that postponed entry into the workforce. When teenagers first emerged in the films and radio programs of the late 1930s and early 1940s, adults found them endearing. They were likable characters (Andy Hardy, Corliss Archer, Henry Aldrich) played by engaging young stars (Mickey Rooney, Judy Garland, Deanna Durbin, Ann Rutherford, and Shirley Temple). Although their language and social conventions were distinctive (jitterbugging, swing music, jive talk), they were hardly considered at odds with the adult world. They eagerly accepted adult responsibilities and seemed at home in their milieu. In one of the final films in the series, Andy Hardy joins the army. Even the Dead End Kids became comedic characters rather than the hoodlums they had first been in *Angels with Dirty Faces* (1938).

They got into jams, had romantic vexations, and mischievously interfered in the lives of their older brothers and sisters, all with no serious consequences. They exhibited no angst or alienation. That was to come in the 1950s, when every problem had a personal psychological dimension. Then there emerged a new character—moody, angry, rebellious, surly, and verging on violence. We see it in Marlon Brando's startling portrayal of the California biker in *The Wild One* (1954). "What are you kids rebelling against?" someone asks Brando's character. "I dunno," he replies. "What ya got?"

In his memorable film debut in *East of Eden* and then in *Rebel without a Cause* (both 1955), James Dean struck a similar chord. He and

Brando, both introspective to the point of self-absorption, became cultural icons for young people. Dean's films gave audiences an early glimpse of the young at war with their elders, in particular sons against fathers. In *East of Eden*, his character cannot relate to his father's rigid moralism; in *Rebel without a Cause* he finds his father a pusillanimous wimp dominated by a shrewish mother. In both he is misunderstood and tormented. Perhaps the silent generation, accustomed to obedience to their parents and raised to eschew self-assertion, found an outlet in Dean's unabashedly emotional persona, the antithesis of 1950s cool. As Nora Sayre, a member of the silent generation, explains in her book about the films of the 1950s, "Dean did personify the defiance that many subdued adolescents kept hidden. . . . He also seemed to have binges of exuberance with no stimulant but himself. And he *did it in public,* even in front of strangers; for us, that was almost inconceivable."[57]

Brando and Dean emerged along with a music that distinctively belonged to the young: rock and roll. This genre produced its own restless, moody, and narcissistic cultural hero in Elvis Presley. Elvis's music, like the characters played by Brando and Dean, had incipient sexual overtones, hinting at rebellion. His hip-shaking gyrations made older folks fret that he was subverting the morals of their children. As music historian Martha Bayles puts it, "To the worried opinion makers of the 1950s, Elvis was, along with James Dean and Marlon Brando, a quintessential juvenile delinquent."[58] Elvis and Chuck Berry, a black rock and roller from the same period, combined a mixture of sounds from white country-and-western music and black rhythm and blues. Unlike the angry heavy metal, punk, and grunge rock that followed, the music of Presley and Berry had a degree of gaiety and humor. It drew on the vigorous and uninhibited musical tradition of the black and white Pentecostal churches of the South. An important racial barrier had been crossed: both black and white teenagers were dancing to a new beat, even though they were still in separate dance halls.

A youth culture was emerging, and the concept of a common culture from which adults and teenagers could draw was diminishing. In 1959, *Life* magazine estimated teenage discretionary income at $10 billion, most of it going to entertainment. In sharp contrast to the older audiences of the 1930s and 1940s, approximately three-quarters of the American movie audience were now teenagers. Popular music and television also began to focus on this market. Unlike the romantic and patriotic themes that permeated popular culture in the 1940s, 1950s youth culture spoke of sexual longing and rebellion. It created, says one critic, "an acute sense of difference from the adult world."[59] Youth culture carried the emphasis on the personal over the political into the realm of social rebellion and alienation from the adult world. It was a journey that would eventually lead back to the political in the 1960s, but in the late 1950s it had not yet made that turn. The political overtones were hard to decipher, since the youth had picked up their clues from a largely apolitical culture. In the calm 1950s there were no obvious political avenues for the expression of discontent. As the historian James Patterson describes the atmosphere, "Restless young people in the 1950s tended to rebel on a fairly small stage in which parents and neighbors remained the major impediments to gratification. Except for blacks, who grew increasingly militant in fighting against racial injustice, young people who were unhappy with the status quo did not much concern themselves with larger political or social problems."[60] Yet in Brando, Dean, and Presley, some saw behavior which, if not delinquent, had within it the seeds of a strong antisocial bias: disdain for authority, lack of decorum, elevation of pleasure over work, and unrestrained sexuality.

The rebellious message of this incipient culture did not have the same impact on young women, at least not right away. As male figures became more broodish and rebellious, female anxiety was taking a different form. In the 1930s and early 1940s there had been numerous roles for strong-minded, assertive career women. Rosalind Russell played the no-nonsense female reporter who exposed corruption in high places in *His Girl Friday* (1938); Katharine Hepburn was cast as a world-renowned expert on international relations in *Woman of the Year* (1942); and one should not forget that Vivien Leigh's Scarlett O'Hara restored her family's fortunes through grit and guts out of the wreckage of the Civil War in *Gone with the Wind* (1939). Other actresses of that era—Bette Davis, Joan Crawford, Carol Lombard, Greta Garbo—more than held their own with such strong leading men as Clark Gable, Spencer Tracy, and Humphrey Bogart; indeed, they often carried the film.

By the mid-1950s many of the same actresses were playing neurotic, love-starved females whose only hope for fulfillment was through the love of a man. In *All about Eve* (1950), Bette Davis, as Margo Channing, realizes that despite a triumphant stage career her life at age forty is empty without marriage. As the film ends, she willingly gives away a major part to a conniving ingenue whom she detests in order to marry her director. In *Sunset Boulevard* (1950), Gloria Swanson, a dominant actress of the 1920s, plays a has-been silent film star so desperate for a man that she murders her young lover in a jealous rage. Katharine Hepburn, who more than held her ground with Spencer Tracy in numerous films of the 1940s, played neurotic sex-starved spinsters in *African Queen* (1951), *Summertime* (1955), and *Rainmaker* (1956). Joan Crawford, who had won an Academy Award playing a single mother determined to make a life for her ungrateful daughter in *Mildred Pierce* (1945), took on a slightly different persona after the war. In the 1950s she made a career playing disturbed and sexually repressed middle-aged women in a series of forgettable films.

In contrast to the sex-starved spinsters were the sex goddesses: Marilyn Monroe, Jayne Mansfield, Jane Russell. Their films usually had them in tight sweaters or with low necklines. Even so, their sexuality was kept within limits, and in most of these films they too found their fulfillment in marriage. Hollywood saw no need to be subtle about it: one of Monroe's early films was titled *How to Marry a Millionaire* (1953). The idealization of marriage and motherhood went beyond the movies. Women were marrying earlier, having children younger, and dropping out of college in greater numbers. Fewer were entering professional schools or pursuing advanced degrees.[61]

Feminist writer Betty Friedan in her 1963 best-seller, *The Feminine Mystique*, argued that such idealization of domesticity stunted women's growth, discouraged careers, and denied them opportunities for individual achievement and personal identity. The success of Friedan's book was strong evidence that its themes made sense to many. Nonetheless, the reality for women in the 1950s was more complicated than Friedan's cultural stereotype. Not all women were trapped at home or lost without marriage. Despite the marriage boom, the baby boom, and discriminatory barriers, married and unmarried women were joining the workforce in increasing numbers and were actively participating in politics and community life. A study of popular women's magazines of the 1950s found that "they included stories that glorified domesticity, but they also expressed ambivalence about domesticity, endorsed women's nondomestic activity, and celebrated women's public success."[62]

If there was dissatisfaction during the 1950s, much of it may have come from the inflated hopes that the postwar era would usher in a new age. Peace and prosperity would allow people to find greater meaning and satisfaction in their lives. Against these expectations any reality was bound to be disappointing. Social critics such as William Whyte and David Reisman felt that the culture of large corporations was stamping out the remnants of American individualism. In *The Organization Man*, Whyte wrote of a new American character emerging from the large corporations, the law firms, and the universities, one that prized cooperation and conformity over competition and individualism. In *The Lonely Crowd*, David Reisman described a new "other-directed" personality who, lacking an internalized set of beliefs, was concerned about status, eager to please, and skilled at manipulating others.[63] American suburban life was seen as an extension of the developments that produced the organization man and other-directed personality. Suburbia became a favorite subject of social critics. They thought that housing developments, consumerism, and mindless conformity threatened individuality and diversity. Books titled *Cracks in the Picture Window* and *The Split-Level Trap* appeared on best-seller lists.

A later social historian, Geoffrey Perrett, believes that the social criticism of the period was "little more than the scorn of the educated and the sophisticated for ordinary people doing ordinary things." He argues that the suburban stereotype was broadly overdone: "The spreading of huge organizations, the rapidity of technological change, the rise of suburbia, the standardization of life posed new challenges, but for the most part people coped with them. That may not be very dramatic. But it is the truth of daily life as most people knew it and lived it."[64] Suburban life was not monolithic. Communities varied in style, economic class, and political viewpoint. Friendships were made that lasted lifetimes, and voluntary associations helped to build genuine communities. But the culture of the personal invariably focused on discontent, and discontent, not contentment, was what usually fascinated intellectuals and critics. As is often the case, the popular culture was sending contradictory signals.

The Seeds of
Political and Social Discontent

On the surface, the mid-1950s were an unusually stable period. Much of the anti-Communist hysteria had ebbed; inflation was virtually nonexistent; and the economy was producing jobs and higher wages. Yet the seeds of political and social discontent began to sprout.

In November 1955 a new periodical, *National Review*, made its appearance. Edited by the young William F. Buckley, Jr., its purpose was to revitalize American conservatism and liberate it from the dead hand of Modern Republicanism. In the first issue, Buckley brashly proclaimed that *National Review* "stands athwart history yelling Stop." The magazine soon became a vehicle of conservative criticism of the Eisenhower administration. In 1956, Buckley declared that Eisenhower's first term was distinguished by "its easy and whole-hearted acceptance of the great statist legacy of the New Deal."[65] *National Review*'s persistent criticism of Eisenhower, who remained personally popular throughout both his terms in office, was a reminder that conservatism was still an isolated intellectual movement.

It would take several decades and the election of Ronald Reagan (who was a long-time subscriber to *National Review*) for the movement to become mainstream. Nonetheless, the magazine's appearance at the height of the Eisenhower era was a sign that consensus would not last forever. Throughout the 1950s, *National Review* would be the vehicle for numerous conservative polemics against liberal statism at home and accommodation to communism abroad. As Frank Meyer, one of its editors, claimed, conservatives wanted to roll back both the Iron Curtain and the Roosevelt Revolution.[66]

During his second term, events began to disturb the Eisenhower quietude. The shift began with the Soviet launch of *Sputnik*, the first earth-orbiting satellite, in 1957. This first Cold War challenge to American scientific superiority spawned fears that the Soviets would soon gain the advantage in the emerging ballistic missile technology. Its success emboldened the Soviet Union. In 1958, Soviet leader Nikita Khrushchev demanded that the Allied forces leave West Berlin within six months. Editorial pages and journals of opinion were filled with articles about the loss of American national purpose. Eisenhower's calm leadership, so highly praised by many in the mid-1950s, was now criticized as unfocused and passive, and such criticism was not limited to the pages of *National Review*. A report commissioned by the government and delivered to Eisenhower's National Security Council called for a dramatic increase in defense spending on everything from ballistic missiles to conventional forces to fallout shelters. In the same year as the *Sputnik* launch, Harvard economist John Kenneth Galbraith published *The Affluent Society*, an attack on the conspicuous consumption of Americans at the expense of schools, highways, and scientific research.

Criticism came from all sides. Hard-line anti-Communists were concerned that America was losing the arms race to the Soviet Union and warned of a "missile gap." Liberals, picking up on Galbraith's criticism, felt that the public sector had been ignored and allowed to deteriorate under the Eisenhower administration. Commentators as varied as labor leader George Meany, columnist Walter Lippmann, and Harvard professor Henry Kissinger were lamenting the loss of national purpose.

Ike was increasingly portrayed as lazy and out of touch. Yet despite his increasing age and indirect style of governing, he was anything but. In foreign policy he was actively using the Central Intelligence Agency (CIA) to subvert unfriendly governments in such far-flung places as Laos, Indonesia, and the Congo. He sent marines to Lebanon in the summer of 1958 to prevent a Communist coup (which was in fact a remote possibility). In defense policy he refused to be pressured into spending more than he thought necessary. For one thing, he knew from highly secret air reconnaissance flights that the Soviet Union's missile program posed little threat to American superiority. Nuclear weapons had one purpose in Eisenhower's mind: they would provide a means to prevent all wars. These weapons could serve as a comparatively inexpensive and effective deterrent to future Koreas, as well as to a full-scale nuclear exchange, without the interminable piling on of conventional weapons.

Eisenhower was eager to begin an arms control and diplomatic dialogue with Khrushchev and to reach an agreement on limiting nuclear testing and perhaps resolving the perennial question of Berlin.[67] In 1959 the two leaders met at the Camp David presidential retreat, and Khrushchev agreed to withdraw his Berlin ultimatum. With tension eased, a summit conference of the leaders of the United States, Britain, France, and the Soviet Union was planned for May 1960 in Paris, with the expectation that it could result in a nuclear test ban agreement. In that event, Eisenhower would have outflanked his foreign policy critics and brought about a significant reduction in Cold War tensions.

Such hopes were dashed on May 1, 1960, when a U-2 reconnaissance plane was shot down by Soviet rocket fire. The pilot, a CIA employee named Gary Francis Powers, was captured; when interrogated, he confessed to spying. Khrushchev had known about the flights since their inception in 1956, but since he was powerless to stop them, he had been reluctant to acknowledge their existence. The downing of Powers's plane gave Khrushchev his opening. When he arrived in Paris, he demanded as a precondition for the summit conference that Eisenhower apologize for the flights, suspend them in the future, and punish those connected with them. When Eisenhower rejected these demands, Khrushchev stormed out of the conference and refused to negotiate with the American president during the remainder of his term.

As if the U-2 incident and the failure of the Paris summit were not enough to rekindle Cold War tension, problems were also mounting in Southeast Asia and Cuba. In January 1959, Fidel Castro seized power in Cuba, overthrowing a corrupt but pro-American dictator. Soon Castro was executing his opponents, expropriating American property, denouncing Yankee imperialism, and making diplomatic overtures to the Soviets. In South Vietnam the pro-American government of Ngo Dinh Diem was facing a growing threat from guerrillas supported by the Communist government of Ho Chi Minh in North Vietnam.

Many who were critical of Eisenhower thought he was not pursuing the Cold War with sufficient vigilance. Frank Meyer wrote, "The net balance of 1959, after six years of an administration brought into power by the basic backing of conservative votes, registers an immense slippage of our will to resist Communism and in our position vis-à-vis Communism."[68]

Another group, outside the American cultural and political mainstream, considered the entire culture of the Cold War tiresome and irrelevant. These poets and writers, labeled "Beats" or "Beatniks" and based primarily in San Francisco and New York, expressed in vigorous and often sexually explicit poetry and prose their contempt for the Cold War and the arms race as well as American materialism, conformity, and sexual restrictiveness. Writing in cadences inspired by improvisational jazz, Jack Kerouac's *On the Road* (1957) became a Beat classic. It was a novel of back-road America and back-seat sex. In its most familiar passage, Kerouac wrote, "The only people for me are the mad ones, the ones who are mad to live, mad to talk, mad to be saved, desirous of everything at the same time, the ones who never yawn or say a commonplace thing, but burn, burn, burn like fabulous roman candles exploding like spiders across the stars."[69] Allen Ginsberg's poem *Howl* (1956)—with its often-quoted lines "I have seen the best minds of my generation destroyed by madness, starving hysterical naked / dragging themselves through the negro streets at dawn looking for an angry fix"[70]—was explicit in its homosexual references. Ginsberg, Kerouac, and others became cult heroes to many young followers. *On the Road* received a rave review in the *New York Times* and catapulted onto the best-seller list.

Censorship laws had kept most sexually explicit fiction off the shelves. When Grove Press, in 1959, attempted to distribute an unexpurgated version of D. H. Lawrence's *Lady Chatterley's Lover*, Post-master General Arthur Summerfield sought to have it barred from the mail. When the Supreme Court upheld a lower court order overturning the ban, literary censorship was virtually over in America. The same year, Grove Press published another novel far more shocking than anything D. H. Lawrence might have imagined. It was William Burroughs's *Naked Lunch*, written from the perspective of a deranged drug addict. Pessimistic and violent, Burroughs's novel won notoriety by its sheer audacity and became as important as *On the Road* to the Beat movement.

Despite the favorable *Times* review of *On the Road*, however, most critics ridiculed the Beats and their work. A 1959 article in *Life* sneered at them as the "Only Revolution Around." The poet Edith Sitwell called *Naked Lunch* "psychopathological filth." In one sense the Beats were a cultural freak show for mainstream America. The few who took them more seriously were horrified by what they found. Norman Podhoretz, later a leading voice of neoconservatism, considered them cultural juvenile delinquents. In his view, theirs was "a movement of brute stupidity and know-nothingism that is trying to take over the country from a middle class which is supposed to be the guardian of civilization but which has practically dislocated its shoulder in its eagerness to throw in the towel."[71]

The Beats brought a message that many of Podhoretz's generation could neither understand nor appreciate. The generation of the Great Depression and World War II treasured security and stability. For the next generation, raised on television and accustomed to affluence, security seemed boring. They could not even adopt the same heroes. Eisenhower was curiously remote to them, more a grandfather figure than the inspiring war leader he had been to their parents. The alternative to Eisenhower's Modern Republicanism, the legalistic and programmatic liberalism of the New Deal and Fair Deal, was equally uninspiring to those who danced to rock and roll, dug Elvis, and found the Beats fascinating.

In the late 1950s popular stand-up comedians Lenny Bruce and Mort Sahl made political satire the centerpiece of their acts. They treated the Cold War with a degree of levity and skepticism unheard of during the early 1950s. Sahl quipped that "every time the Russians throw an American in jail, the [House Un-American Activities] Committee throws an American in jail to get even," and that "maybe the Russians will steal all our secrets. Then they'll be two years behind."[72]

Bruce's satire had a harder, more graphic edge. Castro had ruined Cuba for American tourists, he mockingly complained: "You can get no narcotics, no abortions, there's no prostitutes there." Bruce's life and his act became increasingly outrageous. After numerous arrests on obscenity and narcotics charges, Lenny Bruce died in 1966 of causes unknown. Mort Sahl's career continued into the 1960s, but later changes in the culture made his humor seem a bit tame.

Political radicals, marginalized in the Eisenhower years, began to understand the potential for their movement in the Beats' message. David McReynolds, a longtime pacifist and radical, understood this immediately. He wrote in 1959, "The beat generation by its very existence serves notice on all of us who are political that if we want to involve youth in politics we must develop a politics of action. The beat generation can understand Gandhi much better than they can Roosevelt."[73]

McReynolds's reference to Gandhi proved to be prophetic in a region distant from the San Francisco coffeehouses where Ginsberg and others read their poetry to a rapt audience: it was in the South and in the context of race. White southern leadership had steadfastly avoided implementing the Supreme Court's historic *Brown v. Board of Education* (1954) decision that declared state-supported segregation unconstitutional. In 1957 a federal court had ordered that nine black students be admitted to Central High School in Little Rock, Arkansas. Governor Orval Faubus, playing to white fears and racial hatreds, ordered the Arkansas National Guard to surround the school on opening day to prevent the black students from entering. President Eisenhower, after unsuccessfully haggling with Governor Faubus, was eventually forced to send troops into Little Rock to enforce the court order. It was an awkward moment for Eisenhower, who had never publicly endorsed *Brown* or taken an unequivocal position against school segregation. Although he later signed two modest civil rights bills affecting voting rights, neither the president nor the Congress had any taste for confronting the broad question of racial segregation and discrimination.

The patience of black Americans, however, was running out. A new generation of black people was prepared to move the issue out of the courtroom—where most civil rights battles had been fought—and into the streets, where real pressure might be brought to bear. The 1955 Montgomery, Alabama, bus boycott had been only a slight glimmer of what was to come. Boycotts and court suits were one thing; frontal assaults on public accommodations (restaurants, hotels, theaters, sports arenas) that practiced racial discrimination were another. Precisely such a challenge occurred on February 1, 1960, in Greensboro, North Carolina. Four students from North Carolina A&T, an all-black state school, became instant heroes on campus when they staged a sit-in at the whites-only lunch counter of the local Woolworth store. The action electrified black students across the South. By the end of the month sit-in campaigns had been organized in thirty-one southern cities. Committed to a nonviolent approach, the movement was soon under the leadership of Dr. Martin Luther King, Jr., and his Southern Christian Leadership Conference. The Reverend Douglas Moore, one of King's close associates, commented, "If Woolworth and the other stores think this is just another panty raid, they haven't had their sociologists in the field."[74] These were indeed no panty raids. Breaking the mold of their apolitical white contemporaries and discomforting older civil rights leaders, black students soon formed their own organization, the Student Nonviolent Coordinating Committee (SNCC).

Several months after the Greensboro sit-ins a group of primarily white students in San Francisco gave another warning that the silent generation was about to find its voice. They gathered at the city hall on May 13, 1960, to protest the scheduled hearings of the House Un-American Activities Committee; when denied the right to attend the hearings, they adopted the tactic of the black students and sat down in the rotunda. The police attacked the student protesters with fire hoses and clubs and even hurled some down the marble steps of the building. The event was startling. No one had previously dared confront HUAC so brazenly; most Americans were terrified of even coming into contact with the committee. But in Greensboro and San Francisco a new spirit of defiance was born. The formless and apolitical nature of youth rebellion was beginning to take on a clear political cast. As sociologist Todd Gitlin explains it, "Between the sit-ins and the anti-HUAC demonstration, the Fifties expired."[75]

Historians differ as to the significance of the 1950s. William Chafe sees the decade as time of contradictions and paradoxes, "diversity in the face of uniformity, the creation of close-knit communities despite massive mobility, changes in sex roles occurring in the face of the 'feminine mystique,' the emergence of cultural rebels in the midst of chilling conformity."[76] William L. O'Neill has written that critics failed to understand much of what happened in the 1950s. The arts flowered, inflation was brought under control, people were better fed and housed, and schools were built to keep up with the baby boom. O'Neill concludes, "It is true that the popular culture was unexciting . . . and the family-oriented, suburban style of living wanting in charm or distinction. The fact remains that these were years of real progress for ordinary Americans."[77]

The 1960s and the Rebirth of Reform

In the 1960 Democratic presidential nominating contest, Sen. John F. Kennedy of Massachusetts was the candidate of the political center—slightly to the right of Adlai Stevenson and slightly to the left of Lyndon Johnson. Kennedy had carefully staked out mainstream positions on civil rights, economic growth, and foreign policy. Although many of the party elders, including former President Truman, were wary of this rich, young, ambitious senator, and others feared the country would not elect a Catholic president, his appeal defied rational politics and spoke to the emerging spirit of the decade. When he entered the party convention in Los Angeles, his well-oiled political organization rolled over the opposition, and he was nominated on the first ballot. Kennedy intrigued even the novelist Norman Mailer, who has admired few politicians. Writing about the Democratic National Convention for *Esquire* in a piece entitled, "Superman Comes to the Supermarket," he presented Kennedy as an existential hero who would help the country "recover its imagination, its pioneer lust for the unexpected and incalculable."[78] Mailer saw that Kennedy the politician was far less interesting than Kennedy the celebrity—the war hero and PT boat captain swimming five miles to shore carrying one of his injured crew, the glamorous politician escorting his dazzling young wife, the Catholic politician going face to face with a group of Baptist ministers on the issue of church and state and winning them over, the author recovering from a near fatal back operation to write the Pulitzer Prize-winning historical biography *Profiles in Courage* (1956).

It cannot be said that John Kennedy's victory over Richard Nixon in the 1960 presidential election was a triumph of ideas or a major advance for American liberalism. Kennedy's call for a New Frontier sounded more exciting than Nixon's dogged prose, but in reality the two disagreed on precious little. Both supported more defense spending and modest growth of the welfare state. The religious issue neutralized itself, with Kennedy winning as many Republican Catholics as he lost Democratic Protestants. But his eloquence, self-confidence, and dash as demonstrated in the television debates were in sharp contrast to the dourness of Richard Nixon, who was actually only several years older yet was characterized as a "young fogy." Kennedy instinctively understood the new medium that would transform American politics. He was not a passionate orator in the style of nineteenth- and early-twentieth-century politicians. Such histrionics were not suited for television. He was cool, understated, self-confident, articulate, and terse. As president, he was the first to hold live televised press conferences and invite network anchors into the White House for televised interviews.

JFK brought the term "style" into the political lexicon and sought to elevate the nation's cultural tastes, which many liberals thought were symbolized by President Eisenhower's affinity for detective and western novels and music by Fred Waring. It was common for artists and intellectuals to belittle the state of American culture in the late 1950s. Nobel Prize author William Faulkner lamented in 1958, "The artist has no more actual value in the American culture than he has in the American economy of today, no place at all in the warp and woof, the thews and sinews, the mosaic of the American dream."[79] Kennedy invited more than fifty prominent writers, composers, and painters— including John Steinbeck, W. H. Auden, Alexis Leger, John Hersey, and Robert Lowell—to his inaugural and asked Robert Frost to read a poem for the occasion.

In a conscious effort to elevate the role of the arts in American life, President and Mrs. Kennedy invited the noted cellist Pablo Casals to perform at the White House and hosted dinners honoring the Western Hemisphere's Nobel laureates, the French writer André Malraux, and the composer Igor Stravinsky. The composer Leonard Bernstein was so impressed by the party for Casals that he lauded the Kennedy administration as "a remarkable combination of informality and stateliness . . . casualness and majesty."[80] Kennedy brought the intellectual elite into the corridors of power and used the influence of the presidency to elevate their status. He staffed his administration with numerous academics and Rhodes scholars; prestigious appointments were given to two leading liberal intellectuals: Arthur Schlesinger, Jr. (special adviser to the president), and John Kenneth Galbraith (ambassador to India). In contrast, the Eisenhower administration had been peopled largely by businessmen, lawyers, and bankers.

Not all intellectuals were impressed. The literary critic Alfred Kazin wrote in the American Scholar that "Kennedy's shrewd awareness of what intellectuals can do, even his undoubted inner respect for certain writers, scholars and thinkers, is irrelevant to the tragic issues and contributes nothing to their solution. To be an 'intellectual' is the latest style in American success, the mark of our manipulable society."[81]

Despite its early love affair with liberal intellectuals, the Kennedy administration's contribution to the liberal agenda, measured by its legislative achievements, was modest. A few measures did pass—an increase in the minimum wage, an economic development program for Appalachia, the Peace Corps, and an extension of unemployment insurance—but they did not substantially enlarge or transform the nature of the welfare state. Those that would—aid to education and Medicare—languished in the Congress, which was still controlled by the conservative coalition of Republicans and Southern Democrats that had kept the New Deal and Fair Deal under wraps since 1938. Despite the blandishments of civil rights leaders, his own campaign pledges, the depth of southern resistance, and the persistence of the sit-in movement, Kennedy refused to invest his political capital in civil rights.

Much of Kennedy's domestic program was designed to gain the confidence of business leaders, many of whom had been suspicious of him and his liberal advisers. Before he considered any reduction in personal income taxes, Kennedy proposed a business tax credit whereby companies could deduct from their taxes up to 7 percent of the cost of new investment. In 1962 he put the full force of his administration behind the Trade Expansion Act, which gave the president authority to negotiate tariff reductions with the European Common Market. Export-minded companies such as IBM, Ford, Heinz, Standard Oil, and Pillsbury worked closely with the president.

Kennedy's relations with the business community received a serious setback as the result of an unpleasant confrontation with the leaders of the steel industry. In April 1962, infuriated by the decision of Roger Blough, the president of U.S. Steel, and other companies to raise the price of steel six dollars per ton, Kennedy took the industry to task. In a televised statement he lacerated "a tiny handful of steel executives whose pursuit of private power and profit exceeds their sense of public responsibility."[82] He threatened a price-fixing investigation and a review of their defense contracts. The companies capitulated, and all withdrew the increase. It was a Pyrrhic victory for the administration, however. The president was branded as "anti-business," and on May 25, 1962, the Dow-Jones average went into a decline; by June it had lost 27 percent of its December 1961 value.

Fearing that the economy was headed for a downturn that some would surely call the "Kennedy recession" and eager to soothe the businessmen, Kennedy proposed a tax cut that would reduce the corporate income tax from 52 to 47 percent and the top marginal tax rate from 91 to 70 percent. Soon the business community was working closely with the administration to push the tax bill through Congress. Medicare, aid to education, and civil rights were on the back burner, and Kennedy was pursuing an economic policy focused more on increasing economic growth and retaining business confidence than on advancing liberal reform. (Thirty-five years later, conservative Republicans were holding up his reduction of the top marginal tax rates as a model of supply-side economics.)

Kennedy's foreign and defense policies were slightly more hawkish than Eisenhower's, and Cold War tensions heightened. In the face of clear evidence, also known to Ike, that no missile gap existed, Kennedy began a substantial defense buildup and accelerated the ballistic missile program. He also approved (and later regretted) the CIA plan for the Bay of Pigs invasion of Cuba and increased American military presence in Vietnam. When Kennedy and Khrushchev met in the summer of 1961 in Vienna, they made no progress on any issues, and neither side showed any flexibility in negotiations over a nuclear test ban. In August, Soviet-American relations worsened: the Soviets began the construction of the Berlin Wall, and Kennedy responded by calling up army reserve units and further increasing the defense budget.

With the possible exception of the Peace Corps program, the first two years of the Kennedy administration did not capture the energy and imagination of disaffected youth, particularly college students fascinated by the Beats and the energy of the black students' sit-ins. Like Truman's and Eisenhower's, Kennedy's cautious centrism continued to leave ideologues, on both the left and the right, outside the circles of power and influence. Vital center liberalism had excluded many on the left who desired both radical domestic change and accommodation with the Soviets. Those on the right saw even the modest liberal accomplishments of the Kennedy administration as moving the country inexorably toward greater state control of American life. Modern Republicanism under the Eisenhower administration had given little solace to those who wished to see a rollback of the welfare state and the Soviet Empire. There was more conservative dissatisfaction with the state of the Republican Party than with the Kennedy administration, from which they expected little. Richard Nixon, as the 1960 Republican nominee, had spent much of his time wooing Governor Nelson Rockefeller of New York, the leader of the party's liberal wing. The two had met prior to the national convention at Governor Rockefeller's Fifth Avenue apartment and issued a statement known as the Compact of Fifth Avenue. It was marked by Nixon's acceptance of Rockefeller's suggestions for the party platform, calling for a more activist economic policy and greater support for civil rights.[83] In addition to that capitulation, Nixon rubbed salt in conservative wounds by selecting as his running mate UN Ambassador Henry Cabot Lodge, who as senator from Massachusetts had been a leader in the 1952 presidential nomination campaign for Eisenhower against the conservative hero Sen. Robert A. Taft.

Disappointed by Nixon's behavior and the general direction of the Republican Party, William F. Buckley, Jr., in September 1960 invited eighty young conservatives to meet at his home in Sharon, Connecticut. Out of that conference came a new organization known as Young Americans for Freedom (YAF) and a new statement of conservative principles called the Sharon Statement. Written by Yale student M. Stanton Evans and edited by Buckley, the statement was an effort to fuse three elements within the conservative movements: traditionalists who sought to anchor society in a transcendent moral order based on religious commitment; libertarians who regarded economic and personal freedom from state control as the supreme value; and anti-Communists who demanded not an accommodation with but a triumph over Marxism.

Eisenhower had steered the Republican Party toward the center of American politics. Under such conditions, it was difficult for a major Republican to take on the mantle of conservative leadership and oppose the popular president. No such figure had emerged since Taft's death in 1953. Nixon's appeasement of the Rockefeller wing and his subsequent defeat by John Kennedy changed all that. About the same time that YAF was founded and the Sharon Statement was written, Sen. Barry Goldwater (R-AZ) wrote (with the assistance of Buckley's brother-in-law, L. Brent Bozell) *Conscience of a Conservative*. The book was an effort to develop a coherent conservative critique that would reach a broad audience and perhaps galvanize a movement. In it Goldwater denounced "the natural tendency of government to expand in the direction of absolutism."[84] He called for a strict construction of the Constitution and a new respect for the Tenth Amendment's protection of states' rights. Being a good party man, Goldwater refused to challenge Nixon and agreed to endorse him at the Republican National Convention. But in a dramatic moment he took the podium and addressed the disaffected delegates: "Let's grow up, conservatives. If we want to take this party back, and I think we can some day, let's get to work."[85] By 1964 his book had gone into twenty printings and sold over three million copies. A new conservative hero had emerged, but the movement was still on the fringes.

The growing tension of the nuclear arms buildup and the civil rights movement eventually forced Kennedy out of his cautious centrism. The Cuban missile crisis of October 1962 brought the United States and the Soviet Union to the brink of nuclear war. Only a last-minute compromise, whereby Khrushchev agreed to remove the Soviet missiles from Cuba and Kennedy pledged not to sponsor an invasion of the island, averted possible catastrophe. The crisis chastened Kennedy and increased his concern about the dangers of a continual arms race. In June 1963 at American University he delivered a major address on the dangers of nuclear war. The United States and the Soviet Union, he told his audience, had "a mutually deep interest in a just and genuine peace and in halting the arms race. . . . And if we cannot end now our differences, at least we can help make the world safe for diversity. For, in the final analysis, our most basic common link is that we all inhabit this small planet. We all breathe the same air. We all cherish our children's future. And we are all mortal."[86]

That summer Kennedy and Khrushchev negotiated the Limited Nuclear Test Ban Treaty banning all such tests in the atmosphere, outer space, and under water. Although the treaty had only a marginal impact on the development of nuclear technology, it was signed by more than one hundred nations and helped to retard the proliferation of nuclear weapons in nonnuclear states. Yet this first major nuclear arms control agreement of the Cold War had chiefly symbolic importance. It did not alleviate the growing fear of nuclear war that, in the minds of many Americans, was assuming an even greater importance than the fear of communism.

During 1961 and 1962, Kennedy had frustrated the leaders of the civil rights movement, who had expected him to make their cause a major priority of his administration. He told Martin Luther King, Jr., Roy Wilkins, and others that any effort to push civil rights legislation would only alienate Southern Democrats, whose support he needed for aid to education and an increased minimum wage, both of which would be of benefit to blacks. Still, in those years Kennedy did take a number of civil rights steps through executive action. He placed a larger number of blacks in senior positions, issued a strong executive order against racial discrimination in government hiring, and brought more government suits against voter discrimination. When the governor of Mississippi, Ross Barnett, refused to obey a federal order allowing a black student, James Meredith, to attend the University of Mississippi, Kennedy ordered troops to the campus to enforce the order and protect Meredith from mob violence. Yet the intractable problems remained untouched: most schools in the South were still segregated; the voting rights bill had done little for Negro enfranchisement; public accommodations, despite the sit-in movements, remained closed to blacks. Martin Luther King, Jr., feared that unless there was a dramatic breakthrough in the struggle for civil rights, his campaign of non-violence would lose support among a younger generation of blacks.

In November 1962 the prominent black writer James Baldwin published an essay in *The New Yorker* titled "Letter from a Region of My Mind." Baldwin wrote eloquently of the depth of black anger and warned of future violent confrontation: "There is no reason that black men should be expected to be more patient, more forbearing, more farseeing than whites; indeed, quite the contrary."[87] Baldwin's words would prove prophetic.

In the spring of 1963 the tensions escalated when King had organized a massive campaign against discrimination in Birmingham, Alabama. The city police commissioner, Eugene "Bull" Connor, proved at great cost to be a perfect foil. He arrested King twice, and during an Easter weekend while incarcerated, King wrote one of his most memorable statements, "Letter from Birmingham Jail." Infuriated by the persistence of the civil rights marchers, Connor used attack dogs on long leashes and high-pressure fire hoses against crowds that included many young children. He actually hauled two thousand children off to jail.

As the scene of the first major racial demonstration to be carried live on television, Birmingham brought the issue to the forefront of American life. Kennedy realized he could no longer argue that the rest of his program took precedence. The civil rights movement now held the potential for violence that would, among other things, do great damage to America's image as the leader of the free world. In a June 11, 1963, national television address, therefore, the president announced his support for a new civil rights bill whose major provision would eliminate racial discrimination in public accommodations. Although the content of the bill was modest (it did not include sections on employment or voting rights), Kennedy's speech established a clear moral context. This was, he said, "a moral issue as old as the scriptures and as clear as the American Constitution. . . . A great change is at hand, and our task is that revolution, that change, be peaceful and constructive for all." He would ask Congress to make the commitment "that race has no place in American life or law."[88] In response, Dr. King, who had been critical of Kennedy's caution, praised the speech as "one of the most eloquent, profound, and unequivocal pleas for Justice and Freedom of all men ever made by any president. You spoke passionately to the moral issues involved in the integration struggle."[89] Tragically, the next evening, NAACP field secretary Medgar Evers was assassinated by a sniper in front of his home as he was returning from a meeting.

The Birmingham demonstrations, the Kennedy speech, and the Medgar Evers murder had turned the civil rights issue into a national crisis. During the early summer of 1963 there had been 758 racial demonstrations and 14,733 arrests in 186 American cities. To focus national attention, unify the movement, and increase the pressure on Kennedy and the Congress, major civil rights leaders organized the March on Washington for August 28. The march, which attracted around 250,000 people of whom about 20 percent were white, was the occasion for Dr. King's famous "I Have a Dream" speech. Attended by numerous celebrities, the event was nonviolent and inspiring, but it did little to move Kennedy's civil rights bill through Congress.

At the time of his assassination on November 22, 1963, not only was President Kennedy's civil rights bill bogged down in the Congress but so were his other programs—Medicare, federal aid to education, and even his tax bill. The assassination in Dallas had repercussions that have affected Americans for decades, deepening our sense of vulnerability, heightening our paranoia and susceptibility to conspiracy theories, and perhaps diminishing our self-confidence. Yet in the short run his death gave a boost to his programs and to the overall liberal agenda. Although Kennedy's visit to Texas had nothing to do with civil rights, his assassination made him a martyr to that cause. His successor, Vice President Lyndon Baines Johnson, was a former Senate majority leader and a gifted practitioner of Washington politics. The son of a progressive Texas state senator, he wanted to make his mark in history as a friend of the little people. Johnson knew that in the wake of Kennedy's assassination those issues attached to his name would be considered tributes to his memory. Johnson reenergized the legislative struggle for civil rights, strengthened Kennedy's original bill by adding a fair employment section, garnered moderate Republican support, broke the southern filibuster in the Senate, and gained its passage in early 1964.

Johnson, far more than Kennedy, had faith in the capacity of government to alleviate, if not solve, the problems of society. He wanted to take full advantage of the opportunity and set his sights on fulfilling the liberal agenda. He was eager to have his name placed beside that of Franklin D. Roosevelt, of whom as a young congressman he had been a loyal follower and protégé. On the very evening following Kennedy's assassination, Johnson said to his advisers, "Do you realize that every issue that is on my desk tonight was on my desk when I came to Congress in 1937?"[90]

Johnson may have been exaggerating, as was his habit, but he was not far off the mark. No second act had yet followed Roosevelt's New Deal. Even though both Truman's Fair Deal and Kennedy's New Frontier contained the same essential elements—aid to education, civil rights, and federal health insurance—neither president saw any of these measures reach his desk. Johnson, as a legislative leader, had won a reputation for building consensus and finding points of agreement. As president, he wished to build a new political consensus around a liberal agenda. Unlike Roosevelt, who had branded his opponents in the business community as "economic royalists," Johnson sought to persuade them that an effective social policy could create stability and enhance the system. The early 1960s was a time of prosperity and abundance that made the country more receptive to liberal ideas. The Kennedy tax cut that Johnson steered through Congress in 1964 helped to trigger an economic boom that lasted throughout the decade. Such conditions, combined with the Democratic congressional majorities, gave Johnson his opportunity.

In 1962, Michael Harrington, a young social democrat, had written *The Other America*, graphic tales of the impoverished in Appalachia, New York's Bowery, and the barrios of the Southwest. Harrington claimed that as many as a quarter of Americans were still mired in poverty. The book received numerous laudatory reviews; in particular, one from the critic Dwight Macdonald in *The New Yorker* came to the attention of President Kennedy. Harrington's book and Kennedy's interest in it had brought the subject to public notice. Kennedy had asked his advisers to develop programs to deal with the problem of poverty, but at the time of his death nothing had been formulated.

Johnson called on his advisers to construct a legislative program and announced in 1964 his "War on Poverty." He presented the project not as an act of class warfare but as a method of turning dependent people into productive citizens. He even dubbed the bill the Economic Opportunity Act. In the Johnson style he mobilized the labor movement, civil rights leaders, big-city mayors, the National Council of Churches, and even the Chamber of Commerce. Cleverly, he funded the program at only $970 million, less than 1 percent of the federal budget. The bill, passed that fall, included a panoply of programs—Job Corps centers for training, a Neighborhood Youth Corps providing low-wage jobs for teens, a domestic peace corps, loans for small business and rural development, and community action programs for local initiatives— all under a new Office of Economic Opportunity.[91]

The bill was the embodiment of the belief that government intervention could solve the age-old problem of poverty without great cost or social division. What distinguished this effort from the New Deal was more than programmatic. The New Deal had sprung from bottom-up, grassroots demands for labor legislation, banking reform, and old age pensions. The antipoverty effort was the product of a new class of policy intellectuals: social scientists, lawyers, and social workers who had flocked to Washington in the Kennedy-Johnson years. Poverty, they assumed, resulted from behavioral pathologies that could be ameliorated by the right mix of interventionist strategies. For example, the Jobs Corps would provide remedial programs to make troubled teenagers employable; the Manpower Development program would train unemployed workers; Head Start would provide preschool education for poor children; Legal Services would give the poor access to the courts for class-action suits; and the Community Action Program would allow the federal government to contract with community groups to administer local antipoverty programs.[92]

In 1964 these hopes seemed reasonable. Disappointments would come later. Then, liberalism, with its generous and optimistic impulses, sat well with the American people, and many of its adherents assumed that it was about to enshrine itself, at last, as the centerpiece of the American political consensus. The 1964 election gave them every reason to believe that their hopes would be realized. The conservative wing of the Republican Party, largely based in the South and West, was responding to Goldwater's 1960 admonition to build its influence. The leading moderate candidate, Gov. Nelson A. Rockefeller of New York, had been tarnished by a somewhat scandalous divorce and lost to Goldwater in the crucial California primary. With Rockefeller out of the running, the moderate wing of the party could find no other champion, and Goldwater became the Republican nominee. He ran as a true believer in the conservative cause of small government. Opposed to the civil rights laws and the antipoverty program, disdainful even of the New Deal, he was the perfect foil for Lyndon Johnson.

Goldwater criticized such sacred New Deal cows as Social Security, the Tennessee Valley Authority (TVA), and farm price supports. "My aim," he openly admitted, "is not to pass laws but to repeal them." The major function of government, Goldwater believed, was national defense, and he thought the United States should pursue a policy of victory over communism even at the risk of war. Against Goldwater's radicalism, Johnson portrayed himself as the defender of the great American consensus. In a televised campaign speech he asserted, "We must decide whether we will move ahead by building on the solid structure of achievement created by forward looking men of both parties over the past thirty years. Or whether we will begin to tear down this structure and move in a radically new direction."[93]

The country apparently bought Johnson's argument and gave him a fifteen-million-vote victory over Goldwater. Equally important, the Democratic Party had gained 2 to 1 margins in both the House and the Senate, giving liberals in the Eighty-ninth Congress their first working majority since 1936. The stage was set for a major advance of their agenda. Having passed Kennedy's tax cut, the civil rights bill, and the antipoverty program in 1964, and now armed with his new congressional majority, Johnson had plans that would outstrip the New Deal, the Fair Deal, and the New Frontier in their scope. In a 1964 commencement address at the University of Michigan he unveiled his ambitious vision. "We have the opportunity," he told the graduates, "to move not only toward the rich society and the powerful society but upward to the Great Society. . . . It is a place where the city of man serves not only the needs of the body and the demands of commerce but the desire for beauty and the hunger for community. . . . It is a place where men are more concerned with the quality of their goals than the quantity of their goods."[94] Johnson believed that if government could end poverty, eliminate racial barriers, and stimulate economic growth, it could also provide clean air and water, consumer protection, arts and humanities support, more wilderness areas, college loans, and highway beautification. His legislative agenda, passed by a willing Congress, was designed to do precisely those things.

Despite the tragic death of John Kennedy, the early years of Lyndon Johnson's presidency marked the high point of twentieth-century

American liberalism. In a bountiful country such as America, much seemed possible. With enough resources, intelligence, and good will the Great Society could be constructed. Vietnam was still a minor insurgency requiring a relatively small military commitment and a modest percentage of the defense budget. After the Cuban missile crisis, relations with the Soviet Union had improved. No major crisis loomed between the two superpowers. The Berlin Wall, despite its grotesqueness, had prevented a mass exodus from East Germany and removed the city's potential to become a flash point in the Cold War. Negotiations on a treaty limiting the spread of nuclear weapons were also going forward.

Johnson seized this opportunity to push a large body of legislation through the cooperative Eighty-ninth Congress. At the top of the list were Medicare and federal aid to education—long-awaited promises dating back to President Truman. But as a man of sweeping ambition, Johnson was not content simply to fulfill the older agenda; he wanted to put his own stamp on American liberalism. During these heady months he signed a voting rights bill that guaranteed and protected black suffrage in the South; an immigration law that ended the bias in favor of northern Europeans; a housing bill that created a cabinet-level Department of Housing and Urban Development and included rent supplements for the poor; a higher-education bill that made grants to libraries and insured loan programs for college students. Having declared in his Great Society speech that Americans should be concerned with the quality of life as well as material conditions, he pushed through Congress the Water Quality Act of 1965, which mandated strict federal standards, and a bill establishing the National Endowment for the Arts and Humanities to subsidize deserving individuals and organizations.

As the historian Irwin Unger describes it, "The first session of the Eighty-ninth Congress was the high water mark of the Great Society." Columnist Tom Wicker put it more graphically in the summer of 1965: "They are rolling the bills out of Congress these days the way Detroit turns supersleek, souped-up autos off the assembly line. . . . The list of achievements is so long that it reads better than the legislative achievements of most two-term presidents."[95] The next year Congress added several more bills to Johnson's impressive list. The National Traffic and Motor Vehicle Safety Act authorized the Transportation Department to set auto safety standards; the Model Cities program was created to revitalize the social and physical environment of the inner cities; the Fair Packaging and Labeling Act was designed to protect the public from false advertising and shoddy goods. Great Society programs benefited the middle class as well as the poor and created new expectations and constituencies for government services. Medicare, environmental laws, consumer protection laws, aid to education, and subsidies for the arts and humanities appealed to a broad constituency. Medicare would become one of the most important and expensive entitlement programs ever designed—and a future budgetary headache.

Conservative critics of the Great Society argued that its programs undermined the values of hard work and self-reliance. Charles Murray, in his book *Losing Ground*, asserted that the expansion of welfare benefits such as Aid to Families with Dependent Children, Medicaid, and food stamps gave benefits to single mothers that a working-class husband might not be able to provide; consequently, the poor developed habits that trapped them in a life of poverty. The political scientist Lawrence Mead claimed that the education and training programs produced disappointing results and had little impact on "the skill of the recipients." On the other hand, Irwin Unger believes that the decline in poverty from 17.3 percent in 1965 to 12 percent in 1969 would not have occurred without the Great Society programs.[96] John E. Schwarz has argued that higher Social Security benefits and the Medicare program reduced poverty among the elderly by one-third and that Medicaid contributed substantially to the decline in black infant mortality from 1965 to 1972.[97]

Rebels at the Gates

Popular as his Great Society programs were at first, especially Medicare and aid to education, Johnson was riding a consensus that contained deep cracks, not immediately visible. Forces that had been bubbling beneath the surface since the late 1950s needed only a few flash points to erupt. The elements of combustibility were in place. The increasingly militant black leadership would not be satisfied with the passage of laws and the enforcement of constitutional rights. A backlash movement was taking root among working-class whites who gradually perceived the Great Society as indifferent to their concerns and catering instead to the special needs of the black community and to the favored causes (environmentalism and consumerism) of a liberal upper-middle-class elite. A growing left-radical youth movement held utopian visions of a participatory democracy and challenged the conservative social and sexual mores of the World War II generation. A more ideologically minded conservative movement was willing to challenge the very fundamentals of government-led social reform. Books, movies, and music were reflecting a tendency toward cultural iconoclasm. So long as the country was prosperous and at peace, these forces could be kept at bay, but it did not take a prophet to see their potential.

During the summer of 1962, inspired by the San Francisco HUAC demonstration and the boldness of SNCC, a group of students known as Students for a Democratic Society (SDS), under the tutelage of the social democratic League for Industrial Democracy, had met at a labor resort in Port Huron, Michigan. Led by two University of Michigan students, Al Haber and Tom Hayden, the group composed a manifesto for the student left. The Port Huron Statement began with a declaration designed to end the silence of the silent generation: "We are of the people of this generation, bred in at least modest comfort, housed now in universities, looking uncomfortably to the world we inherit." It showed a determination to break with both the old left ("the dreams of the older left were perverted by Stalinism and never recreated") and the end-of-ideology liberals ("the decline of utopia and hope is in fact one of the defining features of social life today"). In their place the authors called for a participatory democracy defined by two principles: "that the individual share in those social decisions determining the quality and direction of his life; that society be organized to encourage independence in men and provide the media for their common participation."

It was difficult to translate this romantic declaration into a workable political ideology and program. But these students were influenced by the audacity of the Beats, the existential heroes of Camus's novels, and the courage of the Greensboro sit-ins. As Tom Hayden later explained, "We believed in action. . . . Active participation. Citizenship. . . . By personally committing yourself and taking risks, you could enter history and try to change it."[98] They also attempted to reduce the attachment of the left to its European socialist roots and to cast it as a uniquely American phenomenon. Their vision of a decentralized and nonbureaucratic egalitarian society drew upon the mythology of late-eighteenth-century American democracy—the Jeffersonian self-governing village and the New England town meeting. In this break with the past traditions of the left, the Port Huron Statement and its SDS authors were creating what would be known as the New Left, or what they liked to call "the Movement."

Their first effort at organized participatory action came in the summer of 1964, when the SDS National Convention authorized the Economic Research and Action Project. Some 125 students went into the slums of several northern cities, including Newark, Boston, Cleveland, and Baltimore, to organize blacks around a radical political agenda. The disappointment was immediate. Few students could live on their meager allowance, and black activists were less and less inclined to accept white leadership. In most cities the project did not outlast the summer.[99]

Leaders of the student left soon realized that they would not have to journey into the inner city to find their most promising followers. The revelation came that fall at the University of California, Berkeley. After university officials decided to bar political activity from a part of the campus that had long been set aside for such advocacy, a worker from the Congress of Racial Equality (CORE) was arrested for setting up a table and soliciting funds. The students responded not with petitions and rallies but with the direct action techniques of the civil rights movement—sit-ins and the occupation of university facilities. That dispute ended peaceably with a compromise, but the student radicals had discovered a constituency among their own peers.

The Berkeley Free Speech Movement (FSM), as it was called, tapped a source of middle-class student alienation allegedly derived from the impersonality and bureaucratization of life in a large university. Although they did not actually use the term, what the students were asking for sounded like participatory democracy. As one defined it, "The students' basic demand is a demand to be heard, to be considered, to be taken into account when decisions concerning their education and their life in the university community are being made."[100] The cure for such alienation was action—direct and dramatic. Mario Savio, a leader of FSM, put it graphically in what was to become one of the most quoted speeches of the decade: "There is a time when the operation of the machine becomes so odious, makes you so sick at heart, that you can't take part; you can't even passively take part, and you've got to put your bodies upon the gears and upon the wheels, upon the levers, upon all the apparatus and you've got to make it stop." Still, despite the excitement and publicity surrounding the Berkeley demonstrations, student radicalism remained on the far fringes of American life, even campus life.

Other strands of cultural disrepair emerged during the presidential campaign of 1964. At the Democratic National Convention a largely black insurgent group of Mississippi delegates, known as the Mississippi Freedom Democratic Party, challenged the all-white regular delegation. The convention, under Johnson's orders, allowed only two of their delegates to be seated at large but promised that racial discrimination would be eliminated in the selection of delegates in the future. The agreement was considered a sellout by the younger and more militant faction of the civil rights movement, led by Stokely Carmichael of SNCC and Floyd McKissick of CORE. Each was deeply influenced by the separatist philosophy of Malcolm X and the radical Marxism of West Indian Frantz Fanon. Fanon's treatise *The Wretched of the Earth* indicted both European and American society for having colonized black people in Africa and America. Carmichael and McKissick were working to take over their respective organizations from leaders closer in spirit to Martin Luther King, Jr. In August 1965 the mood changed in the black community, making it more receptive to the appeals of radicalism and separatism. Rioting broke out in the black neighborhood of Watts in Los Angeles, leaving thirty-four dead, more than one thousand injured, and nearly one thousand buildings destroyed. The Great Society promises had not touched those in the inner cities affected by broken families, inadequate schools, rising crime and drug usage, and deep alienation from the broader white culture. Watts was the beginning of a series of inner-city riots that would plague the nation for the remainder of the decade and would provide a setting in which black radicalism could flourish.

Dissent from consensus in the 1960s was not limited to the left. Important stirrings were also felt on the right. As historian John A. Andrew III describes the decade, "It was not so much a radical decade as a polarized one."[101] Gov. George Wallace of Alabama had mounted an audacious challenge to Lyndon Johnson in presidential primaries in Wisconsin, Indiana, and Maryland, attacking Johnson's civil rights program and winning 30 to 43 percent of the Democratic vote. Wallace's support was found in the Italian, Polish, and Serbian communities of Milwaukee and among the steelworkers of Gary, Indiana, and Baltimore, Maryland. Out of the campaign came the phrase "white backlash" and, more important, powerful evidence that American liberalism was in danger of losing its hold on the white working class.

Many conservatives considered Goldwater's defeat not a humiliation but the beginning of a major political beachhead in the Republican Party. They saw his nomination as a major step in remaking the party into a strong conservative force that would challenge Great Society liberalism, not accommodate it. Despite Goldwater's massive defeat, the 1964 elections contained the elements of a conservative takeover. The Wallace campaign had tapped a source of discontent among northern white working-class voters who had been faithful to the Democrats since the 1930s. The Democrats' support for civil rights had also alienated many white voters in the South. Goldwater, breaking the historical pattern dating back to the Civil War, found his greatest support in that region; he carried Mississippi (with 87 percent of the vote), South Carolina, Louisiana, and Georgia. This was the beginning of a movement of southern whites into the Republican Party that has continued for decades. As the southern wing of the party increased in power and influence, it brought with it none of the Modern Republicanism of the Eisenhower era. With the exception of the defense budget and perhaps the space program, these voters increasingly saw the federal government as an intrusive irritant. Over time, the entire center of gravity in the Republican Party would shift to the right, making impossible the kind of comfortable consensus that prevailed in the 1950s. Ideological conservatives were also emboldened by the Goldwater candidacy. Many of those who had founded YAF in 1960 formed the American Conservative Union in 1964 to act as an organizational and ideological base for a takeover of the Republican Party.

Popular as well as political culture reflected a departure from earlier attitudes. For all the publicity and attention they garnered in the late 1950s, the Beats could be dismissed as a minor cultural sideshow. Nonetheless, their willingness to defy convention and question the values of the past did take root in novels, films, and critical essays of the early 1960s. Joseph Heller's *Catch-22* (1960) rendered World War II not as heroic drama but as theater of the absurd. According to the bombardier Yossarian, Heller's main character, the villain is not the Nazis but war itself. While the Germans are trying to shoot him down from the air, he muses, his own army is sending him up there to be killed: "They all wanted him dead." The novel gained a following even before Vietnam stirred a potent antiwar culture. It was read as a comic satire on a dehumanizing bureaucratized society, dealing with tragedy so as to make it a harbinger of a new cultural perspective. The existential hero of the 1950s was isolated in a despair considered endemic to the human condition. In *Catch-22*, tragedy is the product of a society in which the individual is a functionary, not an end in himself; thus, authority should be demystified and overturned. Although no character in the novel heeds this call, the implication is that only through collective action can humanity be restored. *Catch-22* became an inspiration for the more literate members of the student protest movement.

The military, so savagely satirized by Heller, had usually been treated reverentially by Hollywood or at least with an affectionate comic touch. Until the mid-1960s almost all films dealing with it were produced in cooperation with the military. In 1964, however, director Stanley Kubrick's *Dr. Strangelove or: How I Learned to Stop Worrying and Love the Bomb* brought a fiercely suspicious attitude toward the military and the entire notion of nuclear deterrence. In the film an insane air force general refuses to rescind a senseless nuclear attack order on the Soviets; the technology gets out of control; and the world careens toward nuclear disaster. The Pentagon command center resembles, as one critic put it, "a tour through a Hollywood insane asylum." The characters' names tell all: the chairman of the Joint Chiefs of Staff is an oversexed general, "Buck" Turgidson; the hapless president is Merkin Muffley; the crazed air force general is Jack D. Ripper; and the president's adviser is Dr. Strangelove, a "rehabilitated" Nazi scientist. It was an indication of changing tastes that the film was one of the top box office successes of the year and was nominated for several Academy Awards, including Best Picture and Best Director.

Two other films that same year offered a similarly iconoclastic view of the military: *Fail-Safe* and *Seven Days in May*. In *Fail-Safe*, unlike *Dr. Strangelove*, the same doomsday scenario is played out not by lunatics and fools but, as film critic Bosley Crowther put it in the *New York Times*, "intelligent men trying to use their wits and techniques to correct an error that has occurred through over-reliance on the efficiency of machines."[102] *Seven Days in May* projects a sinister underside to the American military. Burt Lancaster as the chairman of the Joint Chiefs is involved in a plot to overthrow the president, who has just signed a nuclear disarmament treaty. Although Lancaster and his coconspirators are foiled by a loyal marine colonel, played by Kirk Douglas, the very notion that a senior military man could be portrayed as a traitor was no longer unthinkable. If the military could be treated with such disregard, other taboos could be broken as well. And they were.

The Motion Picture Production Code was increasingly being challenged and amended. In 1953, Otto Preminger had the audacity to release *The Moon Is Blue* even though it had been denied the Production Code Seal of Approval because of its use of such unmentionable words as "virgin" and "pregnant." By the 1960s the code's numerous taboos against such subjects as homosexuality, interracial romance, and adultery were weakening under pressures for social change. Films were coming close to the edge without actually shattering the barriers. In *One Potato, Two Potato* (1964) interracial marriage and a passionate kiss were sympathetically portrayed; *Splendor in the Grass* (1961) dealt openly with the subject of teenage sex. In 1966 the code was amended to suggest only restraint in treating sexual themes rather than prohibition of them. That year *Who's Afraid of Virginia Woolf* with Elizabeth Taylor and Richard Burton was released to broad critical praise despite its consistent use of expletives, and *The Pawnbroker* with Rod Steiger included a scene showing a prostitute naked from the waist up. By 1968 the code would be replaced by a rating system that classified films by their suitability for the young but allowed virtually anything for adults. The movie audience, once participants in a common culture and experience, became fractionalized. It was rare that parents could take young children to a serious film, as they had frequently done in the 1940s and 1950s.

Musical taste also evolved, and more popular songs catered to the young. Rock and roll suffered a brief period of decline in the late 1950s and early 1960s with the induction of Elvis Presley into the army, the tragic death in a plane crash of Buddy Holly, Richie Valens, and the Big Bopper, and the scandalous marriage of Jerry Lee Lewis to his fourteen-year-old cousin. Despite the civil rights demonstrations, the New Left, and the Berkeley Free Speech Movement, however, there was little reason to believe, prior to Vietnam, that mainstream American youth was in a rebellious state of mind. As the music historian Ian Mac-Donald describes the state of youthful tastes in the early 1960s, "In the USA, the 'kids' were diverted by cars, bobby-sox heart throbs, and surf music."[103] Then in 1964 the Beatles burst onto the music scene, changing the nature of American popular music and making an indelible imprint on American culture. They brought from England not only an inventive fluid sound, magnetic stage presence, and the unmistakable rock beat but also a disdain for staid British society.

The Beatles would take American youth culture to another level. Their 1964 American tour began with an appearance on the *Ed Sullivan Show* and played to hysterical teenage mobs in New York, Washington, and Miami. By the end of the year Beatles merchandise had grossed over $50 million. Although their appearance and music did not openly menace society, their influence over the young was enormous, and their implicit message was profoundly subversive. As cultural historian Alan Matusow explains it, "Treating the adult world as absurd, they told their fans to kick off their shoes, heed their hormones, and have fun. However harmless initially, the Beatles phenomenon contained the possibility of danger. The frenzied loyalty they inspired endowed the Fab Four with immense potential power—power to alter life styles, change values, and create a new sensibility, a new way of perceiving the world."[104]

Bob Dylan, the young folk singer and composer, had made "Blowin' in the Wind" and "The Times They Are A-Changin'" into anthems of the liberal and civil rights movements. Realizing that the Beatles had touched a core of cultural unrest among the young, Dylan appeared at the Newport Folk Festival in 1966 wearing a black leather jacket and backed by an electric band. His music, moving from liberal protest to cultural radicalism in songs such as "Like a Rolling Stone," "Maggie's Farm," and "Desolation Row," painted a picture of a desolate and corrupt America.

The Fabric Is Rent

It would take earth-shaking events to bring into violent contention the forces that Lyndon Johnson's Great Society had sought to submerge—reenergized conservatism, the white backlash, black nationalism, and student radicalism—and those events would occur ten thousand miles away. The Vietnam War was the seismic upheaval that would blow apart the consensus and place liberalism on the political defensive for the next several decades. Its reverberations in both politics and culture gave each group in the United States an argument against the dominant consensus. Each argument, however, was different from the others. It was difficult to imagine a new consensus emerging from such contentiousness.

America's mobilization and participation in World War II had created an invigorated sense of national unity and a welcomed economic prosperity. In contrast, the escalation of the Vietnam War in 1965 occurred in a political and cultural environment unprepared for a lengthy war in a faraway land. Rising expectations for domestic reform, growing cultural skepticism, newly relaxed relations with the Soviet Union, and an already strong economy were not conducive to the support this effort would eventually require. Johnson's enormously successful 1964 campaign had seemed to grasp the spirit of the time. He focused almost exclusively on domestic issues with a warning against Barry Goldwater's alleged militarism; Vietnam was barely mentioned.

Johnson had clung to the hope that the Communist insurgency could be contained without massive American intervention or any diversion from his plans for the Great Society.

When his top advisers—Secretary of State Dean Rusk, Secretary of Defense Robert McNamara, and National Security Adviser McGeorge Bundy—concluded in the summer of 1965 that American air strikes and increased ground combat support would be necessary, Johnson acceded, but, hoping that the war could be brought to swift conclusion, saw no need to alert the American people to its potential costs. Bundy, in a June 30, 1965, memo, assured the president that the U.S. position was far different from that of the French, who had been forced out of Indo-China in 1954. "At home," Bundy wrote, "we remain politically strong and, in general, politically united. Options, both military and political, remain to us that were no longer available to the French."[105] Bundy and others in the administration seemed oblivious to the cultural forces that threatened the Johnsonian consensus. Above everything else, Johnson did not want anything to interfere with his ambitious legislative agenda—certainly not a rancorous congressional debate on Vietnam in which the full nature of the problem could be aired. While his programs awaited passage, then, Johnson decided not to mobilize the reserves, gain a clear congressional authorization to conduct the war, or publicly disclose the extent of his military commitment. Rather, he told Congress in early 1966, "I believe we can continue the Great Society while we fight in Vietnam." But this line, received with considerable applause, was wishful thinking by both the president and the Congress. Although Johnson sidestepped into the conflict and raised the ante gradually over a three-year period, the war soon became the focal point for the political and cultural clash that had been simmering beneath the surface of American life for almost a decade.

For the student left the Vietnam War occasioned its break with liberalism. Up to that point it had been ambivalent. SDS had endorsed the election of President Johnson with the tepid slogan "Part of the way with LBJ." The SDS Political Education Project had argued that the 1964 Democratic Party platform was "superior to any passed by a major national party since the first New Deal."[106] But as Johnson began his escalation of the war in the spring of 1965, SDS organized an antiwar march on Washington. Speaking to an early cadre of war dissenters, the SDS president, Paul Potter, made a wholesale attack on the political system: "What kind of system is it that justifies the United States or any other country seizing the destinies of the Vietnamese people and using them callously for their own purposes, . . . that puts national values before human values. . . . We must name that system, we must describe it, analyze it, understand it, and change it." It was up to the next SDS president, Carl Oglesby, to take the analysis a step further. In a speech to another antiwar rally in Washington that fall, he named the system: "corporate liberalism." Those who had planned the Vietnam War, Oglesby told the protesters, were not "moral monsters. They are all honorable men. They are all liberals." He also took a swipe at the conformist silent generation, claiming, "We have become a nation of young, bright-eyed, hard-hearted, slim-waisted, bullet-headed make-out artists. A nation . . . of beardless liberals."[107] Throughout the remainder of the 1960s the student left would focus its greatest wrath against the liberals. The students ignored the conservatives, who, having been routed in the 1964 election, were seemingly irrelevant.

As the war escalated in the years 1965–1968, SDS moved further away from its earlier efforts to organize the poor and concentrated on building a student movement. Understanding the need for drama and action as well as the appeal to self-interest, it focused on draft resistance. In New York's Central Park in the spring of 1967, as part of a major antiwar march, a group of SDS leaders from Cornell burned their draft cards in defiance of federal law. The media gravitated to the event. What followed was a coalition of local draft-resistance groups whose tactics were increasingly theatrical and confrontational.

Another indication that the young were more interested in theater than political manifestos came on January 14, 1967, in Golden Gate Park, San Francisco. The "Human Be-In" drew a crowd of about twenty thousand people. On the platform were the Beat poets Allen Ginsberg and Gary Snyder, former Harvard professor turned proponent of the hallucinogenic drug LSD Timothy Leary, and local antiwar leader Jerry Rubin. Ginsberg chanted a Buddhist mantra; Leary urged the crowd to "turn on, tune in, and drop out"; and Rubin tried to squeeze in an antiwar message. This time the media was more interested in the crowd. *Newsweek*, once a staid version of *Time* magazine, photographed the event in color. As Todd Gitlin describes it, "Twenty thousand people, more or less, reveled, dropped acid, burned incense, tootled flutes, jingled tambourines, passed out flowers, admired one another, felt the immensity of their collective spectacle."[108]

Out of the Be-In came the term "hippies" to name those considered descendants of the Beats. The hippie impulse, soon to be dubbed the counterculture, was far more powerful than the programmatic politics of the antiwar movement. Its message, although not always explicit, was even more radical. As Alan Matusow puts it, "Hippies mocked liberal politicians, scorned efforts to repair the social order, and repudiated bourgeois society. In so doing, they became cultural radicals opposed to authority."[109]

In the summer of 1967 thousands of so-called flower children flocked to the Haight-Ashbury neighborhood of San Francisco. They wore garish clothes, dropped acid, lived communally, and engaged in promiscuous sex. The "summer of love" in reality was somewhat darker than its name. Haight-Ashbury had also attracted gangs and a large number of deranged people. By the end of the year the district had witnessed seventeen murders, one hundred rapes, and close to three thousand burglaries.[110] Most of the visitors soon left, but the counterculture spread faster than any political message of the New Left.

The New Left was not prepared to drop out; instead, it adopted more flamboyant and dramatic tactics. In Oakland, California, on October 16, 1967, SDS and other militant groups organized ten thousand people to blockade an army induction center; they tied up traffic and virtually paralyzed the city. The students eventually retreated, but their impressive show of strength had gained national attention. The next week some fifty thousand marchers descended on Washington for another demonstration against the war. Breaking with their moderate leaders, who had hoped for the usual speeches and songs, many of the participants were eager to supply some revolutionary theater. They crossed the Memorial Bridge to the Pentagon, where they provided the spectacle of girls putting flowers in soldiers' gun barrels and troops being implored to "join us." Eventually, those troops and federal marshals cleared the demonstrators away by force.

Since marches and petitions were not enough to attract the media, in the years that followed, the student left—though representing only a fraction of the American public—was able to grab center stage through their politics of theater. The students, acutely conscious of the fact that whether or not people agreed with them, they had the public's attention, thereafter heralded most demonstrations with the slogan THE WHOLE WORLD IS WATCHING. Jerry Rubin and Abbie Hoffman were two of the activists who understood that merging radical politics with cultural rebellion could provide the kind of outrageous theater the young would love and the media would cover. In 1966, Rubin appeared at a House Un-American Activities Committee meeting as Tom Paine, wearing a Revolutionary War uniform and demanding to testify. He was thrown out, but it was a national story. The next year Hoffman stormed the New York Stock Exchange, throwing money on the floor and burning bills.

SDS moved away from participatory democracy and became increasingly enamored of Marxism. It adopted a more radical form of direct action and closer identification with the Communist guerrillas in Vietnam and Castro's Cuba. Its new leaders, Carl Davidson and Greg Calvert, saw in students the new vanguard of the revolution and eventually the workers of a new service economy. In a speech to an SDS group in Princeton, New Jersey, in February 1967, Calvert urged students to organize on their own behalf. They were, he said, "the key group in the creation of the productive forces of the super-technological capitalism, . . . trainees of the new working class."[111] If they hoped that sex, drugs, draft dodging, and rock music would bring the revolution, however, the student radicals were to be disappointed. Although a significant number of the young tuned in to the counterculture and the politics of personal liberation, only a fraction became attracted to revolutionary politics. Those that remained in the student movement turned, as the decade progressed, from protest to resistance to violence and eventually to disillusionment.

The mood that was unleashed in 1967 rippled through the popular culture. Two films of that year, *The Graduate* and *Bonnie and Clyde*, captured the spirit of youthful defiance. *The Graduate* is almost bereft of any explicit politics, but it is biting social commentary. After graduating from college, the hero, Benjamin Braddock, played by Dustin Hoffman, returns to his affluent Los Angeles home to be feted by his parents. In his eyes their world seems intellectually vacuous and vulgar, and he is soon seduced by a sexually rapacious, middle-aged friend of the family, Mrs. Robinson. Benjamin eventually falls in love with Mrs. Robinson's daughter, Elaine, and rescues her from a life and a marriage preordained by her parents. As Benjamin and Elaine flee in the final scene, it is not clear where they are going or why, only that the affluent life they leave behind has been suffocating them.

In *Bonnie and Clyde*, director Arthur Penn and writers Robert Benton and David Newman rendered two of the most notorious bank robbers and killers of the 1930s, Bonnie Parker and Clyde Barrow, as victims of society's cruelty and indifference. The groundbreaking combination of a documentary look with slapstick humor, graphic violence, and sexual innuendo made it an instant cult film for the young. Benton and Newman had consciously constructed the picture to catch their mood. They wrote, "If Bonnie and Clyde were here today, they would be hip. Their values have been assimilated in much of our culture—not robbing banks and killing people, of course, but their style, their sexuality, their bravado, their delicacy, and their cultivated arrogance, their narcissistic insecurity, their curious ambition have relevance to the way we live now."[112] The film historian Peter Biskind notes that *Bonnie and Clyde* reversed the conventional moral polarities: "The bad guys in this film were traditional authority figures: parents, sheriffs."[113] The dean of movie critics, Bosley Crowther of the *New York Times*, called it "another indulgence of a restless and reckless taste and an embarrassing addition to the excess of violence on the screen"— but he was in a distinct minority. Two other major film critics, Andrew Sarris and Pauline Kael, attacked Crowther on the grounds that his opinion would encourage censorship. Kael thought that filmmakers should be free to use violence if it was essential to the story and that society needed no more guardians of morality.[114]

Sarris and Kael had a better feel for popular tastes than the older Crowther; both films received much critical praise and were major box office hits. *Bonnie and Clyde* gained ten Academy Award nominations; *The Graduate*, seven. Hollywood was discovering that older tastes, traditions, and values could be openly flouted with considerable profit. In just four short years, America had witnessed the assassination of a president, an escalated war in Vietnam, a puzzling youth rebellion, black rage, and urban riots. Much of middle America was suffering a crisis of confidence. In 1957, *Bonnie and Clyde* could not and would not have been made; in 1967, many thought it was the picture of the year.

The most dramatic violence in America during the middle and late 1960s, however, came not from white bank robbers on the lam but from something more threatening to domestic tranquillity—black anger erupting in full force. The patience and discipline demanded by Dr. King's nonviolent approach was hard to maintain. The tensions between the older and younger blacks erupted in the summer of 1966 when a white gunman shot James Meredith on a Mississippi highway while he was leading a small civil rights march. At a rally protesting the shooting, Stokely Carmichael of SNCC defied the nonviolent line. He told the crowd, "Every courthouse in Mississippi ought to be burned tomorrow to get rid of the dirt." As he intoned, "What do you want? Black power, black power," the audience echoed his words.[115] Roy Wilkins of the NAACP and Martin Luther King, Jr., who at first disassociated themselves from any hint of black separatism or nationalism, muted their criticism as it became clearer that Carmichael's black power rhetoric had found an audience.

The Watts riots of 1965 had been a harbinger of the violence and disorder that would spread throughout many northern cities. In 1966 there were thirty-eight riots in inner cities, including Chicago, Cleveland, and San Francisco. The next year the violence escalated with more than 150 riots, thirty-three of which required the intervention of the National Guard. The most serious, in Detroit and Newark, lasted a week or more and left buildings destroyed and people homeless. Detroit suffered over $250 million in property losses, and forty-three persons died, many from National Guard gunfire.[116] Traditional civil rights leaders—Roy Wilkins of the NAACP, Whitney Young of the Urban League, and Martin Luther King, Jr.—who had their roots in either the black middle class or church communities in the South could exercise little influence in restraining the riots. These areas had a large number of young men from unstable single-parent families and were also witnessing a decline in relatively high-paying manufacturing jobs.[117]

For a new generation of younger black leaders the riots were a more authentic expression of the black state of mind than Dr. King's philosophy of nonviolent resistance. In May 1967 a group of militants in Oakland formed the Black Panther Party for Self-Defense. Their leaders, Huey Newton, Bobby Seale, and Eldridge Cleaver, organized a march to the capitol building in Sacramento to protest legislation banning citizens from carrying loaded weapons inside city limits. With their own sense of theater to fit the times, the marchers wore black pants, black leather jackets, and black berets, and they brandished rifles and shotguns. The rhetoric of the Panthers moved from nationalism to Marxism and to violence. Newton wrote in 1967, "Only with the power of the gun can the Black masses halt the terror and brutality perpetuated against them by the armed racist power structure."[118]

Carmichael and his successor as head of SNCC, H. "Rap" Brown, saw the riots as nationalist insurrections. Brown told a rally of blacks in Cambridge, Maryland, soon after the Newark riot, "If America don't come around, we are going to burn it down."[119] Carmichael, speaking in Havana, Cuba, that August, talked of solidarity with radical insurgencies in the Third World. "We have no alternative but to take up arms and struggle for our total liberation and total revolution." However offensive this rhetoric may have been to the white majority, it was great media theater, and its coverage overshadowed the progress achieved by their moderate elders.

Unlike King and Wilkins, none of these young militants had the slightest interest in the liberal agenda or even in a dialogue with liberals. Both white and black liberals were caught between the expectations of the Great Society on the one hand and the realities of Vietnam and rising black nationalism on the other. Johnson's Great Society programs were simply empty promises for communities that could see little change in their lives. As the Vietnam War droned on without apparent resolution, Johnson's popularity declined. His congressional liberal majority disappeared in the 1966 congressional elections, when the Democrats lost more than forty seats in the House of Representatives. The war was also draining money from the Great Society project. The president had scheduled a substantial increase in funding for the antipoverty programs in 1967–68, but they received only a token increase for fiscal year 1968.

Johnson responded to the riots by appointing a commission headed by Illinois Governor Otto Kerner, which later issued a report calling for $30 billion more for the poor in the next fiscal year, doubling what was already being spent. Johnson knew this was impossible, as he acknowledged in his memoirs: "I would have been delighted to have had an appropriation of an additional $30 billion to solve the problems of our cities, but I knew it was unrealistic."[120] He could not produce a massive liberal Marshall Plan for the cities, and the Kerner Report was politely shelved. All of this made it increasingly difficult for moderate black leaders to maintain their influence with the black rank and file.

More was at stake than just the passage of one program or the increased funding of another. The black radicals were attacking the notion that we could all become Americans and overcome our class, ethnic, and racial identities. From their perspective, the civil rights movement (a phrase they rarely used) should be not about increasing opportunities for individual blacks in the American political system but about group entitlement. The capitalist system would, in their view, always be weighted against blacks; therefore, blacks as a group should be recognized and rewarded.

Black nationalism also spawned a greater sense of ethnic identity throughout the country, particularly among Polish, Italian, and Jewish Americans. As two scholars of the period have described this change, "By the end of the sixties, despite nearly fifteen years of racial progress and legislative reform, American society seemed about to unravel into a maze of ethnic and self-interest politics."[121] Affirmative action and the proliferation of black studies and other ethnic programs at various colleges and universities were an expression of this development.

The Year of
America's Nervous Breakdown

When 1968 was over, few regretted its passing. The accumulation of tensions and divisions and two tragic assassinations brought the American political system close to the breaking point. Even though the country survived and went on to see better days, it was in many ways a different country. The common culture of the 1940s and the conservative conformity of the 1950s began to seem like a distant past. The strands of the political and cultural fabric become unwound. Black nationalism grew in intensity; student radicalism became more strident and even violent; a conservative populist working-class backlash was building against civil rights, the counterculture, and the antiwar movement; and the Democratic Party flew apart over Vietnam. It was hard to locate a political center of gravity.

Traumatic events punctuated the year and accelerated the sense of coming apart: the February Tet offensive in Vietnam; President Johnson's March announcement that he would not seek another term and would pursue a political settlement in Vietnam; the April assassination of Dr. Martin Luther King, Jr., and the June assassination of Sen. Robert F. Kennedy; the August riots in Chicago during the Democratic National Convention; the independent candidacy of George C. Wallace and the photo-finish victory of Richard Nixon in the November presidential election.

In retrospect, the Tet offensive can be seen as a desperate effort by the Communist guerrilla forces in South Vietnam to drive the Americans and their Vietnamese allies from a number of the major cities along the coast. It was a military failure, for American and Vietnamese forces eventually drove the Communists out of the cities of Hue, Danang, and Saigon and inflicted heavy casualties on them. Nonetheless, the Communists had been able to penetrate these cities and had even held some of them for a short time, convincing many that America could not win the war without paying an unacceptable price. Walter Cronkite, the popular CBS anchorman and icon of television journalism, visited Vietnam and declared the war unwinnable. In early March a story was leaked to the *New York Times* that Gen. William Westmoreland, the commander in Vietnam, had requested 206,000 troops in addition to the 550,000 already there.

Sen. Eugene McCarthy (D-MN), who had been running a largely symbolic and seemingly futile campaign against President Johnson for the Democratic nomination, found himself flooded with volunteers from college campuses. Many students even cut their hair and dressed neatly; "Clean for Gene" was the slogan. After having been considered a joke in the fall of 1967 when he announced his candidacy, McCarthy came close to defeating Johnson in the March 12 New Hampshire primary, losing only by 50 to 42 percent. Johnson's approval ratings were plummeting, and polls for the upcoming April Wisconsin primary showed McCarthy in the lead. Four days after the New Hampshire primary, Sen. Robert F. Kennedy of New York, the oldest surviving Kennedy brother and former attorney general, announced his candidacy for the presidential nomination. The announcement stirred hostility among McCarthy supporters, many of whom had been turned down by Kennedy in 1967 when they had asked him to run. McCarthy had taken up the cause against difficult odds, and now it seemed that Robert Kennedy was going to cash in on McCarthy's improbable success.

Whatever the merits of that argument, Kennedy's candidacy complicated Lyndon Johnson's life and made the forces he had to contend with considerably more formidable. For one thing, he feared the Kennedy mystique. Of greater consequence, Kennedy and McCarthy appealed to different constituencies—McCarthy to the college students and suburban liberals; Kennedy to white working-class and black and Hispanic communities—a combination that would be difficult to fend off. Moreover, the world seemed to be closing in on the beleaguered president. His advisers were divided about what to do in Vietnam, and the current strategy of attrition had lost much of its popular support. More and more Americans thought we should either "win or get out." Consequently, in a dramatic announcement on March 31—two days before the primary in Wisconsin, where he was running far behind McCarthy—Johnson declared, "I shall not seek, and I will not accept the nomination of my party for another term as your president."

Four days later, Martin Luther King, Jr., in Memphis to support a sanitation workers' strike and prevent it from becoming violent, was assassinated by a white man, James Earl Ray. King had been working to regain the momentum of his nonviolent movement, which was under siege from both conservative whites and black power advocates. He wanted to build a coalition of black and white poor and working people behind a new "Economic Bill of Rights" that would guarantee employment for all. He had planned a "Poor People's Campaign" with a march on Washington. His assassination led to another wave of riots in the nation's inner cities, the most severe in Washington, DC, where seventy-five thousand troops had to patrol the streets, city blocks were burnt out, three thousand people were injured, five were killed, and twenty-one thousand arrested. Despite the riots and the rising tide of black militancy, King had set the tone for the civil rights movement with his emphasis on nonviolence and a black-white coalition. Todd Gitlin has written, "When he was murdered, it seemed that nonviolence went to the grave with him, and the movement was 'free at last' from restraint."[122]

Just as King's death tore at the strands of racial unity, the events of the following months weakened the remaining elements of political unity. Following Johnson's withdrawal, Vice President Hubert Humphrey entered the presidential race, but too late for the primaries; he had to count on Johnson's support in the nonprimary states where party regulars controlled the delegates. In the meantime, Kennedy and McCarthy battled it out in the primaries. Kennedy won in Indiana and Nebraska, McCarthy in Oregon. In California, the climactic battle, Kennedy won by 46 to 42 percent. On the evening of his victory, Robert Kennedy spoke to supporters in the Ambassador Hotel in Los Angeles. As he was leaving through the kitchen, he was shot by Sirhan Sirhan, an aggrieved Palestinian offended by the senator's support of Israel. The death of Robert Kennedy horrified the nation and eliminated the only mainstream Democratic politician who might have melded the student activists, the black community, and the white working class into a coherent constituency. McCarthy's ironic intellectualism had little to communicate to ethnic whites and blacks; Humphrey, whatever his private feelings, was kept on a short leash by Lyndon Johnson, who expected him to support the Vietnam War.

George Wallace had decided to forgo the Democratic primaries in 1968 and run as a third-party candidate in November. The polls showed that he could garner substantial support from both poor rural whites in the South and many working-class ethnics in the North. Wallace spoke a new populist rhetoric. Unlike the populists of the late nineteenth century, who had railed against monopolists, bankers, and commodity traders, Wallace assaulted a cultural elite that glamorized antiwar demonstrators, hippies, and black radicals and attacked government bureaucrats who imposed forced busing on neighborhood schools. He told the National Press Club in 1968 that he spoke for "the bus driver, the beautician, the fireman, the policeman, and the steelworker, the plumber, and the communications worker, and the oil worker and the little businessman."[123] His litany of working-class people evoked images that were obviously white.

The resentment that Wallace directed at the cultural elite was returned in kind. Some intellectuals feared that the populist impulse bore the seeds of fascism. The intellectual left treated Wallace and his white working-class followers with contempt. Writing in the *New York Review of Books*, the major intellectual outlet of the 1960s, Elizabeth Hardwick described Wallace in "his plastic-like ill-cut suits, his graying drip-dry shirts, with his sour, dark unprepossessing look, carrying the scent of hurry and hair oil" as a man whose "natural home would seem to be a seedy hotel with a lot of people in the lobby, and his relaxation a cheap diner." His supporters were "joyless, sore and miserable."[124]

White working-class people increasingly felt the contempt of the New Left and the counterculture. According to the historian David Farber, "Protesters paid little mind to the history of white working people in the United States—conceding little to their struggle to make ends meet. . . . They seemed to give no respect to the hard work it had taken and still took most Americans to earn pleasant life-styles." As the media gave more attention to student protests and black radicals, white working people believed that their place on the social hierarchy was threatened. Those who followed Wallace saw the government not as an ally but as an impediment, and the media as an enemy. Farber explains, "George Wallace, in 1968, tried to mutate a racist populist impulse of the Old South into a national politics of resentment."[125]

Wallace's campaign accentuated the black-white divide and the alienation of the white working class from the counterculture, American liberalism, and the antiwar movement. At the Democratic National Convention in Chicago that summer the various elements clashed, with disastrous results for the party. Gene McCarthy was strangely detached from the contest after Robert Kennedy's death, his candidacy no longer a magnet for young people or a vehicle for their antiwar fury. Without a candidate, the student antiwar movement focused its efforts on disrupting the Democratic convention. Delegates who had backed either Kennedy or McCarthy attempted to add a peace plank to the Democratic platform. Since McCarthy had made only a lame effort to gain the support of the Kennedy delegates, many of them rallied around Sen. George McGovern of South Dakota, who agreed to serve as a stand-in for the late senator. All of this was more symbolic than substantive. Lyndon Johnson, working with his operatives in the Democratic Party and Mayor Richard Daley of Chicago, had the convention scripted and under tight control. Humphrey was destined to be the nominee, and there would be no plank in the platform even remotely critical of Johnson's Vietnam policy.

Regardless of this preordained outcome, the convention exposed divisions within the Democratic Party and the constituents of American liberalism that would deepen over the next two decades. Older and more traditional Democrats were instinctively patriotic and would not openly oppose an American military effort. Although many had their own doubts about the Vietnam War, they were united in their detestation of the antiwar movement and they took strong offense at the coarse language, sexual openness, and bizarre antics of the counterculture. This group was at the heart of the old Democratic coalition of union leaders, urban machine politicians, southern white Democrats, and Eastern and Central European ethnics.

The Kennedy and McCarthy campaigns had tapped into constituencies with weaker loyalties to that coalition. McCarthy attracted the younger, better-educated voters who were likely to be found in university towns and upscale suburban communities. They were opposed to the war, were relatively affluent, had no sentimental attachment to the New Deal, and were more likely than their elders to question established authority. Many of those who had supported Robert Kennedy, particularly in the California primary, were black and Hispanic. These two minority communities were developing more outspoken and nontraditional political leaders such as Cesar Chávez and younger followers of Dr. King such as Jesse Jackson and Andrew Young, who were less likely to be co-opted into the traditional party structure.

Outside the convention hall, war protesters gathered to embarrass and disrupt Johnson's scripted and controlled convention. There were two major groups: the Youth International Party, or Yippies, led by Jerry Rubin and Abbie Hoffman; and a more self-consciously political organization called the Mobilization, organized by Tom Hayden and Rennie Davis of the SDS. The Yippies, in the spirit of the counterculture, wanted to make outrageous mayhem, and the leaders of the "Mobe" had dreams of leading a new revolutionary movement. The Yippies' platform was full of glorious generalities, but their heart was in their humor, designed to infuriate straight America. Along with full employment and elimination of pollution, they demanded the abolition of money and pay toilets. Hayden and Davis were more serious and may have wanted a violent confrontation with Mayor Daley's police in order to expose the brutality of the system and radicalize more Americans. What followed was chaos on the streets of Chicago and disastrous political strife in the convention hall.

On the eve of the convention the Yippies had refused to leave Lincoln Park on Chicago's North Side where they were holding a "Festival of Life." The police, goaded by taunts, attempted to clear the park with tear gas and clubs. This melee continued on and off for several days. In Grant Park across from the Conrad Hilton Hotel, where many delegates stayed, other demonstrators clashed with police before network television cameras. At the convention itself, the peace platform, calling for a bombing halt in Vietnam and an early withdrawal of "a significant number of troops," was easily defeated. But Humphrey would be nominated by a party ripped apart over the war. Sen. Abraham Ribicoff of Connecticut, making the nominating speech for George McGovern, stared at Mayor Daley as he denounced the "Gestapo tactics on the streets of Chicago." Daley hurled insults back that were lip-read by some watching on television as "F—— you, you Jew son of a bitch."

The "Battle of Chicago" was about more than the war in Vietnam or the Democratic presidential nomination. It was a chilling manifestation of a deep cultural divide. Regardless of their feelings about the war, many Americans backed the Chicago police, placed Support Your Local Police bumper stickers on their cars, wore American flags in their lapels, and demanded more law and order. On several levels the war exacerbated class tensions. It was far easier for privileged and college-educated young men to find ways of avoiding military service or at least Vietnam duty—through educational or job deferments, alleged medical disabilities, or National Guard membership—than for young men from poor and working-class backgrounds. Between 1965 and 1972, 45 percent of male high school graduates served in the military as opposed to 23 percent of college graduates.[126] Consequently, many working- and lower-middle-class Americans despised the antiwar movement "as an elitist attack on American troops by people who could avoid war."[127] That most of the visible antiwar activity had been at elite universities such as Berkeley, Columbia, Michigan, and Harvard only reinforced this perception. Both George Wallace and Richard Nixon, who won the Republican presidential nomination that year, sensed in these angry voters a potential political constituency.

The Republican Party, with an increasingly influential southern wing, had moved substantially to the right since 1960. Nixon shifted with the tide. In order to secure the nomination he enlisted the support of Barry Goldwater and Strom Thurmond to nail down southern delegates and staved off a last-minute challenge from California's Governor Ronald Reagan. In order to defeat Humphrey in November he had to attract a significant percentage of Wallace voters without appearing too extreme. Cleverly, Nixon campaigned in calmer terms that avoided Wallace's overheated rhetoric yet captured much of his message. In his set speech, Nixon claimed to speak for "the forgotten Americans, those who did not indulge in violence, those who did not break the law, people pay who their taxes and go to work, people who send their children to school, who go to their churches, people who are not haters, people who love this country."[128]

Wallace made a major blunder in picking Air Force Chief of Staff Curtis LeMay as his vice-presidential running mate. General LeMay's careless comments about nuclear weapons frightened many Wallace supporters. LeMay claimed that after the hydrogen bomb tests in the South Pacific, the rats on the Bikini atoll were "bigger, fatter, and healthier than they ever were before." Wallace faltered in the polls, and Humphrey regained much of his traditional Democratic support after Lyndon Johnson announced a bombing halt just days before the election. Nevertheless, according to polls on the eve of the election, the race was a toss-up.

Nixon won, but with only a 510,000 margin in the popular vote. The election results revealed the fractures in the Democratic Party's once dominant coalition. In the Deep South, the bedrock of Democratic strength, Humphrey received only 10 percent of the white vote. Wallace's support, once as high as 21 percent in the polls, had shrunk to 13.6 percent. Most of it came from the South, although he won significant backing among Catholic voters in the Northeast and the industrialized Midwest who normally voted Democratic and drew strong support in the blue-collar districts of those cities where racial polarization was most acute, such as Newark, New Jersey, Flint, Michigan, and Cleveland. Wallace had benefited from the growing racial polarization, but in general his snarling rhetoric was too strong and threatening for those who wanted a return to calmer days.

It was difficult to imagine how the Wallace and McCarthy voters could continue to coexist within the same party. McCarthy had discovered a constituency of upscale professionals, later dubbed the New

Class, from education, the media, government, and the law. They were sympathetic to the New Left's call for a more open and tolerant society, hostile to the Vietnam War, and supportive of the Great Society's effort to improve the lot of the poor, but their heart was largely in environmentalism and consumer protection. Wallace's constituency was concentrated in the South; the liberalism of the New Class seemed strongest in the Northeast, which became the bedrock of support in national elections and the last bastion of Modern Republicanism.

The Nixon Paradox: Liberal Policies in Conservative Drapery

Nixon faced the complex challenge of finding and holding the political center. He had talked about "bringing us together," but neither the times nor his temperament seemed conducive to such an effort. He needed an early end to the Vietnam War to give him the same boost that Eisenhower had received in 1953 when he ended the Korean War. Sadly, Nixon found Vietnam more intractable than Korea and the North Vietnamese inflexible, holding out for peace terms that were unacceptable to him. Compounding his problem was a Democratic Congress, many of whose members were hostile to him and unlikely to pass a Nixon-stamped legislative agenda.

Nixon's approach displayed a degree of subtlety that kept his opponents off balance. He was culturally conservative and economically liberal. He fanned the flames of resentment against black militants, student protesters, the antiwar movement, and the emerging counterculture to soothe Wallace voters and most middle-American Republicans. As the Vietnam War dragged on without resolution, the student movement was growing in strength and also becoming more militant and violent. In the process it provided Nixon with a foil and a target for his rhetoric. In 1968 students at Columbia, to protest the university's government contracts and its alleged complicity in the war, occupied its president's office and rifled his files; at Cornell black students armed with machine guns took over the student center; and at San Francisco State its president (later a U.S. senator) S. I. Hayakawa gained instant fame by calling out the police and the National Guard to put down the demonstrations.

Most painful and memorable was the incident at Kent State University in Ohio. In May 1970, when Nixon authorized an invasion into technically neutral Cambodia, demonstrations erupted around the country. As he left a Pentagon briefing, Nixon referred to the students as "bums." On May 4, after Kent State students had thrown bottles at police cars, smashed store windows, and firebombed the Reserve Officers' Training Corps (ROTC) building, Gov. James Rhodes sent in the National Guard. About five hundred students gathered on campus in protest; some threw rocks; and some Guardsmen opened fire, killing four students. Vivid pictures of the event captured national attention. Several days later two more students were killed at Jackson State in Mississippi, a predominantly black school, when police fired at dormitory windows to suppress a potential demonstration. Protests followed at more than three hundred campuses. Thirty ROTC buildings were firebombed, and some seventy-five colleges had to close before the spring semester ended. The tragedy at Kent State did not elicit broad public sympathy for the students. A *Newsweek* poll showed that an overwhelming majority blamed the students rather than the National Guard for the killings and that 50 to 39 percent of Americans supported the invasion of Cambodia.[129] Public exasperation with the students was translated into sympathy for Nixon and his policies.

On domestic issues Nixon was equally adept. Working with a Democratic Congress driven by an environmental and consumer agenda, he presided over a remarkable growth of the entitlement and regulatory state. Regulatory legislation reached into hitherto untouched aspects of American life. During his administration Nixon signed into law the Poison Prevention Packaging Act, the Occupational Safety and Health Act, the Equal Opportunity Act, the Consumer Product Safety Act, the Vocational Rehabilitation Act, the Noise Pollution and Control Act, the Safe Drinking Water Act, and the Hazardous Material Transportation Act. The pages in the *Federal Register*, where regulations are published, tripled during his administration.[130]

Nixon had neither the ideological interest nor the political desire to oppose the torrent of environmental activity—teach-ins, marches, and vigils—unleashed by Earth Day in April 1970. His state-of-the-union address that year was a virtual charter of environmentalism: "Clean air, clean water, open spaces, these once again should be the birthright of every American." The address included a recommendation for $10 billion to clear the nation's water supplies. Next he proclaimed the first Earth Week and introduced thirty-six environmental proposals. Most became law, including the National Environmental Protection Act (which established the Environmental Protection Agency), the Clean Air Act, the Oil Spill Act, the Clean Water Act, the

Coastal Zone Management Act, and other antipollution regulations of pesticides and various chemicals.[131]

Despite his personal hostility to liberals, Nixon had no intention of rolling back the Great Society. John Ehrlichman, Nixon's top domestic policy adviser, wrote in 1970, "In terms of social programs, e.g., manpower training, anti-poverty, environment, health and education, we are doing as much or more than Johnson or Kennedy." Ehrlichman was not exaggerating. In 1972, Nixon signed a bill granting a 20 percent increase in Social Security benefits and set the stage for the future indexing of benefits. During the eight years of the Nixon and Ford administrations, entitlement and discretionary domestic spending rose from 9.7 percent of the GNP to 15.4 percent.[132]

Concerned that rising unemployment and inflation could endanger his reelection prospects in 1972, Nixon unveiled in August 1971 a "New Economic Policy" reminiscent of the wartime policies of Roosevelt and Truman: he announced a ninety-day freeze on wages and prices to be administered by a pay board, a price board, and a cost-of-living council. Effective in the short run, the controls produced low inflation and unemployment in 1972 and no doubt assisted Nixon's landslide victory over George McGovern that year.[133]

Unable to end the Vietnam War during his first term, Nixon was still able to diffuse much of the opposition in a series of bold foreign policy strokes. He reduced American forces in Vietnam from 550,000 to 50,000 by late 1972 while refusing to sign an armistice that would endanger the South Vietnamese government; he signed a major Strategic Arms Limitation Treaty (SALT I), which included the Anti-Ballistic Missile Treaty and an executive agreement limiting offensive nuclear missiles; and he opened American relations with China by making a dramatic trip there in February 1972.

During a summit meeting in Moscow with Soviet leader Leonid Brezhnev in May 1972, Nixon engaged in a complex diplomatic minuet. He was attempting to contain the Soviet Union in the face of the American war-weariness (and Cold War-weariness) as a consequence of the protracted struggle in Vietnam. The result was an arrangement with the Soviets allowing them access to U.S. markets and technology and gaining from them an arms control agreement and restraint in supporting Third World revolutions. His penchant for secrecy and control, shared by his national security adviser Dr. Henry Kissinger, prevented Nixon from explaining in full detail the exact nature of his diplomacy, a fact that would haunt his successors, Gerald Ford and

Jimmy Carter, when détente began to unravel. Instead, Nixon talked in generalities about "a generation of peace." In the short run, however, his strategy worked. His diplomatic efforts gained considerable support and siphoned off much of the frustration over Vietnam.

As Nixon was adapting to the liberal agenda in domestic policy and pursuing a less militarized foreign policy, Wallace voters and conservative Republicans had to be satisfied with the rhetoric of cultural conservatism. Their "social issue," made popular by demographers Richard Scammon and Ben Wattenberg in their book *The Real Majority*, had little programmatic content. Rather, the social issue was a mélange of middle-class attitudes toward law and order, hippies, drug culture, and the general flouting of authority. The average voter, said Scammon and Wattenberg, was symbolized by a forty-seven-year-old Dayton housewife whose husband was a machinist: "To know that lady in Dayton is afraid to walk the streets at night, to know that she has a mixed view about blacks and civil rights because before moving to the suburbs, she lived in a neighborhood that became all black, to know that she does not have the money to move if her new neighborhood deteriorates, to know that she is deeply distressed that her son is going to community junior college where LSD was found on the campus—to know all this is the beginning of wisdom."[134]

Nixon took Scammon and Wattenberg's advice to heart. He wrote in his memoirs of his belief that "we should aim our strategy primarily at disaffected Democrats, at blue-collar workers, and at working-class white ethnics. We should set out to capture the vote of the forty-seven-year-old Dayton housewife."[135] Carefully developing his strategy to exploit cultural divisions, he talked of the "silent majority" and fanned the flames of cultural and racial resentment. Through his attorney general and former campaign manager John Mitchell, Nixon attempted to slow down the federal government's efforts to desegregate southern schools. He was rebuffed by a series of Supreme Court decisions mandating an immediate end to the dual school system and authorizing the use of court-ordered busing to achieve that end.[136] Nonetheless, he vigorously opposed busing with the knowledge that it was increasingly unpopular in both the North and the South. He asked Congress to prohibit any funding for such purposes and made the issue a centerpiece of both the 1970 and 1972 campaigns.

When Justice Abe Fortas resigned from the Supreme Court in 1969, Nixon attempted to fill the vacancy—a seat held by a Jewish American since 1916—with a southern conservative. The first nominee, Federal Judge Clement Haynsworth of South Carolina, was turned down by the Senate for his one-time segregationist views and an apparent conflict of interest concerning textile companies in which he held stock. Nixon then nominated another southern federal judge, G. Harrold Carswell, whose views on segregation and treatment of civil rights petitioners in his court betrayed an openly hostile attitude toward black people. After the Senate defeated this nominee, Nixon claimed that the reason for both rejections was "the accident of their birth, the fact that both were born in the South." He declared, "I will not nominate another southerner and let him be subjected to this kind of malicious character assassination accorded both Judges Haynsworth and Carswell."[137] On the recommendation of Chief Justice Warren Burger, whom Nixon had appointed to replace Earl Warren, he then nominated Harry Blackmun from Minnesota, who was easily confirmed. To the possible surprise and dismay of Nixon, Blackmun would become a leading liberal voice on the Court. For his efforts on their behalf during the confirmation battle, however, Nixon did score some political points with southerners.

Vice President Spiro Agnew served as an attack dog for the general strategy, ridiculing the "nattering nabobs of negativism" and the "hopeless hypochondriacs of history." Agnew was not just talking about the antiwar movement. As historian James T. Patterson explains, "His targets included a host of people: opponents of school prayers, advocates of busing, hippies, counterculturalists, radical feminists, pushy blacks, spoiled university students, and intellectuals." During the 1970 congressional election campaign, Nixon himself accused protesters of "violence, lawlessness and permissiveness." In one appearance in San Jose he virtually goaded demonstrators into stoning his armored car.[138]

The effective use of the cultural issue, the existence of a strong economy, a de-escalating war in Vietnam, and a divided Democratic Party provided the basis for Nixon's massive reelection victory over Sen. George McGovern of South Dakota in 1972. With Wallace out of the race, McGovern had the most committed constituency standing on the other side of the cultural issue. He had inherited Gene McCarthy's and Robert Kennedy's workers and constituents. In addition, he took full advantage of a new set of party rules that opened up the nomination process to more grassroots participation and exploited the techniques of direct mail fund raising to appeal to New Class liberals. There were fewer state party conventions controlled by the regulars and in their place a proliferation of primaries and open caucuses in which all registered party members could participate. Consequently, he won the remaining key primaries and took the nomination away from Sens. Ed Muskie and Hubert Humphrey, who had the support of the labor unions and most of the elected Democratic officials.

The new 1972 convention rules further weakened the old Democratic Party establishment by calling for greater representation of women, minorities, and youth. When the delegates gathered in Miami Beach, 38 percent were women, 15 percent were black, and 23 percent were under the age of thirty. The delegates may have been more representative of the party in race and gender but not in economic class. One survey showed that 39 percent held postgraduate degrees, 31 percent had incomes in or over the upper-middle-class range, and the black delegates were affluent and well educated.[139] The convention witnessed an effort by feminist delegates to insert a legalized-abortion plank in the platform. In a year before the famous *Roe v. Wade* decision, with abortion still largely taboo, the McGovern forces defeated the effort, fearing to alienate mainstream America. They need not have bothered; much of the traditional Democratic constituency had already been turned off by McGovern and the cultural liberals. The AFL-CIO refused to endorse him and stayed neutral. The Teamsters and several construction workers' unions actually endorsed Nixon.

George Wallace had decided to forgo an independent run in 1972 and compete within the Democratic Party. He won the Florida primary with about 60 percent of the white vote. During the same election Florida voters approved an antibusing constitutional amendment by a 3-to-1 margin and another to reinstate school prayer by 10 to 1. Wallace was riding a wave of cultural conservatism. According to his biographer Dan T. Carter, "The governor from Alabama understood and voiced the longings of millions of white middle-class and working-class voters for a stable world in which work was rewarded, laziness punished, blacks knew their place, men headed the household, women were men's loyal helpmates, and children were safe from vulgar language."[140] But Wallace's effort in the primaries was cut short by an assassination attempt in Maryland that left him paralyzed from the waist down and unable to pursue the nomination. Had he been able to continue, he might have come to the Democratic National Convention with enough delegates to influence both the selection of the nominee and the nature of the platform. As it was, his constituency had nowhere else to go in November but to Richard Nixon.

Nixon used the cultural issue against McGovern to great advantage. Republican Senator Hugh Scott of Pennsylvania charged, "The McGovern campaign is the campaign of acid, abortion, and amnesty."[141] In attacking the social and cultural attitudes of the Democratic nominee and his supporters, Nixon was offering no specific program but providing those who resented the cultural rebels with the red meat of rhetoric. In fact, his domestic record was moderate to liberal, and his foreign policy achievements—détente with the Soviets, the opening to China, the SALT I agreement, and the winding down of the Vietnam War—were those that a liberal Democratic president might have been proud to defend.

Nixon won one of the greatest landslides in American political history, gaining over 60 percent of the vote and carrying every state save Massachusetts and the District of Columbia. He captured the core of the old Democratic coalition, carrying the South, the union vote, the urban ethnic vote, and the Catholic vote. At the congressional level, however, where the cultural issue seemed to have less salience, the Democrats maintained their strong majority in both the House (242 to 192) and the Senate (57 to 43).

Soon after Nixon began his second term, an armistice ended American participation in the Vietnam War, but he had little time to exploit his landslide victory and new-found personal popularity. Vice President Agnew was forced to resign after pleading nolo contendere to charges that he had avoided paying taxes on kickback money he had accepted as governor of Maryland. Of greater consequence, a burglary of the Democratic National Committee's offices in the Watergate Hotel in Washington was soon traced back to the White House and eventually involved Nixon himself in the cover-up. He resigned the presidency in disgrace with his efforts to reshape American politics in disarray. It would be left to Ronald Reagan, some eight years later, to resume the task. Nevertheless, Nixon's politics predicted the future. The cleavage developing in American cultural life would shape attitudes and behavior for another generation. The cultural questions went beyond the Vietnam War, the immediate issues of the 1972 campaign, and the personality and fate of Richard Nixon. Cultural divisions, virtually nonexistent in the 1940s and 1950s, would become a permanent part of the political landscape.

Films and television reflected both the cynicism brought about by Vietnam and Watergate and the openness to a socially critical perspective. On network television, in both drama and comedy, black performers took featured roles. In *Julia* (1968–1971), Diahann Carroll sympathetically portrayed the problems of a hard-working, black single mother; *The Mod Squad* (1968–1974) featured a countercultural interracial trio, including a female, who worked as a police undercover unit; and *The Flip Wilson Show* (1970–1974) featured the black comedian in a series of skits that often mocked ethnic stereotypes. *All in the Family* (1971–1983) was a breakthrough situation comedy in which Archie Bunker, a frustrated blue-collar conservative played by Carroll O'Connor, fought the generational wars against his liberal daughter and son-in-law. Although Archie could be bigoted and narrow-minded, he garnered audience sympathy as someone trapped in an inadequate life and bewildered by recent social changes.

In the movies a more iconoclastic, countercultural spirit was beginning to take hold. Studio moguls such as Jack Warner and Darryl Zanuck were no longer calling the shots, and in the late 1960s and early 1970s several traditional big-budget films bombed at the box office. The financial success of such pictures as *Bonnie and Clyde* and *The Graduate*, with younger actors Warren Beatty and Dustin Hoffman and new directors Arthur Penn and Mike Nichols, opened the doors to a new generation of filmmakers. In 1970 director Robert Altman's *M*A*S*H* (Mobile Army Surgical Hospital), although set in the Korean War, carried a strong anti-Vietnam War message. The villains are not the enemy soldiers but the war itself and an army bureaucracy interested in wealth, power, and sex. The humorous if not cruel antics of the unit are, often at the expense of nurse "Hot-Lips" Houlihan. In some scenes, the blood gushes like geysers in the surgical tents. There were few traditional sensibilities that *M*A*S*H* did not offend. Its themes were antimilitary, anticlerical, and antiauthoritarian. The *New York Times* called it "the first American movie openly to ridicule belief in God," but Pauline Kael claimed that it was "the best American war movie since sound came in."[142]

Like much of the country, though, Hollywood was influenced by cultural and generational divisions, and the more traditional view of the military could still find an audience. Although *M*A*S*H* was nominated for five Academy Awards in 1970, it was *Patton*, the film biography of the famous World War II general, that actually won six Oscars. *Patton* did not take a simple 1940s Hollywood view of war, but neither did it vilify Gen. George S. Patton. He was portrayed as a brilliant commander who could also be cruel and narrow-minded. Richard Nixon, who certainly would have been repelled by *M*A*S*H*, if he ever saw it, considered *Patton* one of his favorite films, having screened it during the time of the Cambodian invasion. Both films, however, were both commercial and artistic successes, reflecting America's own divided mind.

Coda: Living with a Fractured Consensus

The counterculture's more bizarre manifestations—love-ins and the celebration of hallucinogenic drugs—may have affected only a relative few, but it was hard to ignore its broader attitudes: the challenge to the status quo, resistance to traditional authority, tolerance for different racial groups and life-styles, derision of conventionality, disregard of emotional self-restraint, more open sexuality, and skepticism about America's role abroad. Many of the baby boomers would look at American life in ways that fundamentally differed from those of their parents. Without such a challenge to the dominant culture it is doubtful that the feminist movement, the environmental movement, and the consumer movement would have flourished.

Both the New Left and the counterculture were also important to the rebirth of conservatism in the post-Watergate years. Ironically, the New Left's disdain for centralized power and distrust of the state became a theme of conservatism. The New Left opposed the military-industrial complex, drug laws, abortion laws, and censorship laws. The conservatives opposed excessive economic regulations, high income taxes, the expansion of the welfare state, intrusive environmental laws, and new gun control laws. E. J. Dionne concludes, "Many young voters who had been drawn to the New Left and the counterculture because it attacked authority were drawn to conservatism because it attacked the state. Thus did the New Left wage war against the paternalistic liberal state and defeat it. The right picked up the pieces."[143]

If the economic libertarian strain of conservatism could trace some of its roots to the New Left, the religious right was galvanized, in part, by the counterculture. Many in the South and in America's heartland whose lives were bound by tradition, churchgoing, and patriotism found the messages of the counterculture disturbing and even threatening. The economic shocks of the 1970s, spurred by the rise in energy prices and increased foreign competition, served to deepen the insecurity of the American middle and working classes. As social pathologies began to increase—teenage pregnancies, drug usage, poor educational performance, and violent crime—they demanded more traditional authority, not less.

In another twist of irony, the political adherents of such cultural conservatism—the religious right, the pro-life movement, the opponents of affirmative action—adopted the techniques employed by the civil rights movement and the student left in the 1960s, including marches, demonstrations, and grassroots organizing. In states such as California, Washington, and Colorado, where it was possible, cultural conservatives would resort to ballot initiative and referendum. Talk radio, a growing phenomenon in the 1990s, became a voice of a conservative populism. The conservative movement, once the exclusive province of the upper-middle class and a few intellectual ideologues, gained its support from the Wallace voters and Nixon's silent majority.

The tumult of the 1960s and early 1970s thus ended the notion of a dominant common culture confronting a counterculture. Instead, we now have differing cultural perspectives in constant tension but no dominant perspective. The result is an America far more complicated and diverse than could have been imagined at the end of World War II. As David Chalmers puts it, "Every classic social question erupted into the streets of the nation as challenges to social stasis and stability: individual versus society; integration versus separation; self-expression versus authority; social justice versus order; change versus stability; reform versus revolution; nonviolence versus violence; spiritual values versus materialism; rationality versus the irrational."[144]

The culture wars that erupted and the deeper ideological fault line that appeared in the 1980s and 1990s were an inevitable result. Without a prevailing cultural consensus, less can be assumed about what is acceptable in politics, entertainment, art, and even personal relationships. We cannot sort through these battles on our way to perhaps a new consensus until we better understand how and why the old one collapsed.

During the mid-1970s the Republicans paid the price for the Watergate scandals and a skittish economy. In the 1974 congressional elections they lost forty-eight seats in the House and four in the Senate. Nixon's successor, Gerald R. Ford, who had issued a presidential pardon for the disgraced former president, lost the 1976 presidential election to Georgia's former governor, Jimmy Carter.

Carter approached the presidency as a chastened liberal without an overarching agenda or a dramatic label (New Deal, New Frontier, Great Society). In the 1976 Democratic primaries he presented himself as something of a populist, focusing on the problems of unemployment and inflation and minimizing the more divisive social issues. He sounded what later became known as neoliberal themes: the reorganization of government, the reduction of bureaucracy, reform of the tax code, and a balanced budget. In the Florida primary he attracted enough white working-class and black voters to defeat George Wallace; and in the Pennsylvania primary, he defeated labor's candidate, Sen. Henry Jackson (D-WA), and the liberal favorite, Rep. Morris Udall (D-AZ).

Carter soon learned the limits of neoliberalism and how far it could carry him with the liberal base of the Democratic Party. In order to secure the nomination he promised the National Education Association a new Department of Education; the United Auto Workers, a government-sponsored health-care plan; and the Democratic mayors, an urban economic development initiative and public works jobs to provide fiscal relief.[145] He was able to keep his black-white populist constituency together long enough to defeat Gerald Ford, carrying the vast majority of southern Wallace voters and all the southern states except Florida and Virginia. Once in office, however, Carter could not reconcile his neoliberalism with the demands of the liberal Democrats. The welfare reform proposals that came to his desk from Health, Education and Welfare Secretary Joseph Califano involved more federal spending for jobs or cash assistance; and the recommendation of Housing and Urban Development Secretary Patricia Harris for a national urban policy called for adding another $8 to $10 billion to the $50 billion of government aid to the cities.[146] Carter rejected both proposals and could develop neither a welfare policy nor an urban policy that pleased the core Democratic constituency.

When faced with double-digit inflation in 1979–80, Carter reverted to budgetary austerity, further eroding his support in the Democratic Party. His fiscal year 1979 budget called for virtually no increase in discretionary domestic spending. Other problems—the Soviet invasion of Afghanistan, a sharp increase in oil prices, the Tehran hostage crisis, and a rise in interest rates—made Carter's political position untenable in 1980. These calamitous events compounded his fundamental political failure. He could not satisfy either middle- or working-class Americans—who were increasingly disenchanted with government—or the poor and minorities, who were convinced that more domestic spending was essential to their needs.

This political failure was not personal. Carter faced a dilemma that no Democratic president could have easily resolved. His inability to build on the biracial populist base he had tapped in 1976 was symptomatic of the changing public perception of American liberalism. Post–New Deal liberalism was linked in the minds of many with military stalemate in Vietnam, campus unrest, double-digit inflation, oil price increases, racial quotas, and now ineffective presidents. The failure of Sen. Ted Kennedy (D-MA), a voice of traditional liberalism, to mount a successful challenge to Carter for the 1980 Democratic nomination was just additional evidence of the difficulty of stoking up the old fires.

All this was in sorry contrast to the 1940s, when liberalism was ascendant and associated with strong presidents (Roosevelt and Truman), victory in World War II, the early foreign policy successes of the Cold War (the Marshall Plan, the Berlin blockade, the North Atlantic Treaty Organization or NATO, the democratization of West Germany and Japan), broad-based prosperity, new opportunities for workers and minorities, and a dramatic increase in the nation's wealth. New Deal liberalism sounded major themes and spawned proposals designed to appeal to a broad base of working- and middle-class Americans: Social Security, the G.I. Bill, regional economic development (the TVA and the Rural Electrification Administratrion). It gained loyalties and kept them for a generation. Liberals in the 1970s and 1980s, facing a more diverse and divided America, stitched together programs designed to appeal to particular communities (blacks, feminists, gays, environmentalists) but often lacking in broader national appeal. Whereas past liberal presidents such as Roosevelt, Kennedy, and Johnson had spoken of America's limitless possibilities, Carter harped upon the theme of limits. At the dedication of the John F. Kennedy Library in Boston, he intoned, "The world of 1980 is as different from the world of 1960 as the world of 1960 was from that of 1940. . . . We have a keener appreciation of limits now, the limits of government, limits on the use of military power. . . . We face centrifugal forces in our society and in our political system—forces of regionalism, forces of ethnicity, of narrow economic interest, of single issue politics—that are testing the resiliency of American pluralism and of our ability to govern."[147]

As the 1970s ended and the 1980s began, Carter's pessimism seemed to fit the times. America had yet to regain its confidence after the disaster of Vietnam. Soviet troops had invaded Afghanistan; Americans were being held hostage in Iran, where a virulent anti-American regime had ousted the pro-American shah; and a Soviet military build-up appeared to have outpaced that of the United States. At home the misery index (a combination of the unemployment and inflation rates that Carter had devised during his 1976 campaign against Gerald Ford, when it stood at 12.5 percent) was at nearly 20 percent. Patrick Caddell, a political consultant to Carter, understood that "there was no way we could survive if we allowed [the 1980 election] to become a referendum on the first three years of the Carter Administration."[148]

Carter's Republican opponent in 1980, Ronald Reagan, turned Carter's pessimism against him, claiming, "All of us recognize that these people who keep talking about the age of limits are really talking about their own limitations, not America's."[149] Gaining substantial numbers of working-class votes, Reagan defeated Carter by a significant margin. An ideological Republican conservative, he was the first president of the post–World War II era to challenge domestic liberalism and sense its weakness. He realized that many working-class and middle-class Americans no longer equated their economic interests with the growth of the state, that much of their anger was directed at the state and the elites. "For the average American, the message is clear," Reagan asserted. "Liberalism is no longer the answer—it is the problem."[150] He also benefited from the discontent over what seemed to many an atmosphere of cultural permissiveness and political pessimism. There was a rising divorce rate, an alarming increase in out-of-wedlock teenage pregnancies, greater drug use, and a steady rise in the incidence of violent crime. Reagan directed his rhetoric toward this unease, promising in a final campaign speech "an era of national renewal that will revitalize the values of family, work, and neighborhood."[151]

During the Reagan presidency (1981–1989) the conservative agenda set the tone for American politics. Reagan's ideological coalition consisted of three groups: the neoconservatives, the supply-side economists, and the religious right. The neoconservatives were disillusioned liberal intellectuals who felt that the Democratic Party was leading a retreat from world leadership. They championed Reagan's efforts to rebuild the military, to reconstruct the arms control process around proposals for deep cuts in nuclear arsenals, to place the Soviets on the ideological defensive, and to support anti-Soviet insurgencies in the Third World. In economic policy the supply-siders argued for steep tax reductions that would encourage savings and investment and thus recharge the American economy. In social policy, where Reagan had the least success, the religious right fought for limits on abortion, the reinstitution of school prayer, and restrictions on pornography.

Reagan had mixed results in domestic policy. He was successful in lowering marginal income tax rates and reducing government regulation of business, and after a steep recession in 1981–82 the economy began a substantial recovery that lasted through his administration. His initial effort to reduce domestic spending became only halfhearted, however, in the face of public support for many programs and Democratic control in the House of Representatives. The Democratic leadership in the House would support domestic spending reductions only if the president agreed to reduce military buildup, which he would not do. As the Reagan historian Dinesh D'Souza puts it, the president "reconciled himself to presiding over a large federal government as the price worth paying for his defense policy."[152] The only programs Reagan succeeded in eliminating were revenue sharing and the Comprehensive Education and Training Act. Tax cuts did contribute to the stimulation of the economy and increased federal revenue, but the increase was offset by the continued growth of domestic spending and a 50 percent rise in the defense budget, which led to record federal deficits and a tripling of the national debt.

Initially, Reagan's hard line in foreign policy seemed to garner few results and much criticism. Arms control negotiations with the Soviet Union brought a virtual collapse of the talks and a rebirth of the antinuclear movement in the United States and Western Europe around the issue of a nuclear freeze; his funding of the contra forces fighting the leftist Sandinista regime in Nicaragua brought serious opposition from many Democrats in Congress; and his announcement of the Strategic Defense Initiative to defend against nuclear attacks was ridiculed as "star wars." Nonetheless, Reagan persisted in the policies. He was convinced, as were few in or out of his administration, that the Soviet system was doomed to collapse and that free markets and democracy were the wave of the future.

In 1985, Mikhail Gorbachev, a younger and more modern figure, assumed power in Moscow. Recognizing that in fact the Soviet Union was a system in economic and social decay, he developed a new domestic strategy comprising *glasnost* (political openness and reform) and *perestroika* (economic restructuring and revitalization), and a foreign policy designed to relax tensions with the United States and reduce the economic burden of the arms race.

After their failure to reach an agreement on comprehensive nuclear arms reduction at a summit meeting in Reykjavik, Iceland, in 1987, Reagan and Gorbachev did conclude a breakthrough agreement to eliminate all intermediate nuclear forces from the continent of Europe. Two years later, in a startling series of events, the Berlin Wall fell, and Communist regimes in Poland, Czechoslovakia, Hungary, Romania, East Germany, and Bulgaria collapsed without any Soviet interference. By 1991 the Soviet Union itself had dissolved, and the Cold War was over. The extent to which Ronald Reagan's policy contributed to that collapse remains a subject of continuing historical debate.

Reagan made the least impact in social policy. He gave only rhetorical support to the pro-life movement and rarely mentioned school prayer. Many of the social pathologies that had concerned the religious right—teenage pregnancies, drug usage, the high divorce rate—continued unabated. The divorce rate from 1980 to 1990 increased 40 percent. The number of children born outside of marriage, which had reached 20 percent by 1980, rose to 25 percent in 1990. The availability in the 1980s of cheap, smokable crack cocaine in the black inner cities was largely responsible for an alarming increase in the crime rate and in the number of the homeless.[153]

At the root of many of these problems was the weakening of the American family. Reagan and other conservatives had blamed liberalism and the welfare state for undermining the family but offered few solutions. Liberals were at an even greater loss and on the political defensive throughout the 1980s. George Bush, Reagan's successor, was able to win the presidency in 1988 by dubbing his opponent, Gov. Michael Dukakis of Massachusetts, a "liberal" whose political values were at odds with those of the American people. Bush's political ads focused on Dukakis's veto of a bill requiring students to pledge allegiance to the flag, his opposition to the death penalty, and his authorization of weekend furloughs for prisoners who had been convicted of violent crimes.

President Bush seemed far more at home in foreign policy than in the domestic arena. As the East European Communist empire disintegrated in 1989, Bush was careful not to push matters too far and to continue good relations with Gorbachev. The results were dramatic. In 1990 the Soviets agreed to a treaty uniting East and West Germany within the NATO alliance and to another that virtually dismantled the Soviet army in Europe. In early 1991 the Soviets, although they did not play a military role in the operation known as Desert Storm, were part of the political coalition led by the United States to force the invading army of Iraq's Saddam Hussein out of Kuwait. Then in August a group of Soviet hard-liners held Gorbachev captive at his summerhouse and attempted to assume power. Boris Yeltsin, the president of Russia, resisted them bravely in Moscow; the coup collapsed; and within months the Soviet Union itself was abolished. The leaders of Russia, Ukraine, and Belarus announced, along with other regions of the former USSR, that they would become separate states. The Cold War had ended.

Despite these historic events and America's swift victory over Iraq, George Bush stumbled politically. In 1991 the American economy drifted into a recession, albeit a relatively mild one, and budget deficits were again ballooning. Bush was forced, in part by a Democratic Congress, to renege on a solemn campaign pledge not to raise taxes. Unemployment rose to 7 percent and many large companies were beginning to founder. Numerous white-collar workers, often immune from past recessions, were forced out of work as companies "restructured." Bush had no dramatic remedies for the situation. His approval rating, at a record 91 percent after Desert Storm, began to plummet.

Bush was opposed for reelection by Gov. Bill Clinton of Arkansas and an independent candidate, billionaire Ross Perot. Clinton presented himself as a "New Democrat" whose emphasis would be not on the old welfare state but on investment in jobs, technology, education, and health care. Perot, a blunt-speaking Texan running largely on his own money, directed much of his criticism at Bush for what seemed an out-of-control federal budget deficit. Clinton survived an early sex scandal when his wife, Hillary, joined him in a *60 Minutes* interview to acknowledge their marital problems and their efforts to overcome them. Clinton's campaign recovered; he gained the Democratic nomination and defeated Bush and Perot with 43 percent of the popular vote.

Early in his first term, Clinton introduced an ambitious health-care bill, which was to be the centerpiece of his reform agenda. Considered too expensive and bureaucratic, it was blocked in Congress. Thrown off balance by a complex real estate scandal known as Whitewater and stymied in his reform efforts, Clinton and the Democrats were rocked by the unexpected Republican capture of both houses of Congress in the 1994 midterm election. Clinton soon regained his political balance and his standing with the public when the Republican Congress was blamed for a temporary shutdown of the federal government following congressional disagreements with the president on a series of funding bills.

Clinton also deftly moved to the right in 1996, signing the Welfare Reform Act, which ended welfare as an entitlement and moved its administration back to the states. That November he easily defeated his opponent, Robert Dole, longtime Republican Senate leader. As the economy boomed in the late 1990s, Clinton's popularity remained high despite his involvement in a sex scandal with a young White House intern, Monica Lewinsky. Although the Republican-controlled House of Representatives voted in 1998 to impeach Clinton for perjury and obstruction of justice, the Senate failed to convict him of any of the charges. The intensity of the debate over the Clinton-Lewinsky sex scandal, which raged for over a year, was another manifestation of the depth and persistence of America's cultural divide.

Throughout the 1980s and 1990s, issues of private morality and public behavior continued to divide the country. Popularly known as the culture wars, these disputes insinuated themselves into numerous aspects of American life—education, the arts, entertainment, law, and politics. There were sharp differences over such matters as restrictions on abortion, gay marriages, prayer in the schools, public funding of sexually explicit art, and approaches to sex education. The liberal or progressive perspective on these issues emphasized tolerance, openness, and diversity. The conservative or orthodox perspective emphasized the imperatives of transcendent religious authority and traditional morality and the importance of self-control over self-expression. As the sociologist James Hunter defines it, "The culture war emerges over fundamentally different conceptions of moral authority, over different ideas and beliefs about truth, the good, obligation to one another, the nature of community. . . . It is, therefore, cultural conflict at its deepest level."[154] As the twenty-first century begins, Americans are once again redefining their politics and culture. Such are the dynamics of a free society.

NOTES

1. James Russell Lowell, "A Few Bits of Roman Mosaic," in *Literary Essays*, 11 vols. (Cambridge, MA: Riverside Press, 1892), 1:189.
2. Michael Barone, *Our Country: The Shaping of America from Roosevelt to Reagan* (New York: Free Press, 1990), 166.
3. Joseph C. Goulden, *The Best Years, 1945–1950* (New York: Antheneum, 1976), 93.
4. Geoffrey Perrett, *Days of Sadness, Years of Triumph: The American People 1939–1945* (Baltimore, MD: Penguin Books, 1974), 334–35.
5. Geoffrey Perret, *A Country Made by War: From the Revolution to Vietnam—The Story of America's Rise to Power* (New York: Random House, 1989), 439.
6. Goulden, *The Best Years*, 67.

7. Alan Brinkley, *The End of Reform: New Deal Liberalism in Recession and War* (New York: Alfred A. Knopf, 1995), 170.
8. Ibid., 259.
9. *The Gallup Poll: Public Opinion, 1935–1971*, 3 vols. (New York: Random House, 1972), 1:499.
10. Quoted in William L. O'Neill, *A Democracy at War: America's Fight at Home and Abroad in World War II* (Cambridge, MA: Harvard University Press, 1993), 251.
11. *Gallup Poll, 1935–1971*, 1:584, 633.
12. Richard Polenberg, *War and Society: The United States, 1941–1945* (Philadelphia: J. B. Lippincott Company, 1972), 145.
13. Ibid.
14. William M. Tuttle, Jr., *Daddy's Gone to War: The Second World War in the Lives of America's Children* (New York: Oxford University Press, 1993), 241.
15. Nicholas Lemann, *The Promised Land: The Great Black Migration and How it Changed America* (New York: Vintage Books, 1992), 70; O'Neill, *Democracy at War*, 239–40.
16. *The Television Code of the National Association of Broadcasters*, 5th ed. (Washington, DC: National Association of Broadcasters, 1959), 2–4.
17. Clayton R. Koppes and Gregory D. Black, *Hollywood Goes to War: How Politics, Profits, and Propaganda Shaped World War II Movies* (Berkeley: University of California Press, 1990), 68.
18. Neal Gabler, *An Empire of Their Own: How the Jews Invented Hollywood* (New York: Bantam Doubleday Dell Publishing Group, 1988), 6–7.
19. Quoted in Joe Morella, Edward Z. Epstein, and John Griggs, *The Films of World War II* (Secaucus, NJ: Citadel Press, 1973), 133.
20. Koppes and Black, *Hollywood Goes to War,* 258.
21. Ibid., 61.
22. Ibid., 161.
23. Robert J. Bresler, "The Death of Hollywood's Golden Age and the Changing American Character," *USA Today* 125 (1997): 64–67.
24. Stephen J. Whitfield, *The Culture of the Cold War* (Baltimore, MD: Johns Hopkins University Press, 1991), 70; Michael Kazin, *The Populist Persuasion: An American History* (New York: Basic Books, 1995), 168.
25. William H. Chafe, *The Unfinished Journey: America since World War II,* 3d ed. (New York: Oxford University Press, 1995), 112–13.
26. When asked in a January 1947 poll whether they supported government ownership of the banks, rails, coal mines, and electric power, about 65 percent of the public said no. *Gallup Poll, 1935–1971,* 1:623.
27. Quoted in Nelson Lichtenstein, "From Corporatism to Collective Bargaining," in *The Rise and Fall of the New Deal Order, 1930–1980,* ed. Steve Fraser and Gary Gestle (Princeton, NJ: Princeton University Press, 1989), 140.
28. James T. Patterson, *Grand Expectations: The United States, 1945–1974* (New York: Oxford University Press, 1996), 43.
29. *Gallup Poll, 1935–1971,* 1:519.
30. Lichtenstein, "From Corporatism to Collective Bargaining," 122–52.
31. Herbert Stein, *Presidential Economics: The Making of Economic Policy from Roosevelt to Clinton,* 3d rev. ed. (Washington, DC: American Enterprise Institute, 1994), 84.
32. *Gallup Poll, 1935–1971,* 1:495.

33. Stein, *Presidential Economics,* 68.
34. Patterson, *Grand Expectations,* 56.
35. For a discussion of Keyserling's influence, see Alonzo Hamby, *Beyond the New Deal: Harry S. Truman and American Liberalism* (New York: Columbia University Press, 1974), 297–303.
36. Quoted in ibid., 281.
37. Polls taken July 1950; see *Gallup Poll, 1935–1971,* 2:933–34.
38. In addition, the Truman administration had established in 1947 a loyalty program to screen employees in government agencies and to fire any affiliated with groups "designated by the Attorney General as totalitarian, fascistic, communistic or subversive." For a full discussion, see Richard M. Fried, *Nightmare in Red: The McCarthy Era in Perspective* (New York: Oxford University Press, 1990); and Earl Latham, *Communist Controversy in Washington* (Cambridge, MA: Harvard University Press, 1966).
39. Whitfield, *Culture of the Cold War,* 14.
40. Richard Gid Powers, *Not without Honor: The History of American Anticommunism* (New York: Free Press, 1995), 427.
41. David Caute, *The Great Fear: The Anti-Communist Purge under Truman and Eisenhower* (New York: Simon and Schuster, 1978), 505.
42. John Cogley, *Report on Blacklisting I: Movies* (New York: Fund for the Republic, 1956), 282.
43. *Congressional Record,* 81st Cong., 2d sess., p. 3, 96:3281–88.
44. Laurence Leamer, *As Time Goes By: The Life of Ingrid Bergman* (New York: Harper and Row, 1986), 300.
45. Powers, *Not without Honor,* 227.
46. Bernard Crick, *George Orwell: A Life* (Boston: Little, Brown and Company, 1980), 393–94.
47. Quoted in Richard H. Pells, *The Liberal Mind in a Conservative Age: American Intellectuals in the 1940s and 1950s* (New York: Harper and Row, 1985), 133.
48. Ibid., 138.
49. "Our Country and Our Culture: A Symposium," *Partisan Review* 19, (May–June 1952): 282-84.
50. Arthur M. Schlesinger, Jr., *The Vital Center* (Boston: Little, Brown and Company, 1949), 165–70.
51. Adlai E. Stevenson, *A Call to Greatness* (New York: Harper and Brothers, 1954), 35.
52. Quoted in Stephen Ambrose, *Eisenhower, the President* (New York: Simon and Schuster, 1984), 218–20.
53. E. J. Dionne, Jr., *Why Americans Hate Politics* (New York: Simon and Schuster, 1991), 175.
54. Paul Johnson, *Modern Times: The World from the Twenties to the Nineties,* rev. ed. (New York: HarperCollins, 1991), 461.
55. Landon Y. Jones, *Great Expectations: America and the Baby Boom Generation* (New York: Ballantine Books, 1980), 29.
56. Robert Sklar, *Movie-Made America: A Social History of American Movies* (New York: Random House, 1975), 253.
57. Nora Sayre, *Running Time: Films of the Cold War* (New York: Dial Press, 1982), 111.
58. Martha Bayles, *The Hole in Our Soul: The Loss of Beauty and Meaning in American Popular Music* (New York: Free Press, 1994), and "Will the Real Elvis Please Stand Up?" *Wall Street Journal,* August 15, 1997.

58. Wini Breines, *Young, White, and Miserable: Growing Up Female in the Fifties* (Boston: Beacon Press, 1992), 94.

60. Patterson, *Grand Expectations*, 374.

61. Breines, *Young, White, and Miserable*, 51; and Steven Mintz and Susan Kellogg, *Domestic Revolutions: A Social History of American Family Life* (New York: Free Press, 1988), 178.

62. Joanne Meyerowitz, "Beyond the Feminine Mystique: A Reassessment of Postwar Mass Culture," *Journal of American History* 79 (1993), 1455–82.

63. William H. Whyte, *The Organization Man* (New York: Simon and Schuster, 1956); David Riesman with Reuel Denney and Nathan Glazer, *The Lonely Crowd: A Study of the American Character* (New Haven, CN: Yale University Press, 1950).

64. Geoffrey Perrett, *A Dream of Greatness: The American People, 1945–1963* (New York: Coward, McCann and Geoghegan, 1979), 307.

65. William F. Buckley, Jr., "Reflections on Election Eve," *National Review,* November 3, 1956, 6–7; and George H. Nash, *The Conservative Intellectual Movement in America since 1945* (New York: Basic Books, 1976), 253–55.

66. Frank S. Meyer, "The Politics of 'The Impossible,' " *National Review,* November 7, 1959, 459.

67. For a discussion of Eisenhower's thinking, see John Lewis Gaddis, *We Now Know: Rethinking Cold War History* (New York: Oxford University Press, 1997), 221–259.

68. Quoted in Nash, *The Conservative Intellectual Movement*, 254.

69. Jack Kerouac, *On the Road* (New York: Viking Press, 1957), 8.

70. Allen Ginsberg, *Howl and Other Poems* (San Francisco: City Lights Press, 1956), 9.

71. Paul O'Neil, "The Only Revolution Around," *Life*, November 30, 1959; Norman Podhoretz, "Where Is the Beat Generation Going?" *Esquire,* December 1958, 148–50.

72. "Mort Sahl at the Hungry i," Verve Records, 1960.

73. David McReynolds, "The Beat Generation," *Village Voice*, March 11, 1959.

74. Quoted in Taylor Branch, *Parting the Waters: America in the King Years, 1954–1963* (New York: Simon and Schuster, 1988), 275.

75. Todd Gitlin, *The Sixties: Years of Hope, Days of Rage* (New York: Bantam Books, 1987), 83.

76. Chafe, *Unfinished Journey*, 144.

77. William L. O'Neill, *Coming Apart: An Informal History of America in the 1960s* (New York: New York Times Book Company, 1971), 4.

78. Norman Mailer, "Superman Comes to the Supermarket: Hipster as Presidential Candidate," in *Some Honorable Men: Political Conventions, 1960–1972* (Boston: Little, Brown and Company, 1976), 21–26.

79. Quoted in Arthur Schlesinger, Jr., *A Thousand Days: John F. Kennedy in the White House* (Boston: Houghton Mifflin Company, 1965), 729.

80. Quoted in Allen J. Matusow, *The Unraveling of America: A History of Liberalism in the 1960s* (New York: Harper and Row, 1984), 31.

81. Alfred Kazin, "The President and Other Intellectuals," *American Scholar* 30 (1961): 498–516.

82. Quoted in Matusow, *The Unraveling of America*, 40.

83. Theodore H. White, *The Making of a President, 1960* (New York: New American Library, 1962), 215–20.

84. Barry Goldwater, *Conscience of a Conservative* (New York: Victor Publishing Company, 1960), 18.

85. Quoted in Theodore H. White, *The Making of a President, 1964* (New York: New American Library, 1966), 112.

86. Commencement address at American University in Washington, DC, June 10, 1963, in *Public Papers of the Presidents: John F. Kennedy* (Washington, DC: Government Printing Office, 1964), 459–64.

87. The essay was published the next year as a book: James Baldwin, *The Fire Next Time* (New York: Dell Publishing Company, 1963).

88. Television address, June 11, 1963, in *Public Papers of the Presidents: John F. Kennedy*, 468–71.

89. Quoted in Branch, *Parting the Waters*, 824.

90. Quoted in Stephen Skowronek, *The Politics Presidents Make: Leadership from John Adams to George Bush* (Cambridge, MA: Harvard University Press, 1993), 335.

91. Irwin Unger, *The Best of Intentions: The Triumph and Failure of the Great Society under Kennedy, Johnson, and Nixon* (New York: Doubleday and Company, 1996), 85–100.

92. Robert J. Bresler, "The End of the Cold War and the Collapse of Conservative and Liberal Statism," *Religion and Public Life* 30 (1997): 41–42.

93. Quoted in Frederick F. Siesel, *Troubled Journey: From Pearl Harbor to Ronald Reagan* (New York: Hill and Wang, 1984), 158, and in Skowronek, *The Politics Presidents Make*, 339.

94. Commencement address at the University of Michigan, May 22, 1964, in *Public Papers of the Presidents of the United States: Lyndon B. Johnson, 1963–1964* (Washington, DC: Government Printing Office, 1964), 704–6.

95. Unger, *The Best of Intentions*, 145.

96. Ibid., 349–51.

97. John E. Schwarz, *America's Hidden Success: A Reassessment of Twenty Years of Public Policy* (New York: W. W. Norton, 1983), 39, 47.

98. Quoted in James Miller, *Democracy Is in the Streets: From Port Huron to the Siege of Chicago* (New York: Simon and Schuster, 1987), 144.

99. Matusow, *The Unraveling of America*, 315.

100. Ibid., 317.

101. John A. Andrew III, *The Other Side of the Sixties: Young Americans for Freedom and the Rise of Conservative Politics* (New Brunswick, NJ: Rutgers University Press, 1997), 2.

102. Quoted in Lawrence Suid, "The Pentagon and Hollywood: Dr. Strangelove," in *American History/American Film*, ed. John E. O'Connor and Martin A. Jackson (New York: Ungar Publishing Company, 1988), 233.

103. Ian MacDonald, *Revolution in the Head: The Beatles' Records and the Sixties* (London: Fourth Estate Limited, 1994), 7.

104. Matusow, *The Unraveling of America*, 294.

105. Quoted in Larry Berman, *Planning a Tragedy: The Americanization of the War in Vietnam* (New York: W. W. Norton, 1982), 149.

106. Miller, *Democracy Is in the Streets*, 223.

107. Carl Oglesby, "Trapped in a System," in *Takin' It to the Streets: A Sixties Reader*, ed. Alexander Bloom and Wini Breines (New York: Oxford University Press, 1995), 220–25.

108. Gitlin, *The Sixties*, 210.

109. Matusow, *The Unraveling of America*, 277.

110. Ibid., 302.

111. Gregory Calvert, "In White America: Radical Consciousness and Social Change," in Bloom and Breines, *Takin' It to the Streets*, 130.

112. Quoted in Lawrence I. Murray, "Hollywood, Nihilism, and the Youth Culture of the Sixties," in O'Connor and Jackson, *American History/American Film*, 249.

113. Peter Biskind, *Easy Riders, Raging Bulls: How the Sex-Drug-and-Rock-'n'-Roll Generation Saved Hollywood* (New York: Simon and Schuster, 1998), 49.

114. Robert Brent Toplin, *History by Hollywood: The Use and Abuse of the American Past* (Urbana: University of Illinois Press, 1996), 134.

115. Patterson, *Grand Expectations*, 656.

116. Unger, *Best of Intentions*, 247.

117. William Julius Wilson, *The Truly Disadvantaged: The Inner City, the Underclass, and Public Policy* (Chicago: University of Chicago Press, 1987).

118. Quoted in Terry H. Anderson, *The Movement and the Sixties* (New York: Oxford University Press, 1995), 176–77.

119. Quoted in Matusow, *The Unraveling of America*, 365–66.

120. Lyndon Baines Johnson, *The Vantage Point: Perspectives of the Presidency, 1963–1969* (New York: Popular Library, 1971), 173.

121. David H. Colburn and George E. Pozzetta, "Race, Ethnicity, and the Evolution of Political Legitimacy," in *The Sixties from Memory to History*, ed. David Farber (Chapel Hill: University of North Carolina Press, 1994), 120.

122. Gitlin, *The Sixties*, 305–6.

123. Quoted in Kazin, *The Populist Persuasion*, 234–35.

124. Ibid., 235

125. David Farber, "The Silent Majority and Talk about Revolution," in Farber, *The Sixties*, 300.

126. Lawrence Baskir and William Strauss, *Chance and Circumstance: The Draft, the War, and the Vietnam Generation* (New York: Alfred A. Knopf, 1978), 1–11.

127. Michael S. Sherry, *In the Shadow of War: The United States since the 1930s*, (New Haven, CT: Yale University Press, 1995), 295.

128. Quoted in John Morton Blum, *Years of Discord: American Politics and Society, 1961–1974* (New York: W. W. Norton, 1991), 313–14.

129. Patterson, *Grand Expectations*, 754–55.

130. Jonathan Rauch, "What Nixon Wrought," *New Republic*, May 16, 1994, 31.

131. Joan Hoff, *Nixon Reconsidered* (New York: Basic Books, 1994), 22; and Jonathan Aitken, *Nixon: A Life* (Washington, DC: Regnery Publishing Company, 1993), 397–98.

132. Bresler, "The End of the Cold War," 44.

133. Stein, *Presidential Economics*, 195.

134. Richard Scammon and Ben Wattenberg, *The Real Majority* (New York: Coward-McCann, 1970).

135. Richard M. Nixon, *RN: The Memoirs of Richard Nixon*, 2 vols. (New York: Warner Books, 1978), 1:608.

136. *Alexander v. Holmes County Board of Education*, 396 U.S. 19 (1969); and *Swann v. Charlotte-Mecklenburg County Board of Education*, 402 U.S. 1 (1971).

137. Quoted in Stephen F. Ambrose, *Nixon: The Triumph of a Politician, 1962–1972* (New York: Simon and Schuster, 1989), 337–38.

138. Patterson, *Grand Expectations*, 736.

139. Peter N. Carroll, *It Seemed Like Nothing Happened: The Tragedy and Promise of America in the 1970s* (New York: Holt, Rinehart and Winston, 1982), 86.

140. Dan T. Carter, *The Politics of Rage: George Wallace, the Origins of the New Conservatism, and the Transformation of American Politics* (New York: Simon and Schuster, 1995), 424.

141. Quoted in Ambrose, *Nixon*, 605.

142. Quoted in Biskind, *Easy Riders, Raging Bulls*, 97.

143. Dionne, *Why Americans Hate Politics*, 54.

144. David Chalmers, *And the Crooked Places Made Straight: The Struggle for Social Change in the 1960s*, 2d ed. (Baltimore, MD: Johns Hopkins University Press, 1996), 192.

145. Stuart E. Eizenstat, "President Carter, the Democratic Party, and the Making of Domestic Policy," in *The Presidency and Domestic Politics of Jimmy Carter*, ed. Herbert D. Rosenbaum and Alexej Ugrinsky (Westport, CT: Greenwood Press, 1994), 7.

146. Burton I. Kaufman, *The Presidency of James Earl Carter* (Lawrence: University Press of Kansas, 1993), 52–54.

147. David Broder et al., *Pursuit of the Presidency, 1980* (New York: Berkley Books, 1980), 233–34.

148. Quoted in John Kenneth White, *The New Politics of Old Values* (Hanover, NH: University Press of New England, 1988), 55.

149. Quoted in Gary Wills, *Reagan's America: Innocents at Home* (Garden City, NY: Doubleday and Company, 1987), 385.

150. Quoted in Carroll, *It Seemed Like Nothing Happened*, 324.

151. Ronald Reagan, "Vision for America," television broadcast, November 3, 1980, quoted in John Kenneth White, *The New Politics of Old Values* (Hanover, NH: University Press of New England, 1988), 5.

152. Dinesh D'Souza, *Ronald Reagan: How an Ordinary Man Became an Extraordinary Leader* (New York: Free Press, 1997), 102.

153. David Frum, *Dead Right* (New York: Basic Books, 1994), 69–70.

154. James Davison Hunter, *Culture Wars: The Struggle to Define America* (New York: Basic Books, 1991), 49.

Suggestions for Further Reading

GENERAL HISTORY

For a comprehensive overview of the era, see James T. Patterson, *Grand Expectations: The United States, 1945–1974* (New York: Oxford University Press, 1996); and William Chafe, *The Unfinished Journey: America since World War II*, 3d ed. (New York: Oxford University Press, 1995). John Patrick Diggins, *The Proud Decades: America in War and Peace, 1941–1960* (New York: W. W. Norton and Company, 1998), is a highly readable and balanced account of the 1940s and 1950s. John Morton Blum, *The Years of Discord, 1961–1974* (New York: W. W. Norton and Company, 1991), is a helpful perspective on the 1960s and early 1970s. Michael Barone, *Our Country: The Shaping of America from Roosevelt to Reagan* (New York: Free Press, 1990), is a good starting point for an understanding of American political history in the second half of the twentieth century. Although it concentrates on working-class politics, Michael Kazin, *The Populist Persuasion: An American History* (New York: Basic Books, 1995), is a good complement to Barone.

AMERICA IN WORLD WAR II

Although written a quarter-century ago, these books remain valuable accounts of home-front America: John Morton Blum, *V Is for Victory: Politics and American Culture during World War II* (New York: Harcourt Brace Jovanovich, 1976); Richard Polenberg, *War and Society: The United States, 1941–1945* (New York: J. B. Lippincott Company, 1972); Geoffrey Perrett, *Days of Sadness, Years of Triumph: The American People, 1939–1945* (Baltimore, MD: Penguin Books, 1974). A more recent addition to the literature is William L. O'Neill, *A Democracy at War: America's Fight at Home and Abroad in World War II* (Cambridge, MA: Harvard University Press, 1993). Among the most valuable books on American movies during World War II is Clayton R. Koppes and Gregory D. Black, *Hollywood Goes to War: How Politics, Profits, and Propaganda Shaped World War II Movies*

(Berkeley: University of California Press, 1990). And no one with any serious interest in films should be without Ephraim Katz, *The Film Encyclopedia,* 3d ed. (New York: HarperCollins, 1998).

THE COLD WAR

Stephen J. Whitfield, *The Culture of the Cold War* (Baltimore, MD: Johns Hopkins University Press, 1991), is a provocative and critical look at American culture with a focus on its anti-Communist obsession, as are the essays in Lary May, ed., *Recasting America: Culture and Politics in the Age of the Cold War* (Chicago: University of Chicago Press, 1989). Richard Gid Powers, *Not without Honor: The History of American Anticommunism* (New York: Free Press, 1995), is a more sympathetic treatment of American anticommunism. For an overview of American foreign policy during the Cold War, see Stephen E. Ambrose and Douglas G. Brinkley, *Rise to Globalism: American Foreign Policy since 1938,* 8th rev. ed. (New York: Penguin Books, 1997). A more analytical look is found in John Lewis Gaddis, *Strategies of Containment: A Critical Appraisal of Postwar American National Security Policy* (New York: Oxford University Press, 1982). Gaddis provides a post–Cold War perspective based on new material from the Russian and Chinese archives in *We Now Know: Rethinking Cold War History* (New York: Oxford University Press, 1997). Melvyn P. Leffler, *A Preponderance of Power: National Security, the Truman Administration, and the Cold War* (Stanford, CA: Stanford University Press, 1992), is an exhaustive history of policymaking in the early Cold War years.

LIBERALISM AND CONSERVATISM

George H. Nash, *The Conservative Intellectual Movement in America since 1945* (New York: Basic Books, 1976), is a comprehensive look at post–World War II conservatism and its major exponents. John Ehrman, *Neoconservatism: Intellectuals and Foreign Affairs, 1945–1954* (New Haven, CT: Yale University Press, 1995), and Gary Dorrien, *The Neoconservative Mind: Politics, Culture, and the War of Ideology* (Philadelphia: Temple University Press, 1993), explain how an important group of Cold War liberals became neoconservatives in the 1960s and 1970s. Alan Brinkley, *The End of Reform: New Deal Liberalism in Recession and War* (New York: Alfred A. Knopf, 1995), is a lucid combination of economic and political history, explaining the New Deal's contribution to postwar liberalism. Richard H. Pells, *The Liberal Mind in a Conservative Age: American Intellectuals in the 1940s and 1950s* (New York: Harper and Row, 1985), is a synthesis of the liberal intellectual response to World War II and the Cold War. Steve Fraser and Gary Gestle, eds., *The Rise and Fall of the New Deal Order, 1930–1980* (Princeton, NJ: Princeton University Press, 1989), is an important collection of essays on the odyssey of American liberalism. E. J. Dionne, Jr., *Why Americans Hate Politics* (New York: Simon and Schuster, 1991), looks at the impact of ideological strife on American politics and public attitudes.

THE LATE 1940s AND 1950s: POLITICS AND CULTURE

Among the overviews of this period are Joseph C. Goulden, *The Best Years, 1945–1950* (New York: Atheneum, 1976); David Halberstam, *The Fifties* (New York: Villard Books, 1993); Douglas T. Miller and Marion Nowak, *The Fifties: The Way We Really Were* (Garden City, NY: Doubleday and Company, 1977); and Geoffrey Perrett, *A Dream of Greatness: The American People, 1945–1963* (New York: Coward, McCann and Geoghegan, 1979). The Truman years are well covered in Alonzo Hamby's *Man of the People: A Life of Harry S. Truman* (New York:

Oxford University Press, 1995); David McCullough's best-selling *Truman* (New York: Simon and Schuster, 1992); and Robert Donovan's two-volume history of the Truman administration: *Conflict and Crisis: The Presidency of Harry S. Truman, 1945–1948* (New York: W. W. Norton and Company, 1977), and *The Tumultuous Years: The Presidency of Harry S. Truman, 1949–1953* (New York: W. W. Norton and Company, 1982). The Eisenhower years are analyzed in Charles Alexander, *Holding the Line: The Eisenhower Era, 1952–1960* (Bloomington: Indiana University Press, 1975); and in Stephen E. Ambrose, *Eisenhower, the President* (New York: Simon and Schuster, 1984). A review of the films of that era can be found in Nora Sayre, *Running Time: Films of the Cold War* (New York: Dial Press, 1982); and Peter Biskind, *Seeing Is Believing: How Hollywood Taught Us to Stop Worrying and Love the Fifties* (New York: Pantheon Books, 1983). Taylor Branch, *Parting the Waters: America in the King Years, 1954–1963* (New York: Simon and Schuster, 1988), is a comprehensive look at the civil rights movement after the Brown desegregation decision. Wini Breines, *Young, White, and Miserable: Growing Up Female in the Fifties* (Boston: Beacon Press, 1992), provides a feminist perspective on that decade.

THE 1960s AND EARLY 1970s

Most of the accounts of this period focus on the protest movements. Topping the list of many worthwhile books is Allen J. Matusow, *The Unraveling of America: A History of Liberalism in the 1960s* (New York: Harper and Row, 1984). Other valuable works are David Chalmers, *And the Crooked Places Made Straight: The Struggle for Social Change in the 1960s*, 2d ed. (Baltimore, MD: Johns Hopkins University Press, 1996); James Miller, *Democracy in the Streets: From Port Huron to the Siege of Chicago;* William L. O'Neill, *Coming Apart: An Informal History of America in the 1960s* (New York: New York Times Book Company, 1971); and Terry H. Anderson, *The Movement and the Sixties* (New York: Oxford University Press, 1995). Todd Gitlin, *The Sixties: Years of Hope, Days of Rage* (New York: Bantam Books, 1987), is helpful as both history and a memoir of a New Left leader. Written from another historical perspective is John A. Andrew III, *The Other Side of the Sixties: Young Americans for Freedom and the Rise of Conservative Politics* (New Brunswick, NJ: Rutgers University Press, 1997). Martha Bayles, *The Hole in Our Soul: The Loss of Beauty and Meaning in American Popular Music* (New York: Free Press, 1994), provides a critical perspective on the evolution of popular tastes.

An important collection of documents and essays is Alexander Bloom and Wini Breines, eds., *Takin' It to the Streets: A Sixties Reader* (New York: Oxford University Press, 1995). David Farber has put together a provocative set of essays in *The Sixties from Memory to History* (Chapel Hill: University of North Carolina Press, 1994). Irwin Unger, *The Best of Intentions: The Triumph and Failure of the Great Society under Kennedy, Johnson, and Nixon* (New York: Doubleday and Company, 1996), is a balanced treatment of one of American liberalism's most important legacies. Peter N. Carroll, *It Seemed Like Nothing Happened: The Tragedy and Promise of America in the 1970s* (New York: Holt, Rinehart and Winston, 1982), is readable early history of that puzzling decade. Peter Biskind, *Easy Riders, Raging Bulls: How the Sex-Drugs-and-Rock-'n'-Roll Generation Saved Hollywood* (New York: Simon and Schuster, 1998), is a fascinating insider's account of the sea change in the film industry in the late 1960s and 1970s.

II

FRANKLIN DELANO ROOSEVELT

1

State of the Union Address

During World War II, President Roosevelt put aside his reform agenda, telling the press that Dr. New Deal had become Dr. Win the War. On January 11, 1944, however, in his eleventh State of the Union address, he sketched his vision of postwar reform and gave his liberal supporters at least a chance to dream. He called for "a second Bill of Rights under which a new basis of security and prosperity can be established for all—regardless of station, race, or creed." In contrast to the original Bill of Rights, which protected individuals from government, this economic Bill of Rights would require an active government. Roosevelt believed that government should assure for everyone the right to a useful and remunerative job, to adequate wages, to decent housing, to adequate medical care, to a good education, and to protection from the economic fears of old age and unemployment. In this address he articulated what would become the heart of postwar liberalism as embodied in Truman's Fair Deal, Kennedy's New Frontier, and Johnson's Great Society.

THE WHITE HOUSE, *January 11, 1944.*

To the Congress of the United States:

This Nation in the past 2 years has become an active partner in the world's greatest war against human slavery.

We have joined with like-minded people in order to defend ourselves in a world that has been gravely threatened with gangster rule. . . .

It is our duty now to begin to lay the plans and determine the strategy for the winning of a lasting peace and the establishment of an

From *State of the Union Messages of the Presidents* (New York: Chelsea House, 1966), 2875, 2880–82.

American standard of living higher than ever before known. We cannot be content, no matter how high that general standard of living may be, if some fraction of our people—whether it be one-third or one-fifth or one-tenth—is ill-fed, ill-clothed, ill-housed, and insecure.

This Republic had its beginning, and grew to its present strength, under the protection of certain inalienable political rights—among them the right of free speech, free press, free worship, trial by jury, freedom from unreasonable searches and seizures. They were our rights to life and liberty.

As our Nation has grown in size and stature, however—as our industrial economy expanded—these political rights proved inadequate to assure us equality in the pursuit of happiness.

We have come to a clear realization of the fact that true individual freedom cannot exist without economic security and independence. "Necessitous men are not freemen." People who are hungry and out of a job are the stuff of which dictatorships are made.

In our day these economic truths have become accepted as self-evident. We have accepted, so to speak, a second Bill of Rights under which a new basis of security and prosperity can be established for all—regardless of station, race, or creed.

Among these are—

The right to a useful and remunerative job in the industries, or shops or farms or mines of the Nation;

The right to earn enough to provide adequate food and clothing and recreation;

The right of every farmer to raise and sell his products at a return which will give him and his family a decent living;

The right of every businessman, large and small, to trade in an atmosphere of freedom from unfair competition and domination by monopolies at home or abroad;

The right of every family to a decent home;

The right to adequate medical care and the opportunity to achieve and enjoy good health;

The right to adequate protection from the economic fears of old age, sickness, accident, and unemployment;

The right to a good education.

All of these rights spell security. And after this war is won we must be prepared to move forward, in the implementation of these rights, to new goals of human happiness and well-being.

America's own rightful place in the world depends in large part upon how fully these and similar rights have been carried into practice for our citizens. For unless there is security here at home there cannot be lasting peace in the world.

One of the great American industrialists of our day—a man who has rendered yeoman service to his country in this crisis—recently emphasized the grave dangers of "rightist reaction" in this Nation. All clear-thinking businessmen share his concern. Indeed, if such reaction should develop—if history were to repeat itself and we were to return to the so-called normalcy of the 1920's—then it is certain that even though we shall have conquered our enemies on the battlefields abroad, we shall have yielded to the spirit of fascism here at home.

I ask the Congress to explore the means for implementing this economic bill of rights—for it is definitely the responsibility of the Congress so to do. Many of these problems are already before committees of the Congress in the form of proposed legislation. I shall from time to time communicate with the Congress with respect to these and further proposals. In the event that no adequate program of progress is evolved, I am certain that the Nation will be conscious of the fact.

Our fighting men abroad—and their families at home—expect such a program and have the right to insist upon it. It is to their demands that this Government should pay heed rather than to the whining demands of selfish pressure groups who seek to feather their nests while young Americans are dying.

The foreign policy that we have been following—the policy that guided us at Moscow, Cairo, and Tehran—is based on the common sense principle which was best expressed by Benjamin Franklin on July 4, 1776: "We must all hang together, or assuredly we shall all hang separately."

I have often said that there are no two fronts for America in this war. There is only one front. There is one line of unity which extends from the hearts of the people at home to the men of our attacking forces in our farthest outposts. When we speak of our total effort, we speak of the factory and the field and the mine as well as of the battleground—we speak of the soldier and the civilian, the citizen and his Government.

Each and every one of us has a solemn obligation under God to serve this Nation in its most critical hour—to keep this Nation great—to make this Nation greater in a better world.

ARTHUR SCHLESINGER, JR.

2 The Vital Center

Arthur Schlesinger, Jr., was not only a leading American historian and adviser to President John F. Kennedy but also a major voice of postwar liberalism and cofounder of the Americans for Democratic Action. In *The Vital Center* he attempted to place liberalism in the context of the Cold War. Schlesinger added to Roosevelt's vision a profound anti-Communist cast: liberalism must reject all forms of totalitarianism and stand for "a belief in the integrity of the individual, in the limited state, in due process of law, in empiricism and gradualism." Schlesinger believed that President Truman's policy of containing Soviet expansion abroad and promoting liberal reform at home could be the basis of a broad national consensus, a consensus around which liberals, unions, and enlightened capitalists could rally.

Introduction [to the 1962 Edition]

The Vital Center was written in the autumn and winter of 1948–49. This was a moment of transition in the post-war history of American liberalism—a moment when the liberal community was engaged in the double task of redefining its attitude toward the phenomenon of Communism and, partly in consequence, of reconstructing the bases of liberal political philosophy.

In the years since, the process of redefinition has been completed: I believe that all American liberals recognize today that liberalism has nothing in common with Communism, either as to means or as to ends.

As for the process of reconstruction, this is by its nature continuous: if liberalism should ever harden into ideology, then, like all ideologies, it would be overwhelmed by the turbulence and unpredictability of history—especially in an age when science and technology

From *The Vital Center* (Boston: Houghton Mifflin, 1949, 1962), ix–xvii, 1–10, 243–56. Reprinted by permission of Arthur Schlesinger, Jr.

have made the velocity of history so much greater than ever before. The continuing enterprise of reconstruction has consequently brought new phases of liberal thought to the forefront in the thirteen years since this book was published. It may be worthwhile to note some of these later developments.

So far as Communism is concerned, in the confused years immediately after the end of the Second World War, and in spite of Stalin's notable record in the thirties of internal terror and international betrayal, the Soviet Union retained for some people traces of the idealistic fervor of the Russian Revolution. By 1962, it seems safe to say that postwar Soviet policy has extinguished any remaining elements of idealism in the Communist appeal. No one with any knowledge of history can believe in the Soviet Union on the supposition that Communist victory would usher in a generous and beneficent society. Where people believe in the Soviet Union today, it is on quite other grounds: it is basically because they are persuaded that, whether they like it or not, Communism is going to win, and that they had therefore better make their terms with a Communist world. The essence of contemporary Soviet policy is to enhance this impression of the inevitability of Communist triumph, to employ every resource of science and politics to identify Communism with the future and to convince people everywhere that they must accept the necessity of Communism or face the certainty of obliteration. They have addressed this policy especially to the southern half of the world where the awakening of underdeveloped countries from centuries of oblivion is discharging new and incalculable energies into human society.

The irony is that the very eagerness with which the intellectuals in emergent nations often embrace Communism itself suggests that Communism is *not* the wave of the future and is, if it is anything, a passing stage to which some may temporarily turn in the quest for modernity. Where Marx portrayed Communism as the fulfillment of the process of modernization, history seems abundantly to show that, if the world avoids thermonuclear suicide, the modernization process, contrary to Marxist prophecy, will vindicate the mixed society and render Communism obsolete.

The Marxist contention has been (a) that capitalism is the predestined casualty of the modernization process, and (b) that Communism is its predestined culmination. In these terms Communism has boasted the certification of history. But history quite plainly refutes the

Communist case. It shows (a) that the mixed society, as it modernizes itself, can overcome the internal contradictions which in Marx's view doomed it to destruction, and (b) that Communism is historically a function of the prefatory rather than the concluding stages of the modernization process.

Marx rested his case for the inevitability of Communist triumph on the theory that capitalism contained the seeds of its own destruction. He argued that the capitalist economy generated inexorable inner tendencies—"contradictions"—which would infallibly bring about its downfall. One inexorable tendency was the increasing wealth of the rich and the increasing poverty of the poor. Another was the increasing frequency and severity of economic crisis. Together these tendencies would infallibly carry society to a point of revolutionary "ripeness" when the proletariat would rise in its wrath, overthrow the possessing classes, and install a classless society. Marx saw no way of denying this process, because he believed that the capitalist state could never be anything but the executive committee of the capitalist class.

This was Marx's fatal error. The capitalist state in developed societies, far from being the helpless instrument of the possessing class, has become the means by which other groups in society have redressed the balance of social power against those whom Hamilton called the "rich and well-born." This has been true in the United States, for example, since the age of Jackson. The liberal democratic state has accomplished two things in particular. It has brought about a redistribution of wealth which has defeated Marx's prediction of progressive immiseration; and it has brought about an economic stabilization which has defeated Marx's prediction of ever worsening economic crisis. What the democratic parties of the developed nations have done, in short, has been to use the state to force capitalism to do what both the classical capitalists and the classical Marxists declared was impossible: to control the business cycle and to reapportion income in favor of those whom Jackson called the "humble members of society."

The champions of the affirmative state, in their determination to avert Marxist revolution, had to fight conservatism at every step along the way. Nonetheless, they persevered; and the twentieth century in America and Great Britain saw the rejection of laissez-faire, the subjugation of the business cycle, the drowning of revolution in a torrent of consumer goods, and the establishment of the "affluent society." The revolutionary fires within capitalism, lit by the great industrialists in the nineteenth century, were put out in the twentieth by the triumphs of industry—and by the liberal politicians, by Theodore Roosevelt and Woodrow Wilson and Franklin D. Roosevelt. Such men ignored the dogmatists, the philosophers of either/or, and created the mixed society. Both classical socialism and classical capitalism were products of the nineteenth century, and their day is over. As a result, capitalism can no longer be relied upon to dig its own grave; and Communism, if it ever comes to developed countries, will come not as a consequence of social evolution but only on the bayonets of the Red Army.

At the same time, history has thrown sharp light on the actual function of Communism. Marx, regarding Communism as the climax of the development process, prophesied that it would come first in the most developed nations. On the contrary, it has come to nations in the early phases of development, like Russia and China; and it has appealed to activists in such nations precisely because they see it as the means of rapid and effective modernization. Instead of being the culmination of the modernization effort, Communism would seem to be a form of social organization to which some countries aspiring to development have resorted in the hope of speeding the pace of modernization. We do not know what will happen to Communism in a Communist state which achieves full development; but if it should then survive in anything like its present form, it would be because of the efficiency of its apparatus of control and terror, not because it is the natural organizational expression of the institutions of affluence.

History thus shows plainly that Communism is not the form of social organization toward which all societies are irresistibly evolving. Rather it is a phenomenon of the transition from stagnation to development, a "disease" (in Walt Rostow's phrase) of the modernization process. Democratic, regulated capitalism—the mixed society—will be far more capable of coping with the long-term consequences of modernization. "The wave of the future," Walter Lippmann has well said, "is not Communist domination of the world. The wave of the future is social reform and social revolution driving us toward the goal of national independence and equality of personal status."

If this is so, it emphasizes more than ever the need to keep abreast of history in our own social ideas and programs. We are all indebted to J. K. Galbraith for his demonstration that the affluent society compels a sweeping reconsideration of social and economic policies. The problems of the New Deal were essentially quantitative problems—problems of meeting stark human needs for food, clothing, shelter, and employment. Most of these needs are now effectively met for most Americans, but a sense of spiritual disquietude remains nevertheless. A full dinner pail turns out to be something less than the promised land. The final lesson of the affluent society is surely that affluence is not enough—that solving the quantitative problems of living only increases the importance of the quality of the life lived. These qualitative problems seem next on the American agenda.

The qualitative aspects of life are only marginally within the reach of government. Yet public policy surely has its contribution to make to the elevation of American civilization. "The great object of the institution of civil government," said John Quincy Adams in his first message to Congress, "is the improvement of the condition of those who are parties to the social compact, and no government, in whatever form constituted, can accomplish the lawful end of its institution but in proportion as it improves the condition of those over whom it is established. . . . Moral, political, intellectual improvement are duties assigned by the Author of Our Existence to social no less than to individual man. For the fulfillment of those duties governments are invested with power, and to the attainment of the end—the progressive improvement of the condition of the governed—the exercise of delegated powers is a duty as sacred and indispensable as the usurpation of powers not granted is criminal and odious."

A central issue of contemporary domestic polity is a variation on the question which concerned Adams—that is, the question of the balance between the amount of our national wealth we reserve for private satisfaction and the amount we dedicate to public need. In the thirties "recovery" was the catchword of our national economic philosophy; in the forties, "full employment"; in the fifties, "economic growth"; in the future, it is likely to become "allocation of resources." No one would argue that steering more resources into the public sector would cure the spiritual ailments of the affluent society; but it seems possible that the resulting improvements in opportunities in education, medical care, social welfare, community planning, culture, and the arts will improve the chances for the individual to win his own spiritual fulfillment.

The impending shift from quantitative to qualitative liberalism emphasizes once again the hazards involved in the degeneration of liberalism into ideology. By tradition American liberalism is humane, experimental, and pragmatic; it has no sense of messianic mission and no faith that all problems have final solutions. It assumes that freedom implies conflict. It agrees with Madison, in the Tenth Federalist, that the competition among economic interests is inherent in a free society. It also agrees with George Bancroft, who wrote: "The feud between the capitalist and laborer, the house of Have and the house of Want, is as old as social union, and can never be entirely quieted; but he who will act with moderation, prefer fact to theory, and remember that everything in the world is relative and not absolute, will see that the violence of the contest may be stilled."

Its empirical temper means that American liberalism stands in sharp contrast to the millennial nostalgia which still characterizes both the American right and the European left—the notion that the day will come when all conflict will pass, when Satan will be cast into the lake of fire and brimstone, and mankind will behold a new heaven and a new earth. José Figueres, the Latin American patriot, calls his finca in the Costa Rican uplands "La Lucha Sin Fin"—the struggle without end. Freedom is inseparable from struggle; and freedom, as Brandeis said, is the great developer; it is both the means employed and the end attained. This, I believe, states the essence of the progressive hope—this and the understanding that the struggle itself offers not only better opportunities for others but a measure of fulfillment for oneself. . . .

Politics in an Age of Anxiety

Western man in the middle of the twentieth century is tense, uncertain, adrift. We look upon our epoch as a time of troubles, an age of anxiety. The grounds of our civilization, of our certitude, are breaking up under our feet, and familiar ideas and institutions vanish as we reach for them, like shadows in the falling dusk. Most of the world has reconciled itself to this half-light, to the reign of insecurity. Even those peoples who hastily traded their insecurities for a mirage of security are finding themselves no better off than the rest. Only the United States still has buffers between itself and the anxieties of our age: buffers of time, of distance, of natural wealth, of national ingenuity, of a stubborn tradition of hope.

A nation which has made a religion of success ought to find it hard to acclimate itself to the middle of the twentieth century. For frustration is increasingly the hallmark of this century—the frustration of triumphant science and rampant technology, the frustration of the most generous hopes and of the most splendid dreams. Nineteen hundred looked forward to the irresistible expansion of freedom, democracy, and abundance; 1950 will look back to totalitarianism, to concentration camps, to mass starvation, to atomic war. Yet for the United States the world tragedy still has the flickering unreality of a motion picture. It grips us as we see it; but, lingering over the familiar milkshake in the bright drugstore, we forget the nightmare in the resurgence of warmth and comfort. Anxiety is something we hear about. It is not yet part of our lives—not of enough of our lives, anyway, to inform our national decisions.

The world tragedy, as it impinges upon Americans, strikes us in relatively simple terms. It is we or they; the United States or the Soviet Union; capitalism or Communism; let us resolve this conflict, and all problems will be solved. These choices are, indeed, the terms of the immediate problem, and it is only in these terms that steps can be taken toward enduring solutions. But let us not deceive ourselves into regarding the American-Russian rivalry as the source of world troubles.

Neither capitalism nor Communism is the cause of the contemporary upsurge of anxiety. Indeed, to a considerable degree, unhappy people have registered the same complaints against both. Each system is charged with having dehumanized the worker, fettered the lower classes, and destroyed personal and political liberty. Before the First War the case against Communism was generally made in terms of efficiency, the case against capitalism in terms of morality: that is, Communism was conceded to be enlightened in principle but was held not to work; capitalism was conceded to work but was held not to be enlightened in principle. After the Soviet experience, the Great Depression, and the Second War, we see a reverse tendency—a disposition to admit the inefficiency of capitalism and justify it as providing the margin on which liberty and democracy subsist; a disposition to believe that the very completeness of Communist control necessarily squeezes out freedom.

In a sense, the arguments are interchangeable, the indictments cancel out. Does not this suggest that both sides have indulged in what Whitehead calls the "fallacy of misplaced concreteness"—the error of mistaking abstractions for concrete realities? We have seen identical criticisms lodged with heat and fervor against the abstractions "capitalism" and "Communism." But these criticisms may perhaps be lodged more profoundly not against any particular system of ownership but against industrial organization and the post-industrial state, whatever the system of ownership.

The human race in the last three centuries has been going through a global change-of-life. Science and technology have ushered man into a new cycle of civilization, and the consequence has been a terrifying problem of adjustment. In two centuries science and technology have narrowed the seas, ravaged the forests, and irrigated the deserts. They have leveled national frontiers, undermined national self-sufficiencies, and infinitely increased man's power to build and to destroy. The velocity of life has entered into a new phase. With it has come the imperative need for a social structure to contain that velocity—a social structure within which the individual can achieve some measure of self-fulfillment.

This new social structure must succeed where the ancient jurisdictions of the family, the clan, the guild, and the nation-state have failed. It must solve the problems created by the speed-up of time, the reduction of space, and the increase in tension. It must develop new equivalents for the sanctions once imposed by custom and by religion. The specifications for the new society cannot but strain to the utmost the emotional and moral resources of the individual and the community.

In retrospect, these demands seem to have been too severe and exhausting. Civilization has not met them, which is why today it is consumed by anxiety and fear. Failing to create a new social structure, it has become the victim rather than the master of industrialism. The liberation of the individual during the Renaissance and Reformation set the Industrial Revolution in motion; in its course, industrialism has given people new freedom and opportunity. Yet its ultimate tendency under whatever system of ownership—a tendency inherent in its very technical structure—is to impersonalize economic relationships. In the end industrialism drives the free individual to the wall.

A static and decentralized society, based on agriculture and handicraft, was a society dependent on personal ties and governed by a personal ethic. Industrialism shattered the ties and consequently the ethic. A new code arose to cope with the remote and statistical units of the modern economy, and the gap between economic practice and personal morality widened swiftly and alarmingly. The industrial manager dealt not in familiar personal relationships but in impersonal magnitudes over great stretches of time and distance. The corporation was almost as much a device to solve moral as economic problems. It gave the new impersonality an institutional embodiment; a corporation, as the saying went, had neither a body to be kicked nor a soul to be damned. "Corporations will do what individuals would not dare to do," the richest man in Boston wrote with candor a century ago. "—Where the dishonesty is the work of *all* the Members, every *one* can say with Macbeth in the murder of Banquo, 'Thou canst not say I did it.'"[1]

The impersonality of the new economic system meant, in brief, that no one had to feel a direct responsibility for the obvious and terrible costs in human suffering. Doubtless there was a lurking sense of guilt, but the very mechanism of organization provided solace and remission. As organization became more elaborate and comprehensive, it became increasingly the instrumentality through which moral man could indulge his natural weakness for immoral deeds. All organization suffered from this internal tendency. What was true of the competitive corporation became all the more true of the monopoly; and what was true even to a degree of the democratic state (which, after all, was responsive to popular control as the corporation was not) became horribly true of the totalitarian state. "A crime which would press quite heavily on the conscience of one man, becomes quite endurable when divided among many."[2]

The impersonality of the system, in other words, brought out not the best but the worst in the men who operated it. Industrialism, at the same time that it released vast new energies, imposed on the world a sinister new structure of relationships. The result was to give potent weapons to the pride and the greed of man, the sadism and the masochism, the ecstasy in power and the ecstasy in submission; and it thereby increased man's sense of guilt. The result was to create problems of organization to which man has not risen and which threaten to engulf him, and it thereby multiplied man's anxieties. The result was to devitalize the old religions while producing nothing new capable of controlling pride and power, and it thereby heightened both guilt and anxiety.

Man today must organize beyond his moral and emotional means: this is the fundamental cause of our distempers. This basic dilemma projects itself to us in the middle of the twentieth century in terms of the conflict between the United States and the Soviet Union. But the USA and the USSR are not the alternatives today because either nation has solved the basic problem—because either nation has succeeded in squaring the temptations of power and the corruptions of organization with the weaknesses of man. They are centers of hope because they are centers of power; and they are centers of power less because of political or social wisdom than because of natural endowments in population, in fertility of the soil and in treasures beneath it, in geographical size and geographical remoteness. Their power makes them the inevitable focus of the tensions of the age. But they are not the cause of the tensions. Nor does either nation have the secret of their solution. Nor will the destruction of one by the other usher in utopia.

The fact that the contest between the USA and the USSR is not the source of the contemporary crisis does not, however, alter the fact that the crisis must be met in terms of this contest. Enthusiasts have suggested other strategies. If organization is the basic trouble, for example, one can sympathize with the anarchist rejection of organization. One can dally with the distributist dream of decentralization and the restoration of feudalism. One can admire the serenity of those who follow Gandhi's faith in nonviolence. But one must face the fact that none of these "solutions" solves very much except the complexes of the individual who adopts them. They raise questions which must be raised; they provide the basis perhaps for a searching moral criticism of the existing order; but they leave the main forces of social chaos untouched. A Thoreau or a Gandhi, who has gone himself through intense moral ordeals, has earned the most profound moral respect. But it is a far cry from Thoreau or Gandhi to the ineffectual escapists who in their name engage in such practices as conscientious objection in time of war.

You cannot flee from science and technology into a quietist dreamworld. The state and the factory are inexorable: bad men will run them if good abdicate the job. The USA, the USSR, the strength of industrialism, and the weakness of man cannot be evaded; they make up the problem; and there is no point, in General Marshall's phrase, in "fighting the problem." We must understand that the terms of the problem do not exhaust the dilemma of history, but we must understand equally that men in the middle of the twentieth century can strike at the dilemma of history only in terms of the problem.

We can act, in consequence, only in terms of imperfect alternatives. But, though the choice the alternatives present may be imperfect, it is nonetheless a real choice. Even if capitalism and Communism are both the children of the Industrial Revolution, there remain crucial differences between the USA and the USSR. These can be defined as basically the differences between free society and totalitarianism. This is a choice we cannot escape.

The conception of the free society—a society committed to the protection of the liberties of conscience, expression, and political opposition—is the crowning glory of western history. Centuries of struggle have drawn a ring of freedom around the individual, a ring secured by law, by custom, and by institutions. Here is a classic statement of the tests of freedom:

1. Is there the right to free expression of opinion and of opposition and criticism of the Government of the day?
2. Have the people the right to turn out a Government of which they disapprove, and are constitutional means provided by which they can make their will apparent?
3. Are there courts of justice free from violence by the Executive and free of all threats of mob violence and all association with any particular political parties?
4. Will these courts administer open and well-established laws which are associated in the human mind with the broad principles of decency and justice?
5. Will there be fair play for poor as well as for rich, for private persons as well as Government officials?
6. Will the rights of the individual, subject to his duties to the state, be maintained and asserted and exalted?
7. Is the ordinary peasant or workman, earning a living by daily toil and striving to bring up his family, free from the fear that some grim police organization under the control of a single party, like the Gestapo, started by the Nazi and Fascist parties, will tap him on the shoulder and pack him off without fair or open trial to bondage or ill-treatment?[3]

A conception of unequaled grandeur (modern liberals will, I trust, forgive the fact that the quotation is from Winston Churchill)—yet this conception has broken down at vital points under the pressures of industrial organization. Its failure has created its totalitarian enemy—which professes to meet these needs and moves to do so, proudly and even flagrantly, at the expense of the liberties which define free society.

Is there reason to believe that totalitarianism will be any more effective a master of the pressures of industrial society? The evidence suggests rather that the totalitarian enterprise brings in its wake a whole series of new and intolerable evils. Far from solving the problems of organization, totalitarianism raises them to a climax. A man like Thoreau could find the liberal state of free society a "semihuman tiger or ox, stalking over the earth, with its heart taken out and the top of its brain shot away."[4] But the liberal state acknowledged many limitations in its demands upon men; the total state acknowledges none. It systematically annihilates the gaps and rivalries which make for freedom in a more loosely organized society. It dispenses with liberty without providing security. If organization corrupts, total organization corrupts totally.

Free society and totalitarianism today struggle for the minds and hearts of men. If the USA and the USSR were in entire ideological agreement, the imperatives of power—of geography and of economic competition—would still tend to create rivalries; but the ideological conflict has now detonated the power conflict. There is no easy answer to this double polarization. If we believe in free society hard enough to keep on fighting for it, we are pledged to a permanent crisis which will test the moral, the political, and very possibly the military strength of each side. A "permanent" crisis? Well, a generation or two anyway, permanent in one's own lifetime, permanent in the sense that no international miracle, no political sleight-of-hand will do away overnight with the tensions between ourselves and Russia.

Indeed, we have no assurance that any solution is possible. The twentieth century has at least relieved us of the illusion that progress is inevitable. This age is straining all the capacities of man. At best, it is an age of transition; at worst, an age of catastrophe. And even an age of transition, as John C. Calhoun has reminded us, "must always necessarily be one of uncertainty, confusion, error and wild and fierce fanaticism."[5] There is no more exciting time in which to live—no time more crucial or more tragic. We must recognize that this is the nature of our age: that the womb has irrevocably closed behind us, that security is a foolish dream of old men, that crisis will always be with us.

Our own objective is clear. We must defend and strengthen free society. The means are somewhat more difficult. Surrender to totalitarianism—whether the surrender of military strong points or the surrender of standards and values—is the most certain road to the destruction of free society. War is the next most certain road. The first question is how to protect free society short of war. The answer will involve all dimensions of activity—political, economic, moral, and military.

We must first understand more clearly *why* free society has failed. Then we must examine the nature of the totalitarian challenge. Then we may acquire some notion of the strategy and tactics of a democratic counteroffensive. . . .

Freedom: A Fighting Faith

Industrialism is the benefactor and the villain of our time: it has burned up the mortgage, but at the same time sealed us in a subtler slavery. It has created wealth and comfort in undreamed-of abundance. But in the wake of its incomparable economic achievement it has left the thin, deadly trail of anxiety. The connecting fluids of industrial society begin to dry up; the seams harden and crack; and society is transformed into a parched desert, "a heap of broken images, where the sun beats, and the dead tree gives no shelter, the cricket no relief, and the dry stone no sound of water"—that state of social purgatory which Durkheim called "anomie" and where Eliot saw fear in a handful of dust.

Under industrialism the social order ceases to be society in faith and brotherhood. It becomes the waste land, "asocial society," in Alex Comfort's phrase—"a society of onlookers, congested but lonely, technically advanced but utterly insecure, subject to a complicated mechanism of order but individually irresponsible."[6] We live on from day to day, persisting mechanically in the routine of a morality and a social pattern which has been switched off but which continues to run from its earlier momentum. Our lives are empty of belief. They are lives of quiet desperation.

Who can live without desperation in a society turned asocial—in a social system which represents organized frustration instead of organized fulfillment? Freedom has lost its foundation in community and become a torment; "individualism" strips the individual of layer after layer of protective tissue. Reduced to panic, industrial man joins the lemming migration, the convulsive mass escape from freedom to totalitarianism, hurling himself from the bleak and rocky cliffs into the deep, womb-dark sea below. In free society, as at present constituted, the falcon cannot hear the falconer, the center cannot hold. Anarchy is loosed upon the world; and, as in Yeats's terrible vision, some rough beast, its hour come round at last, slouches toward Bethlehem to be born.

Through this century, free society has been on the defensive, demoralized by the infection of anxiety, staggering under the body blows of fascism and Communism. Free society alienates the lonely and uprooted masses, while totalitarianism, building on their frustrations and cravings, provides a structure of belief, men to worship and men to hate and rites which guarantee salvation. The crisis of free society has assumed the form of international collisions between the democracies and the totalitarian powers, but this fact should not blind us to the fact that in its essence this crisis is internal.

Free society will survive, in the last resort, only if enough people believe in it deeply enough to die for it. However reluctant peace-loving people are to recognize that fact, history's warning is clear and cold;

civilizations which cannot man their walls in times of alarm are doomed to destruction by the barbarians. We have deeply believed only when the issue of war has reduced our future to the stark problem of self-preservation. Franklin Roosevelt read the American people with his usual uncanny accuracy when he named the Second War not the "war for freedom" but the "war for survival." Our democracy has still to generate a living emotional content, rich enough to overcome the anxieties incited by industrialism, deep enough to rally its members to battle for freedom—not just for self preservation. Freedom must become, in Holmes's phrase, a "fighting faith."

Why does not democracy believe in itself with passion? Why is freedom not a fighting faith? In part because democracy, by its nature, dissipates rather than concentrates its internal moral force. The thrust of the democratic faith is away from fanaticism; it is toward compromise, persuasion, and consent in politics, toward tolerance and diversity in society; its economic foundation lies in the easily frightened middle class. Its love of variety discourages dogmatism, and its love of skepticism discourages hero worship. In place of theology and ritual, of hierarchy and demonology, it sets up a belief in intellectual freedom and unrestricted inquiry. The advocate of free society defines himself by telling what he is against; what he is for turns out to be certain *means*, and he leaves other people to charge the means with content. Today democracy is paying the price for its systematic cultivation of the peaceful and rational virtues. "Many a man will live and die upon a dogma; no man will be a martyr for a conclusion."[7]

Democracy, moreover, has not worn too well as a philosophy of life in an industrial age. It seemed more solid at the high noon of success than it does in the uncertainties of falling dusk. In its traditional form it has presupposed emotional and psychological stability in the individual. It has assumed, much too confidently, that the gnawing problems of doubt and anxiety would be banished by the advance of science or cured by a rise in the standard of living. The spectacular reopening of these problems in our time finds the democratic faith lacking in the profounder emotional resources. Democracy has no defense-in-depth against the neuroses of industrialism. When philosophies of blood and violence arise to take up the slack between democracy's thin optimism and the bitter agonies of experience, democracy by comparison appears pale and feeble.

Yet it seems doubtful whether democracy could itself be transformed into a political religion, like totalitarianism, without losing its characteristic belief in individual dignity and freedom. Does this mean that democracy is destined to defeat, sooner or later, by one or another of the totalitarian sects?

The death pallor will indeed come over free society unless it can recharge the deepest sources of its moral energy. And we cannot make democracy a fighting faith merely by exhortation or by self-flagellation, and certainly not by renouncing the values which distinguish free society from totalitarianism. Yet we must somehow dissolve the anxieties which drive people in free society to become traitors to freedom. We must somehow give the lonely masses a sense of individual human function; we must restore community to the industrial order.

There is on our side, of course, the long-run impossibility of totalitarianism. A totalitarian order offers no legitimate solution to the problem of freedom and anxiety. It does not restore basic securities; it does not create a world where men may expect lives of self-fulfillment. It enables man not to face himself but to flee himself by diving into the Party and the state. Only he cannot stay there; he must either come up for air or drown. Totalitarianism has scotched the snake of anxiety but not killed it, and anxiety will be its undoing.

An enduring social order must base itself upon the emotional energies and needs of man. Totalitarianism thwarts and represses too much of man ever to become in any sense a "good society." Terror is the essence of totalitarianism; and normal man, in the long run, instinctively organizes himself against terror. This fact gives the champions of freedom their great opportunity. But let no one deceive himself about the short-run efficacy of totalitarian methods. Modern technology has placed in the hands of "totalitarian man" the power to accomplish most of his ends of human subjection. He may have no enduring solution, but neither, for example, did the Dark Ages. Yet the darkness lasted a longer time than the period which has elapsed since the discovery of America.

We cannot count upon totalitarian dynamism running down of its own accord in a single generation. Man is instinctively antitotalitarian, but it is necessary for wise policies to mobilize these instincts early enough to do some good. Our problem is to make democracy the fighting faith not of some future underground movement but of us all here today in the middle of the twentieth century.

The essential strength of democracy as against totalitarianism lies in its startling insight into the value of the individual. Yet, as we have seen, this insight can become abstract and sterile; arrogant forms of individualism sometimes discredit the basic faith in the value of the individual. It is only so far as that insight can achieve a full social dimension, so far as individualism derives freely from community, that democracy will be immune to the virus of totalitarianism.

For all the magnificent triumphs of individualism, we survive only as we remain members of one another. The individual requires a social context, not one imposed by coercion but one freely emerging in response to his own needs and initiatives. Industrialism has inflicted savage wounds on the human sensibility; the cuts and gashes are to be healed only by a conviction of trust and solidarity with other human beings.

It is in these fundamental terms that we must reconstruct our democracy. Optimism about man is not enough. The formalities of democracy are not enough. The fact that a man can cast a secret ballot or shop in Woolworth's rather than Kresge's is more important to those free from anxiety than it is to the casualties of the industrial order. And the casualties multiply: the possessors are corrupted by power, the middling undone by boredom, the dispossessed demoralized by fear. Chamber-of-commerce banalities will no longer console industrial man.

We require individualism which does not wall man off from community; we require community which sustains but does not suffocate the individual. The historic methods of free society are correct so far as they go, but they concentrate on the individual; they do not go far enough. It would be fatal to abandon Winston Churchill's seven tests of freedom. But these tests are inadequate to create free society because they define means, not ends. We know now that man is not sufficiently perfect to shape good means infallibly to good ends. So we no longer describe free society in terms of means alone; we must place ends as well in the forefront of our philosophy of democracy.

An adequate philosophy of free society would have to supplement the Churchill tests by such questions as these:

Do the people have a relative security against the ravages of hunger, sickness, and want?
Do they freely unite in continuous and intimate association with like-minded people for common purposes?
Do they as individuals have a feeling of initiative, function, and fulfillment in the social order?

It has become the duty of free society to answer these questions—and to answer them affirmatively if it would survive. The rise of the social welfare state is an expression of that sense of duty. But the social welfare state is not enough. The sense of duty must be expressed specifically and passionately in the heart and will of men, in their daily decisions and their daily existence, if free men are to remain free.

The contemporary schism between the individual and the community has weakened the will of man. Social conditions cannot, of course, make moral decisions. But they can create conditions where moral decisions are more or less likely to be made. Some social arrangements bring out the evil in man more quickly than others. Slavery, as we knew well in America, corrupts the masters; totalitarian society, placing unbearable strains on man's self-restraint, produces the most violent reactions of fanaticism and hatred; the unchecked rule of the business community encourages greed and oppression. So the reform of institutions becomes an indispensable part of the enterprise of democracy. But the reform of institutions can never be a substitute for the reform of man.

The inadequacy of our institutions only intensifies the tribute that society levies from man: it but exacerbates the moral crisis. The rise of totalitarianism, in other words, signifies more than an internal crisis for democratic society. It signifies an internal crisis for democratic man. There is a Hitler, a Stalin in every breast. "Each of us has the plague within him," cries Tarrou in the Camus novel; "no one, no one on earth is free from it. And I know, too, that we must keep endless watch on ourselves lest in a careless moment we breathe in somebody's face and fasten the infection on him. What's natural is the microbe. All the rest— health, integrity, purity (if you like)—is a product of the human will, of a vigilance that must never falter."[8]

How to produce a vigilance that never falters? How to strengthen the human will? Walt Whitman in his later years grew obsessed with the moral indolence of democracy. Once he had hymned its possibilities with unequaled fervor. Now he looked about him and saw people "with hearts of rags and souls of chalk." As he pondered "the shallowness and miserable selfism of these crowds of men, with all their minds so blank of high humanity and aspiration," then came "the terrible query. . . . Is not Democracy of human rights humbug after all?" The expansion of the powers of government provided no solution. "I have little hope of any man or any community of men, that looks to some civil or military power to defend its vital rights. —If we have it not in ourselves to defend what belongs to us, then the citadel and heart of the towns are taken."

Wherein lies the hope? In "the exercise of Democracy," Whitman finally answered. ". . . to work for Democracy is good, the exercise is good—strength it makes and lessons it teaches." The hope for free society lies, in the last resort, in the kind of men it creates. "There is no week nor day nor hour," wrote Whitman, "when tyranny may not enter upon this country, if the people lose their supreme confidence in themselves,—and lose their roughness and spirit of defiance—Tyranny may always enter—there is no charm, no bar against it—the only bar against it is a large resolute breed of men."[9]

In times past, when freedom has been a fighting faith, producing a "large resolute breed of men," it has acquired its dynamism from communion in action. "The exercise of Democracy" has quickened the sense of the value of the individual, and in that exercise the individual has found a just and fruitful relation to the community. We require today exactly such a rededication to concrete democratic ends so that the exercise of democracy can bring about a reconciliation between the individual and the community, a revival of the *élan* of democracy, and a resurgence of the democratic faith.

The expansion of the powers of government may often be an essential part of society's attack on evils of want and injustice. The industrial economy, for example, has become largely inaccessible to the control of the individual; and, even in the field of civil freedom, law is the means society has for registering its own best standards. Some of the democratic exhilaration consequently has to be revived by delegation: this is why we need the Franklin Roosevelts. Yet the expansion of the powers of government, the reliance on leadership, as Whitman perceived, have also become a means of dodging personal responsibility. This is the essential importance of the issues of civil rights and civil liberties. Every one of us has a direct, piercing, and inescapable responsibility in our own lives on questions of racial discrimination, of political and intellectual freedom—not just to support legislative programs but to extirpate the prejudices of bigotry in our environment and, above all, in ourselves.

Through this joint democratic effort we can tap once again the spontaneous sources of community in our society. Industrialism has covered over the springs of social brotherhood by accelerating the speed and mobility of existence. Standardization, for example, while it has certainly raised levels not only of consumption but of culture, has at the same time cut the umbilical cord too early; it has reduced life to an anonymity of abundance which brings less personal fulfillment than people once got from labor in their own shop or garden. More people read and write, but what they read and write tends to have less connection with themselves. We have made culture available to all at the expense of making much of it the expression of a common fantasy rather than of a common experience. We desperately need a rich emotional life, reflecting actual relations between the individual and the community.

The cultural problem is but one aspect of the larger problem of the role of independent groups, of voluntary associations, in free society. There is an evident thinness in the texture of political democracy, a lack of appeal to those irrational sentiments once mobilized by religion and now by totalitarianism. Democracy, we have argued, is probably inherently incapable of satisfying those emotions in the apparatus of the state without losing its own character. Yet a democratic society, based on a genuine cultural pluralism, on widespread and spontaneous group activity, could go far to supply outlets for the variegated emotions of man, and thus to restore meaning to democratic life. It is the disappearance of effective group activity which leads toward emptiness in the individual, as it also compels the enlargement of the powers of the state.

People deprived of any meaningful role in society, lacking even their own groups to give them a sense of belonging, become cannon fodder for totalitarianism. And groups themselves, once long established, suffer inevitable tendencies toward exclusiveness and bureaucratization, forget their original purpose, and contribute to the downfall of freedom. If the American Medical Association, for example, had given serious attention to the problem of meeting the medical needs of America today, Doctor Fishbein would not be dunning his membership for funds to support a lobby against national health insurance. In the short run, the failure of voluntary initiative invites the spread of state power. In the long run, the disappearance of voluntary association paves the way for the pulverization of the social structure essential to totalitarianism. By the revitalization of voluntary associations we can siphon off emotions which might otherwise be driven to the solutions of despair. We can create strong bulwarks against the totalitarianization of society.[10]

Democracy requires unremitting action on many fronts. It is, in other words, a process, not a conclusion. However painful the thought, it must be recognized that its commitments are unending. The belief in the millennium has dominated our social thinking too long. Our utopian prophets have always supposed that a day would come when all who had not worshiped the beast or received his mark on their foreheads would reign for a thousand years. "And God shall wipe away all tears from their eyes; and there shall be no more death, neither sorrow, nor crying, neither shall there be any more pain: for the former things are passed away."

But the Christian millennium calls for a catastrophic change in human nature. Let us not sentimentalize the millennium by believing we can attain it through scientific discovery or through the revision of our economic system. We must grow up now and forsake the millennial dream. We will not arise one morning to find all problems solved, all need for further strain and struggle ended, while we work two hours a day and spend our leisure eating milk and honey. Given human imperfection, society will continue imperfect. Problems will always torment us, because all important problems are insoluble: that is why they are important. The good comes from the continuing struggle to try and solve them, not from the vain hope of their solution.

This is just as true of the problems of international society. "What men call peace," Gilson has well said, "is never anything but a space between two wars; a precarious equilibrium that lasts as long as mutual fear prevents dissension from declaring itself. This parody of true peace, this armed fear . . . may very well support a kind of order, but never can it bring mankind anything of tranquillity. Not until the social order becomes the spontaneous expression of an interior peace in men's hearts shall we have tranquillity."[11] Does it seem likely (pending the millennium) that we shall ever have an interior peace in the hearts of enough men to transform the nature of human society? The pursuit of peace, Whitehead reminds us, easily passes into its bastard substitute, anesthesia.

So we are forced back on the reality of struggle. So long as society stays free, so long will it continue in its state of tension, breeding contradiction, breeding strife. But we betray ourselves if we accept contradiction and strife as the total meaning of conflict. For conflict is also the guarantee of freedom; it is the instrument of change; it is, above all, the source of discovery, the source of art, the source of love. The choice we face is not between progress with conflict and progress without conflict. The choice is between conflict and stagnation. You cannot expel conflict from society any more than you can from the human mind. When you attempt it, the psychic costs in schizophrenia or torpor are the same.

The totalitarians regard the toleration of conflict as our central weakness. So it may appear to be in an age of anxiety. But we know it to be basically our central strength. The new radicalism derives its power from an acceptance of conflict—an acceptance combined with a determination to create a social framework where conflict issues not in excessive anxiety but in creativity. The center is vital; the center must hold. The object of the new radicalism is to restore the center, to reunite individual and community in fruitful union. The spirit of the new radicalism is the spirit of the center—the spirit of human decency, opposing the extremes of tyranny. Yet, in a more fundamental sense, does not the center itself represent one extreme? while at the other are grouped the forces of corruption—men transformed by pride and power into enemies of humanity.

The new radicalism, drawing strength from a realistic conception of man, dedicates itself to problems as they come, attacking them in terms which best advance the humane and libertarian values, which best secure the freedom and fulfillment of the individual. It believes in attack—and out of attack will come passionate intensity.

Can we win the fight? We must commit ourselves to it with all our vigor in all its dimensions—the struggle within the world against Communism and fascism; the struggle within our country against oppression and stagnation; the struggle within ourselves against pride and corruption—nor can engagement in one dimension exclude responsibility for another. Economic and political action can help restore the balance between individual and community and thereby reduce one great source of anxiety. But even the most favorable social arrangements cannot guarantee individual virtue, and we are far yet from having solved the social problem.

The commitment is complex and rigorous. When has it not been so? If democracy cannot produce the large resolute breed of men capable of the climactic effort, it will founder. Out of the effort, out of the struggle alone, can come the high courage and faith which will preserve freedom.

NOTES

1. Peter C. Brooks to Edward Everett, July 15, 1845, Everett Papers, Massachusetts Historical Society.
2. William M. Gouge, *A Short History of Paper Money and Banking in the United States,* Philadelphia, 1833, Part I, p. 43.
3. Winston Churchill, *London Times,* August 29, 1944.
4. H. D. Thoreau, "Plea for Captain John Brown," *Works,* Boston, 1894, vol. iv, p. 429.
5. John C. Calhoun, *A Disquisition on Government,* New York, 1854, p. 90.
6. Alex Comfort, *The Novel and Our Time,* London, 1948, p. 12.

7. J. H. Newman, *Grammar of Assent*, London, 1930, p. 93. This neglected work remains one of the most valuable of all analyses of the way in which man gives his assent.
8. Albert Camus, *The Plague*, New York, 1948, p. 229.
9. Walt Whitman, "Notes for Lecturers on Democracy and 'Adhesiveness,'" C. J. Furness, *Walt Whitman's Workshop*, Cambridge, MA, 1928, pp. 57, 58.
10. For the role of private associations, see Alexis de Tocqueville, *Democracy in America*, Part I, chap. 12, Part II, bk. i, chaps. 5–7; and the essay, "Biography of a Nation of Joiners," Arthur M. Schlesinger, *Path to the Present*, New York, 1949.
11. Etienne Gilson, *The Spirit of Medieval Philosophy*, New York, 1936, p. 399.

ARTHUR LARSON

3

A Republican Looks at His Party

Arthur Larson, who had served in the Eisenhower
administration as undersecretary of labor, wrote this
brief manifesto for what became known as "Modern
Republicanism" because he wanted his party to recognize the vast changes that had occurred since the
early 1930s, when the Republicans had last held the
White House. He believed that President Eisenhower
had "discovered and established the Authentic American Center in politics" by creating a balance between
the welfare and regulatory state and private enterprise. This new consensus, argued Larson, was a
product of the deradicalization of labor, the willingness of the business community "to accept a wide
range of governmental measures," and "a bipartisan
agreement on the propriety of special measures to
protect farm income." It was now the task of "the
American intellectual . . . to identify, systematize, and
interpret the indigenous American ideology as it has
adapted itself to the mid-twentieth century." When the
1950s ended and the events of the 1960s erupted,
however, few intellectuals were either interested in
or capable of accepting Larson's challenge.

The Question

Is there a distinct and coherent political move-
ment, of which President Eisenhower is the architect and embodiment,
but which is capable of existence and growth independent of him—a
political philosophy with a clear set of principles and objectives,
which one might perhaps call the New Republicanism?

From *A Republican Looks at His Party* (New York: Harper and Bros., 1956), 1–19.
© 1956, 1984 by Arthur Larson. Reprinted by permission of HarperCollins Publishers.

The answer here given is a plain one: there *is* such a distinctive political movement. It is deeply rooted in conscious principle. It knows what it believes and where it is going. It is in the direct line of descent from our oldest political traditions, yet it is quite different in significant ways from anything that has gone before.

The importance of essaying a summary of New Republican principles is magnified by the fact that the pattern does not fit any familiar past formulas.

How can the same philosophy urge the first extension of unemployment insurance by federal action since its beginnings—and at the same time a reduction in the tax on corporate dividends? The greatest government-sponsored road-building project of all time—and a relentless campaign to get the government out of business? The greatest improvements of social security in history—and the return of tidelands oil properties to the states? Increasing and extending the minimum wage—while restoring more of the power business to private enterprise?

All this does not slip comfortably into some well-worn niche like "liberal" or "New Deal" or "prolabor" or "probusiness" or "left" or "right." This is because the New Republicanism is a set of ideas keyed explicitly to contemporary midcentury facts, while the familiar categories, drawn from earlier decades, are now largely obsolete.

New Ideas to Fit New Facts

The fact that the New Republicanism is addressed and adapted to current facts stands out the more sharply when it is contrasted with political philosophies that are competing with it. Its Opposition is divided largely between two ideologies: one which might be said to bear the date 1896 and the other the date 1936.

Adlai Stevenson once remarked that there were a lot of people who had to be dragged, screaming and kicking, into the twentieth century. It is equally true that there are a lot who have to be dragged, kicking and screaming, out of the nineteen-thirties.

In a way, the second out-of-dateness is more subtly dangerous than the first. We know the 1896 ideas are old-fashioned; even their proponents admit this—in fact, that is why they like them. But the 1936 ideas are just as obsolete and invalid, yet they are constantly paraded before us as the product of liberalism and advance-guard thought.

The 1896 ideology, which had adherents in both parties, held that business should have completely free rein; that when working people got together to improve their lot by collective means it was apt to be either a conspiracy or a riot; that the federal government should confine itself to waging an occasional war, delivering the mails, and enforcing the tariff; and that individual suffering unrelated to military or public service was not a proper concern of the general government.

The 1936 ideology, associated with the New Deal, believed that private business was suspect, especially an entity known as Wall Street; that the government's principal concern with economic activity was to avert or alleviate depression and to distribute existing production more equitably; that labor was weak and needed the affirmative aid of government to offset the relative strength of employers; that the central government could, should, and would create a new "economic order"; that all this required that extensive power be centralized in the federal government and a heavy proportion of this federal power in the Executive; and that neither private business nor the states could be relied on to do a major part of the job of improving working conditions, economic growth, or individual security.

There is no use in quarreling about whether either the 1896 or 1936 ideologies were understandable and perhaps even justifiable in 1896 or 1936. It would be unfair, and certainly irrelevant to the present analysis, to pass judgment on the theories and actions of President [William] McKinley or President Grover Cleveland or President Franklin D. Roosevelt on the basis of what we have learned in the meantime or on the basis of changed facts, customs or popular attitudes. The only question that matters is, do these views fit the facts now?

Let us list a few of the many facts which have changed.

1. The greatest change is that we have neither a nationwide depression nor a nationwide war emergency.

Many sincere Democrats have subconsciously embraced the idea of centralization as a solution of our problems solely because the Democratic Administrations were most of the time preoccupied with the necessity of dealing with emergencies which quite legitimately called for strengthened federal action. The facts have now changed—no war, no depression—but the mental habit persists. True, we are committed to a continuing high degree of defense expenditure and are surrounded by world tensions, but this should not be thought inconsistent with the statement that we have a nonwar period. It would be more accurate to say that we are doing what we have always done in some degree—keeping up a peacetime defense establishment. The difference is one of degree: the size of the establishment is many times what we used to think necessary, partly because of our new world responsibility, partly because of the greater degree and extent of tension, and partly because we have learned from experience that earlier establishments were too small. The relevant point here is that we do not have an actual war-type emergency compelling centralization of domestic power.

2. The nature of unemployment has changed.

While we have some unemployment, it is different in character and significance from depression unemployment. In 1936, unemployment was the result and principal symbol of depression. In 1956, such unemployment as persists during prosperity (down to about 4 percent) is the result of special or local causes, requiring various kinds of special or locally adapted measures.

3. The nature of capital has changed.

Capital no longer comes principally from great personal fortunes. It comes from withheld earnings of corporations, from the large trust, insurance, and pension funds, and (third in importance) from publicly issued securities. The widespread modern use of withheld earnings to increase labor productivity and the ownership of the equities in the great insurance and pension funds by the working people of the country mean that labor and capital are becoming merged.

4. Labor has changed.

Labor is not a disinherited, propertyless minority; it comprises the overwhelming majority of Americans. As to organized labor's status, it is now taken for granted in most parts of the country. Moreover, while the process of organizing workers throughout the country is far from complete, the unions now face employers in most instances from a position of roughly equal bargaining strength. Both management and labor representatives, with occasional exceptions, have attained such maturity in labor relations that the expectation of government intervention can have only the effect of preventing or delaying bona fide bargaining and settlement.

5. The idea of the inevitability of inflation has been changed.

The cost of living has been stabilized, and in a period of rapidly rising prosperity and productivity and wages. The old assumption that there must be a certain amount of continuing inflation to keep the economy going has been discredited.

6. *The attitude of business toward government has changed.*

The SEC, FTC, FCC, FPC, ICC, and dozens of other agencies go about their normal routine of applying minimum necessary rules in the public interest, with hardly a voice ever raised any more to question the propriety of their activities. Moreover, the government has learned how to use a whole array of dials which it can turn up or down to influence the course of a business cycle, through credit tightening or easing, tax actions and other fiscal measures, and the business community has accepted these moves as commonplace.

It has also accepted labor relations legislation, social insurance legislation, and various measures to prevent substandard conditions or to alleviate suffering as normal adjuncts of a private enterprise system.

7. *Federal procurement and construction have vastly changed the impact of federal policies on everyday affairs.*

One of the most significant and least understood of all the changes in this list is the existence now of a regular annual expenditure of over thirty billion dollars on federal procurement. In spite of a considerable reduction in such expenditures by the Eisenhower Administration, the sum is still enough to exert a decisive effect in many directions.

Thus, without resorting to legislation but merely by insisting on certain standards as terms in its contracts, the federal government can have a profound influence in such matters as eliminating racial discrimination in employment or maintaining good wage and safety standards.

8. *The economy has changed.*

Ours is no longer an agrarian but an industrial economy, with only about a tenth of our civilian workforce of sixty-seven million people engaged in agriculture. The theory that we have "reached the frontiers" of our industrial expansion has been exploded. New developments not only in automatic technology but in finance, distribution, and industrial planning seem to make our capacity for increased production almost unlimited.

9. *Agriculture has changed.*

Although the number of farmers and farms has decreased with astonishing rapidity, production has soared, due to technological

advances which relatively surpass even those of the industrial establishment. The sharp increase in capital investment and mechanization
accompanying this has altered the essential status of the farmer and
assimilated his problem more to that of other businesses.

10. The character of national issues has changed.

One of the most remarkable changes in our national life is the extent
to which our great national issues are more and more centering on matters which traditionally have been thought of as local in character: water
supply, housing, schools, power, area and urban redevelopment, and
highways. True, there has been some federal interest in these things
in earlier periods, but building roads and water systems and school-
houses has always been a characteristically local responsibility. If
this sort of thing is to be the national political issue of the future, it
means that a major clue to coming political arrangements will be a
new kind of federal-state-local adjustment of governmental relations.
A related change of great significance is that we have become a
metropolitan-urban people, with two-thirds of us living in 168 metro-
politan areas; hence, the big municipality looms as a political entity
of prime importance.

11. The international role of the United States has changed.

We have an awesome responsibility for the fortunes of the Free
World which must have a sobering effect on all political discussion.
Wild "give-'em-hell" political byplay is just as much out of place as café
pseudo-intellectualism in this austere setting. We must have a sincere,
high-level, honest public discussion of issues, for we cannot afford to
be wrong or out of date or biased in our future formulation of policy;
we must be right, or our institutions and freedoms may be lost forever.

Four Tests of a Political Philosophy

The place of a particular movement in the political spectrum is best judged by its domestic policy.

Domestic policy, in turn, can be objectively appraised by the federal government's four main internal relations:

1. To state governments.
2. To private enterprise.
3. To labor.
4. To individual persons and their needs.

Let us apply these tests to the 1896 and 1936 Opposition philosophies.

First, 1896:
1. As to state governments: definitely "state's rights," in the sense that, as against the federal government, states were the lesser of two evils.
2. As to private enterprise: deferential; almost no regulation tolerated.
3. As to labor: hostile and contemptuous.
4. As to individual persons and their needs: indifferent.

Next, 1936:
1. As to state governments: low opinion of their ability to produce much constructive legislation; therefore, centralization favored as a way to get needed legislation.
2. As to private enterprise: inclined to be somewhat hostile and to consider business incapable of operating without government supervision and stimulation.
3. As to labor: solicitous, because labor viewed as needing help of government to overcome bargaining advantage of employers.
4. As to individual persons and their needs: sensitive; perhaps a little inclined to operate in the mass and from a distance.

Now, let us look at the New Republicanism.

It is the genius of the Eisenhower Administration's achievement that it has merged and brought into balance all the positive forces in our country. It is not against any of them. It realizes that they sometimes conflict, but it has found a way to encourage them to work together to a common benefit.

Thus, 1896 was against labor; 1936 was against business; this Administration is against neither but is *for* both.

Eighteen ninety-six mistrusted the federal government; 1936 mistrusted the state governments; this Administration mistrusts neither but assigns each its full role.

What we are now observing is the raw force of nineteenth-century capitalistic private enterprise supplying the driving power to produce a steady prosperity, and the raw force of twentieth-century collective labor action supplying the driving power to improve the wages and working conditions of workers, while the state and federal governments, using the techniques and experience gained over many years, prevent harmful excesses and actions against the public interest and make provision for the hazards and insecurities that are a by-product of free private enterprise. In all this, the key word is *balance*.

In the nineteenth century, there was not enough government regulation and not enough labor strength and freedom; result, unruly business expansion at the expense of the rights of people. In the nineteen-thirties there was too much government regulation and not enough business incentive and freedom; result, deadened business activity and protracted depression, accompanied by much humanitarian concern for the victims of the depression.

Now we have as much government activity as is necessary, but not enough to stifle the normal motivations of private enterprise. And we have a higher degree of government concern for the needs of people than ever before in our history, while at the same time pursuing a policy of maximum restoration of responsibility to individuals and private groups. This balance, together with a gradual restoration of a better balance between federal and state governments, is allowing all these elements in our society to make their maximum contribution to the common good.

The Authentic American Center

By bringing about this consolidation of the best forces in American life, President Eisenhower and his associates have, for the first time in our history, discovered and established the Authentic American Center in politics. This is not a Center in the European sense of an uneasy and precarious midpoint between large and powerful left-wing and right-wing elements of varying degrees of radicalism. It is a Center in the American sense of a common meeting ground of the great majority of our people on our own issues, against a backdrop of our own history, our own current setting, and our own responsibilities for the future.

Throughout this book, the parties to the various controversies are identified by two labels: the New Republicanism and the Opposition. It will be advisable to explain now why these terms have been used, and what they are intended to mean, so that there can be no possible misapprehension.

The term "the New Republicanism" is intended to embrace all the views of the Eisenhower Administration which are relevant to the overall political philosophy here analyzed, whether these views are held by Republicans, Democrats, or Independents. That these views are widely accepted among Democrats and Independents in addition to

Republicans is common knowledge. The fact that many Democrats and Independents voted for Dwight D. Eisenhower, even before his ideas had had a chance to prove themselves in action, is evidence of this. His increasing popularity as his principles have become better known and demonstrated through actual application confirms this fact. It is a fairly safe bet that nine out of ten Americans agree with nine-tenths of what is said and proposed in the 1955 and 1956 State of the Union Messages.

Pitted against the New Republicanism, or the Authentic American Center, will be found the Opposition. What is the Opposition?

This term is intended to include any doctrine, regardless of the party affiliation of the person who asserts it, which is at odds with the American Consensus as here described. It does not refer to the Democratic Party or to Democrats as such.

Most of the time, the Opposition refers either to the 1896 or to the 1936 school of thought on a particular point. It will come as no revelation that the 1896 school still includes, as it did in 1896, some Republicans and some Democrats. The 1936 school includes some Democrats but almost no Republicans.

It will be noted that the two contending sides are identified in terms of ideas, not men. There is a reason for this. It will sometimes happen that a particular Senator or candidate or voter will find himself in emphatic disagreement with some particular principle included as part of the American Consensus. Does this mean that he is outside the pale and must be tagged once and for all as the Opposition? Decidedly not. It would be a poor kind of Center which expelled members for holding reservations on a solitary point. If this man is in agreement with the Consensus on nine points out of ten, we must remember that he is reenforcing that Center nine-tenths of the time and dissenting from it with a relatively small fraction of his political weight.

This kind of Consensus is the distinctive mark of the American party system. It is the sort of thing which drives foreign observers to despair when they try to pin us down to their pattern, with its left-right arrangement of political status and with its regimented voting on all issues by parliamentary majorities. In this country we have alignments formed according to a complex system of sectional, local, traditional, and interest groupings. A working majority on issue A may come about through an alliance between groups who disagree on issue B. We see this process working out in the everyday deliberations of national, state, and local governments as well as in the practical business of elections.

What are the reasons for this recent emergence of the American Consensus? There are at least five.

First should be noted the common social and historical background which makes this high degree of accord possible. We have not entered this period trailing centuries of class consciousness and class warfare. We did not, as a nation, start from a beginning point in which people were divided into aristocrats and serfs, or into rich capitalists and propertyless laborers. Of course, during Revolutionary times there were some "aristocrats" of a sort, but they did their best to play down that fact. And there were struggling laborers, but they in turn never thought of themselves as a fixed "lower class." Above all, the great majority of people, whether farmers, pioneers, woodsmen, workers, craftsmen, or businessmen, viewed themselves as largely identified in the one great enterprise of making their fortunes in a young and expanding country.

Reenforcing this common social origin was a studied ideological position. The American Revolution was part of a period of brilliant thought on political philosophy. The leaders were steeped in the writings of Locke, Hume, Montesquieu, Rousseau, and others and, in turn, themselves wrote prolifically, eloquently, and precisely about their principles and objectives. What with the *Federalist Papers*, the Constitution, and the Declaration of Independence, there was laid down a solid ideological platform upon which all subsequent American thought could build. Unfortunately, this practice of producing comprehensive and systematic analyses of political thought has languished in this country. Communists, Socialists, even Fascists have produced detailed manifestoes and blueprints for action, and imperceptibly we have been drawn into the discussion within the framework and terminology they have chosen. We are now beginning to assert, with a sense of fresh discovery, our own rich ideological heritage.

A third reason for the appearance of the Consensus is the gradual maturing and moving-together of the interests which have provided our principal conflicts. Responsible labor and business leaders are proclaiming the doctrine that labor and management have far-reaching fundamental interests in common. The business community has come to accept a wide range of governmental measures, formerly opposed as "interference," as not only inevitable but highly helpful to business. The antagonism between farmers and "Eastern bankers," which loomed so large some years ago, seems to have dissolved with the increase of ownership by farmers of their own highly capitalized farms, and with the advent of bipartisan agreement on the propriety of special measures to protect farm income.

These are factors of a long-term or gradual kind which have made the Consensus possible. But why has it appeared just now?

For this there are two main reasons.

One is that there has arisen in the world an ideology—that of the Communists—which actively challenges and menaces almost everything we stand for. Principles that we have always taken as much for granted as the air we breathe are now flatly denounced and denied over a large part of the world—the principles, for example, of the preeminence and the freedom and the sovereignty of the individual person. We may even have allowed ourselves at times to think of these principles as downright trite—suitable perhaps for emphasis in a fourth-grade civics course but not the sort of thing you would make the subject of serious discussion among sophisticated adults. Now we suddenly find these familiar ideas to be our rallying point in a grim struggle for the highest stakes in history. A common danger has forced us all to think about what we really think. In doing so, we are finding that we think more like each other than we ever realized, because the essential alikeness of our thoughts shines out against the looming black cloud of a system of thought we abhor.

This is nothing new, for it was also the presence of a common danger which impelled the colonists—North and South, landowner and laborer—to find and define a Consensus with which to go forth together and meet that danger.

Another way in which this worldwide menace to our ideals has strengthened the American Center is by its putting an end to the luxury of toying with extremism. The parlor Communist of the thirties is gone forever. He affects to be hurt and surprised nowadays when the country turns on him unsmilingly and calls him to dead-earnest account, lest he perhaps still be an enemy of his own people. He explains that a lot of well-intentioned young men at about that time joined the Communist Party out of a sort of vague idealism, that there was really no harm intended, and that the whole business should be put down to immature, youthful exuberance.

Whatever may have been the case in the thirties, the march of events has rendered obsolete the café-table Communist and the bull-session Socialist in this country. We are playing for keeps now, with staggering world responsibilities that we cannot escape. The smart young man who announced that he was a Tolstoyan anarchist in order to make a really smashing sensation among his fellows, or the college boxing star who joined the blackshirts because this affiliation provided him with lots of fistfights which he invariably won—these are types which, mercifully, we are no longer breeding in any quantity.

Extremism, then, is being reduced to the hard core of those who really mean business. The dilettantes have been separated from the professionals. As the extremes have, by this process, been shaken down to their true size, the predominance of the Center has become more apparent. This process will gain even greater momentum as the American intellectual increasingly applies his talents to his real task, which is to identify, systematize, and interpret the indigenous American ideology as it has adapted itself to the mid-twentieth century.

The second reason why the American Consensus has now so clearly emerged is that the Eisenhower Administration has defined it, given voice to it, and put it into practice.

This point is of crucial importance. If one were to go no further than to show that a wide area of agreement on fundamentals had been achieved, this would no doubt provide an interesting abstract contribution to the history of political science, but it would have no practical impact on current political events. Under our two-party system the decisive issue becomes, under which party banner does this American Center rally to carry forward these agreed principles?

There is no American Center Party as such, and there will probably never be. Now and then the perennial idea is advanced that our political scene would be more orderly and would make more sense if all the conservatives of both parties would get together in a Conservative Party, and all the liberals of both parties would get together in a Liberal Party. In stubborn defiance of the superficial logic of this proposal, the two major parties keep right on going. One reason for this is the overwhelming preponderance of the Center. Most people do not want to line up on one side or another of an imaginary line separating liberal from conservative. For this and other reasons—historical, sectional, emotional, and practical—the two-party lineup has survived many assaults and, for purposes of any realistic political analysis, must be assumed to continue into the indefinite future.

If, then, the American Consensus is as widespread as it appears to be, every other political question for the future will be dwarfed by the single question, who deserves the credit for marshaling this Consensus, and who will get its political support?

The answer here given is the New Republicanism as exemplified by the Eisenhower Administration.

The primary reason is that it is the Eisenhower Administration that "invented" the successful formula and therefore has a right to the patent. While it is true that some of the component parts have been adapted from the New Deal, as in the case of some social and labor legislation, this only serves to confirm the principal thesis, which is that the genius of the formula lies in consolidating all that is best in American life, whatever its origin. At the same time, let there be no mistake about the fact that a very large part of what is implied by the "New Republicanism" involved a sharp change of direction from that of the Truman and Roosevelt Administrations. In fact, most of this book is devoted to a delineation of this marked change. Moreover, it was not an easy change, for it frequently involved a reversal of a trend that had been going on not only in this country but all over the world for perhaps twenty years.

Another reason why the New Republicanism is properly the party of the American Center is that leading spokesmen for the Democratic Party disavow the Center. Governor [Averell] Harriman was echoing the sentiments of an important, perhaps controlling, segment of Democratic leadership when he said: "There is no such word as 'moderation' or 'middle-of-the-road' in the Democratic vocabulary." This statement is unquestionably in the main tradition of the Democratic Party since 1932.

Historians may someday very well conclude that the Democratic Party was the party adapted to radical reform and freewheeling experimentation at a time when things were badly out of joint, while the Republican Party was the party designed to carry a more mature America forward on a course of steady progress and expansion, backed by the broad support of the American Consensus.

Structurally, the Democratic Party is not set up to be a party of the Center. Its two largest blocks are represented by the most conservative element in the country, the Southern Democrats, and the most radical—the ultra-Fair Dealers. True, there are degrees of conservatism and liberalism within the Republican ranks, too, but there is a difference. Within the Democratic Party the cleavage is abrupt and extreme, and the two segments are ideologically almost not on speaking terms. Within the great bulk of the Republican Party the difference is more one of degree, and as a result it is possible for varying points of view to be merged into a compromise that preserves the best elements of each. The Eisenhower program, in whose preparation and execution Republicans of many shades of opinion had a hand, is the best evidence of this.

It would also be difficult for the Democratic Party to assume the role of party of the Center because a large number of its spokesmen have too long relied on the habit of attacking one part of our American life too large to be excluded from the Center—the business community. It is doubtful whether these spokesmen could ever be persuaded to give up this time-honored weapon. Occasional Democratic leaders have recently announced that they are laying this bludgeon away in the historical weapon collection. But, as of the present writing, they seem to be greatly outnumbered by the Democratic spokesmen who are determined to make an antibusiness "pitch" the main theme of the 1956 campaign.

Given the continued existence of the two-party system, then, the Center will have to express itself in much the way it did in electing President Eisenhower in 1952: that is, by adding to the vote of one party both the independent vote and a considerable portion of the vote of the other party.

If, as seems likely, the Republican Party in 1956, 1960, and later years puts forward candidates who represent the New Republicanism, while Democratic spokesmen are obliged to attack from one extreme position or another, and if some cataclysmic event does not come along which calls all bets off, the Republicans should have a strong chance of staying in power as representatives of the great majority of the voters. But if, as seems unlikely, the Republicans were some day to nominate a candidate for the presidency who was identified with an extreme conservative position, and if, as seems equally unlikely, the Democrats were to seize that moment to choose a nominee who took over the formula of the great middle way, the Democratic candidate would almost certainly win, and thereafter it would be difficult indeed for the Republicans to get back in. The Republicans now hold the Center. If they ever give it up, they may find themselves in a position somewhat like that of the Democrats in 1956—that is, they would be under the uncomfortable political necessity of opposing something that most people are satisfied with, in order to find reasons for a change of Administration.

To summarize: in politics—as in chess—the man who holds the center holds a position of almost unbeatable strength.

ADLAI STEVENSON

4 | A Call to Greatness

After serving as governor of Illinois (1948–1952), Adlai Stevenson was the Democratic presidential nominee in 1952 and 1956. Although he lost to Dwight Eisenhower in both elections, his was one of the most reasoned and moderate voices of midcentury America. In his 1954 Godkin Lectures at Harvard, later published under the title *A Call to Greatness*, Stevenson cautioned against extremism in our anti-Communist fervor. With Joe McCarthy on his mind, he warned against "the contagion of unreason and anti-intellectualism spreading among ourselves, inhibiting thought and initiative in government, distorting the emphasis in our public affairs, moving groups to extremes of intolerance, diverting attention from our great concerns, and provoking division among us." Stevenson saw the Cold War as a long twilight struggle that would require maturity and reason from the American public.

The ordeal of our times, I have suggested, is a challenge to American maturity and American responsibility. Nowhere is this testing more fundamental than in the field of the free mind. For never has an external threat required more clearheaded analysis, more hard and sober thought, and more bold and unterrified vision than the threat we confront today. And yet the very existence of that threat has created strains and tensions, anguish and anxiety, which beat upon the free mind, surround it, torment it, and threaten to smother it. It is an irony that unreason should never be more manifest than in the midst of our great planetary effort to make freedom secure.

Senator Fulbright has called anti-intellectualism "that swinish blight so common in our time." This infection has been epidemic, of course, in the totalitarian states. Antireason is the spirit of the shouting, chanting crowds we remember so well in Hitler's Germany. Almost daily we read of new manifestations of unreason, mob emotion, and violence in some part of the world. In recent years we have even seen the contagion of unreason and anti-intellectualism spreading among ourselves, inhibiting thought and initiative in government, distorting the emphasis in our public affairs, moving groups to extremes of intolerance, diverting attention from our great concerns, and provoking division among us.

Unreason and anti-intellectualism abominate thought. Thinking implies disagreement; and disagreement implies nonconformity; and nonconformity implies heresy; and heresy implies disloyalty— so, obviously, thinking must be stopped. But shouting is not a substitute for thinking, and reason is not the subversion but the salvation of freedom.

Another lesson that we shall have to learn is that we cannot deal with questions of foreign policy in terms of moral absolutes. Compromise is not immoral or treasonable. It is the objective of negotiation, and negotiation is the means of resolving conflict peacefully. But when we negotiate we have to have something to negotiate *with* as well as *for*. If rigidity and absolutist attitudes deprive our representatives of anything to negotiate *with*, then there is nothing they can negotiate *for*. The consequences can be very embarrassing.

We seem to have a current illustration of self-defeating rigidity in the case of China. Because of our justified moral revulsion to the bloodthirsty conspiracy in China, the competition in extreme opinions and arbitrary attitudes among political leaders has virtually deprived us of all flexibility. The Secretary of State was severely criticized by his own party leaders for even agreeing to join our allies in a meeting with the Chinese. And rigidity known publicly in advance not only embarrasses us with our allies but can be seized upon by our enemies and advertised among the uncommitted peoples to prove our obdurate refusal to make any concessions for peace.

The point is not necessarily that we should support the admission to the United Nations of China or grant recognition or something else in exchange for a settlement in Indo-China, Korea, or Formosa. The point is that we must not be imprisoned by our own passions, propaganda, or pronouncements; we should not tie the hands of our representatives and hobble ourselves in advance to the adversary's advantage, not ours.

Times change, and rapidly, in this era of change. John Stuart Mill wrote: "That which seems the height of absurdity in one generation often becomes the height of wisdom in the next." Not very long ago there was a lot of "radical" agitation, so called, in this country. What did the "radicals" want? They wanted social security, old age pensions, regulation of utilities and securities, government aid for housing and education, a nine-hour day, and collective bargaining. Those were heresies not long ago, but in 1953 a Republican President raises the welfare state to Cabinet status and asks for an extension of social security.

Similarly a few years ago we were fighting the Germans and Japanese tooth and toenail and calling them names not fit to print. Today we are nourishing them with our money and arming them with our weapons. A few years ago I was doing savage battle with the Communist Yugoslavs in the United Nations. But last summer the same people entertained me like a long lost friend from one end of Yugoslavia to the other.

Passions rise and subside. Absolutes are few and black and white rare colors in international politics. Keeping an open, flexible mind, shedding our passion for crusades and our taste for absolutes that equate compromise with immorality, will be another hard and useful exercise. As Churchill has said: "Guidance in these mundane matters is granted to us only step by step. . . . There is therefore wisdom in reserving one's decisions as long as possible and until all the facts and forces that will be potent are revealed."

The price of inflexibility in foreign policy will be loss of confidence in our leadership first, then the loss of our allies, or worse. We can't have things all our own way. We shall have to face the necessity of compromise not only with our allies but with our enemies, for power factors are realities. And we shall have to learn to expect something less than total success every time, and not slander our officials as suspicious characters at every setback or failure. For if we do, we shall soon have no successes.

There are limits to the effectiveness of our nation's foreign policy. For foreign policy is concerned with problems which lie beyond our jurisdiction and about which we cannot legislate. There are only two means available for influencing the actions of other states: persuasion and coercion. As a free society, we must rely primarily on persuasion. We can use coercion only rarely, and usually only as a defensive measure.

We cannot have satellites, because this depends on the use of coercion. We cannot employ threats and intimidation effectively, because our actions are open to free discussion and criticism. Great as our power is, we have only a marginal influence on developments outside our boundaries. Guatemala is an example. Our power is almost infinite in comparison to Guatemala's. Yet we have been unable to prevent the emergence of Communist influence there.

Like every great power we are always and simultaneously on both the defensive and the offensive. We must adjust our defense to the adversary's strength and should develop our offense to make the most of our strength. The defensive task is to work with our allies and friends to deny the adversary opportunities to win cheap successes. Communism has yet to gain power in any state through free elections. It must gain control of key positions of power by subversion, penetration, or violence—civil war as in Indo-China or direct aggression as in Korea. The defensive task is in large part a military task: to develop and maintain such strength as to deter general war and to deal with violence in local situations. It is partly a political and economic task; for example, military measures alone are inadequate in Indo-China, and political and economic measures are necessary now to bring stability to Korea.

Offensive task is to work with allied and friendly countries to create a world environment favorable to the steady growth of free institutions. This means political arrangements which will make possible the unity of action essential to survival but which at the same time are consistent with diversity. It means a healthy international economy. The offensive task never ends. Progress will be slow. We hope that we can leave the world in a little better shape than we found it. But to search for a "solution" prematurely is more likely to produce war than peace. There is no such "solution" now, but our problems may fade away with time and cease to have the importance that they now seem to have.

Because of the nature of free societies it is of the utmost importance to prevent war, if possible, and if this is not possible, to keep any future war as severely limited in scope as possible. It is a sign of strength, not of weakness, to be able to keep war limited. To generalize hostilities to a world scale would imperil the very institutions we seek to save by war.

Our objective is not the destruction of communism by war. Our objective is not the incitement of others to violence. Our objective is not to rectify the boundaries and correct the unnatural divisions that afflict the world by force, but by peaceful processes. Our objective is a peace consistent with decency and justice. And our prayer is that history will not say that we led a noble but a lost cause.

It is doubtful whether in all history two ways of life as different and opposed as the Communist way and our way of life have ever come into contact with one another at so many different points without engaging in mortal conflict.

Experience suggests that it has not been easy for men to learn the wisdom and virtue of tolerance for ideas and ways of life which deeply offend the cherished tenets of their own faith. In times past, men of fervent faith regarded religious tolerance as a sign of moral weakness rather than moral strength. It seems that only when warring faiths have become convinced that they must choose between common survival and mutual extinction do they agree to live and let live.

Probably the greatest obstacle in the path of peaceful coexistence is the Soviet belief in the inevitability of conflict between the Communist and the non-Communist worlds. And it is true that Soviet intolerance and unwillingness to abide by the rules of peaceful coexistence have shaken our faith in tolerance and the possibility of peaceful coexistence. But in the atomic era even the most fanatical faith is likely to balk at self-destruction. There is no Iron Curtain that the aggregate sentiments of mankind cannot and will not penetrate in time. Even the most fanatical ambition must adjust itself to demonstrated truth or perish. No faith can long rest on the belief that the world is flat—if its adherents know the world is round. "Great is the truth and mighty above all things."

The hope for peaceful coexistence lies in our ability to convince the rulers of the other world that they cannot extend their system by force, or by stealth, and that unless they use force against us we will not use force against them; that our coalition exists but to serve and to save the imperishable principles of the Charter of the United Nations.

Intolerant power respects power, not weakness. It is imperative therefore to build and better the balance of power. Conspiracy and incitement prosper in disunion and discontent. It is imperative therefore to build and better the unity and well-being of the free world. We cannot do it alone. It is imperative therefore to build and better the coalition. And here we encounter our greatest danger and our final task. A coalition built on expedient reaction to the common danger will not stand, because the Sino-Soviet alliance has the power to blow hot and cold, like Boreas and Phoebus in the fable; it has the power to relax or increase the tension as it sees fit. But our coalition cannot live by fits and starts; it must rest on an enduring community of interest. And successful communal relations mean give and take, cooperation, consultation, accommodation—a decent respect for the opinions of others. Our coalition is a partnership, not a dictatorship. We shall have to listen as well as talk, learn as well as teach. And I sometimes think that what America needs more than anything else is a hearing aid. We can encourage the acceptance of our ideas only as we are willing to accept the ideas and suggestions of others. All of this means a large relinquishment of our freedom of action.

There is not the slightest chance of confidence and mutual trust among the members of the free world's coalition if the United States should fail the test of leadership. We have a great and fortuitous advantage, for if there is nothing the Kremlin wants more than to rule the world, there is nothing the United States wants less than to rule the world. To cling to that truth with clarity, sincerity, and humility will be our greatest strength in the trials of leadership.

America's greatest contribution to human society has come not from her wealth or weapons or ambitions but from her ideas; from the moral sentiments of human liberty and human welfare embodied in the Declaration of Independence and the Bill of Rights. We must cling to these truths, for these are everlasting and universal aspirations. In the words of Lincoln: "It was not the mere separation of the colonies from the motherland, but the sentiment in the Declaration of Independence which gave liberty not alone to the people of this country, but hope to all the world. It was that which gave promise that in due time the weights should be lifted from the shoulders of all men, and that all should have an equal chance." Throughout its history, America has given hope, comfort, and inspiration to freedom's cause in all lands. The reservoir of good will and respect for America was not built up by American arms or intrigue; it was built upon our deep dedication to the cause of human liberty and human welfare.

All through human history runs a struggle between right and wrong, which is destined to endure, perhaps, to the end of time. Some historians during our materialistic years disavowed this theme. But now in our age of anxiety and time of testing, they are bringing it again within their purview. Arthur Schlesinger, Jr., has stated: "If historians are to understand the fullness of the social dilemma they seek to reconstruct, they must understand that sometimes there is no escape from the implacabilities of moral decisions"; while Allan Nevins notes with approval the emergence in historical writing of "a deepened moral sense much needed in our troubled age."

If the record of man's progress is the chronicle of everlasting struggle between right and wrong, it follows that the solutions of our problems lie largely within ourselves, that only with self-mastery can we hope to master history. The scientific mastery of our environment has brought us not tranquillity but rather unrest and new fears. Knowledge alone is not enough. It must be leavened with magnanimity before it becomes wisdom. And "magnanimity in politics," as Burke has reminded us, "is not seldom the truest wisdom."

America's life story is the record of a marvelous growth of body, mind, and character. Now at maturity we shoulder the heaviest burdens of greatness, for in the last analysis the epic struggle for our civilization, for government by consent of the governed, will be determined by what Americans are capable of. In bearing burdens, in ennobling new duties of citizenship, is the greatness of men and nations measured, not in pomp and circumstance.

How shall we bear what Providence has assigned us? In Keats's *Hyperion* are these lines:

> for to bear all naked truths,
> And to envisage circumstances, all calm,
> That is the top of sovereignty. . . .

And so it is.

MARY McCARTHY

5 Mlle. Gulliver en Amérique

Writing in 1952, the noted novelist and essayist Mary McCarthy defended America from the criticisms of Simone de Beauvoir, a leading French left-wing intellectual and feminist who saw it as a country dominated by the "privileged class." McCarthy's views were associated with the left during most of her highly productive literary life. But in this piece, published during the heyday of the great consensus, she joined the chorus with other intellectuals in the defense of America and optimism about its future. "The America invoked by Mlle. de Beauvoir as a country of vast inequalities," she wrote, "is rapidly ceasing to exist."

In January 1947, Simone de Beauvoir, the leading French *femme savante*, alighted from an airplane at LaGuardia Field for a four months' stay in the United States. In her own eyes, this trip had something fabulous about it, of a balloonist's expedition or a descent in a diving bell. Where to Frenchmen of an earlier generation, America was the incredible country of *les peaux rouges* and the novels of Fenimore Cooper, to Mlle. de Beauvoir America was, very simply, movieland—she came to verify for herself the existence of violence, drugstore stools, boy-meets-girl, that she had seen depicted on the screen. Her impressions, which she set down in journal form for the readers of *Les Temps Modernes*, retained therefore the flavor of an eyewitness account, of confirmation of rumor, the object being not so much to assay America as to testify to its reality.

From *On the Contrary: Articles of Belief, 1946–1961* (New York: Noonday Press, 1962), 24–31. Reprinted by permission of the Mary McCarthy Literary Trust.

These impressions, collected into a book, made a certain stir in France; now, three years later, they are appearing in translation in Germany. The book has never been published over here; the few snatches excerpted from it in magazine articles provoked wonder and hostility.

On an American leafing through the pages of an old library copy, the book has a strange effect. It is as though an inhabitant of Lilliput or Brobdingnag, coming upon a copy of *Gulliver's Travels*, sat down to read, in a foreign tongue, of his own local customs codified by an observer of a different species: everything is at once familiar and distorted. The landmarks are there, and some of the institutions and personages—Eighth Avenue, Broadway, Hollywood, the Grand Canyon, Harvard, Yale, Vassar, literary celebrities concealed under initials; here are the drugstores and the cafeterias and the buses and the traffic lights—and yet it is all wrong, schematized, rationalized, like a scale model under glass. Peering down at himself, the American discovers that he has "no sense of *nuance*," that he is always in a good humor, that "in America the individual is nothing," that all Americans think their native town is the most beautiful town in the world, that an office girl cannot go to work in the same dress two days running, that in hotels "illicit" couples are made to swear that they are married, that it almost never happens here that a professor is also a writer, that the majority of American novelists have never been to college, that the middle class has no hold on the country's economic life and very little influence on its political destiny, that the good American citizen is never sick, that racism and reaction grow more menacing every day, that "the appearance, even, of democracy is vanishing from day to day," and that the country is witnessing "the birth of fascism."

From these pages, he discovers, in short, that his country has become, in the eyes of Existentialists, a future which is, so to speak, already a past, a gelid eternity of drugstores, juke boxes, smiles, refrigerators, and "fascism," and that he himself is no longer an individual but a sort of Mars man, a projection of science fiction, the man of 1984. Such a futuristic vision of America was already in Mlle. de Beauvoir's head when she descended from the plane as from a space ship, wearing metaphorical goggles: eager as a little girl to taste the rock-candy delights of this materialistic moon civilization (the orange juice, the ice creams, the jazz, the whiskeys, the martinis, and the lobster). She knows already, nevertheless, that this world is not "real" but only a half-frightening fantasy daydreamed by the Americans.

She has preserved enough of Marxism to be warned that the spun-sugar façade is a device of the "Pullman class" to mask its exploitation and cruelty: while the soda fountains spout, Truman and Marshall prepare an anti-Communist crusade that brings back memories of the Nazis, and Congress plots the ruin of the trade unions. "The collective future is in the hands of a privileged class, the Pullman class, to which are reserved the joys of large-scale enterprise and creation; the others are just wheels in a big steel world; they lack the power to conceive an individual future for themselves; they have no plan or passion, hope or nostalgia, that carries them beyond the present; they know only the unending repetition of the cycle of seasons and hours."

This image of a people from Oz or out of an expressionist ballet, a robot people obedient to a generalization, corresponds, of course, with no reality, either in the United States or anywhere else; it is the petrifaction of a fear very common in Europe today—a fear of the future. Where, in a more hopeful era, America embodied for Europe a certain millennial promise, now in the Atomic Age it embodies an evil presentiment of a millennium just at hand. To Mlle. de Beauvoir, obsessed with memories of Jules Verne, America is a symbol of a mechanical progress once dreamed of and now repudiated with horror; it is a Judgment on itself and on Europe. No friendly experience with Americans can dispel this deep-lying dread. She does not wish to know America but only to ascertain that it is there, just as she had imagined it. She shrinks from involvement in this "big steel world" and makes no attempt to see factories, workers, or political leaders. She prefers the abstraction of "Wall Street."

This recoil from American actuality has the result that might be expected, a result, in fact, so predictable that one might say she willed it. Her book is consistently misinformed in small matters as well as large. She has a gift for visual description which she uses very successfully to evoke certain American phenomena: Hollywood, the Grand Canyon, the Bronx, Chinatown, women's dresses, the stockyards, the Bowery, Golden Gate, auto camps, Hawaiian dinners, etc. In so far as the U.S. is a vast tourist camp, a vacationland, a Stop-in Serv-Urself, she has caught its essence. But in so far as the United States is something more than a caricature of itself conceived by the mind of an ad man or a Western Chamber of Commerce, she has a disinclination to view it. She cannot, for example, take in the names of American writers even when she has their books by her elbow: she speaks repeatedly of James Algee (Agee), of Farrel (Farrell), O'Neil (O'Neill), and of Max Twain—a strange form of compliment to authors whom she professes to like. In the same way, Greenwich Village, which she loves, she speaks of throughout as "Greeniwich," even when she comes to live there.

These are minor distortions. What is more pathetic is her credulity, which amounts to a kind of superstition. She is so eager to appear well informed that she believes anything anybody tells her, especially if it is anti-American and pretends to reveal the inner workings of the capitalist mechanism. The Fifth Avenue shops, she tells us, are "reserved for the capitalist international," and no investigative instinct tempts her to cross the barricade and see for herself. Had she done so, she might have found suburban housewives, file clerks, and stenographers swarming about the racks of Peck & Peck or Best's or Franklin Simon's, and colored girls mingling with white girls at the counters of Saks Fifth Avenue. A Spanish painter assures her that in America you have to hire a press agent to get your paintings shown. An author tells her that in America literary magazines print only favorable reviews. A student tells her that in America private colleges pay better salaries than state universities, so that the best education falls to the privileged classes, who do not want it, and so on. At Vassar, she relates, students are selected "according to their intellectual capacities, family, and fortune." Every item in this catalogue is false. (Private colleges do not pay better salaries—on the contrary, with a few exceptions, they pay notoriously worse; family plays no part in the selection of students at Vassar, and fortune only to the extent that the tuition has to be paid by someone—friend, parent, or scholarship donor; you do not have to hire a press agent; some literary magazines make a positive specialty of printing unfavorable reviews.)

Yet Mlle. de Beauvoir, unsuspecting, continues volubly to pass on "the low-down" to her European readers: there is no friendship between the sexes in America; American whites are "stiff" and "cold"; American society has lost its mobility; capital is in "certain hands," and the worker's task is "carefully laid out." "True, a few accidental successes give the myth of the self-made man a certain support, but they are illusory and tangential. . . ."

The picture of an America that consists of a small ruling class and a vast inert, regimented mass beneath it is elaborated at every opportunity. She sees the dispersion of goods on counters but draws no conclusion from it as to the structure of the economy. The American worker, to her, is invariably the French worker, a consecrated symbol of oppression. She talks a great deal of American conformity but fails to recognize a thing that Tocqueville saw long ago: that this conformity is the expression of a predominantly middle-class society; it is the price paid (as yet) for the spread of plenty. Whether the diffusion of television sets is, in itself, a good is another question; the fact is, however, that they *are* diffused; the "Pullman class," for weal or woe, does not have a corner on them, or on the levers of political power.

The outrage of the upper-class minority at the spectacle of television aerials on the shabby houses of Poverty Row, at the thought of the Frigidaires and washing machines in farmhouse and working-class kitchens, at the new cars parked in ranks outside the factories, at the very thought of installment buying, unemployment compensation, social security, trade-union benefits, veterans' housing, at General Vaughan, above all at Truman the haberdasher, the symbol of this cocky equality—their outrage is perhaps the most striking phenomenon in American life today. Yet Mlle. de Beauvoir remained unaware of it, and unaware also, for all her journal tells us, of income taxes and inheritance taxes, of the expense account and how it has affected buying habits and given a peculiar rashness and transiency to the daily experience of consumption. It can be argued that certain angry elements in American business do not know their own interests, which lie in the consumers' economy; even so, this ignorance and anger are an immense political fact in America.

The society characterized by Mlle. de Beauvoir as "rigid," "frozen," "closed" is in the process of great change. The mansions are torn down and the real-estate "development" takes their place: serried rows of ranch-type houses, painted in pastel colors, each with its picture window and its garden, each equipped with deep-freeze, oil furnace, and automatic washer, spring up in the wilderness. Class barriers disappear or become porous; the factory worker is an economic aristocrat in comparison to the middle-class clerk; even segregation is diminishing; consumption replaces acquisition as an incentive. The America invoked by Mlle. de Beauvoir as a country of vast inequalities and dramatic contrasts is rapidly ceasing to exist.

One can guess that it is the new America, rather than the imaginary America of economic royalism, that creates in Mlle. de Beauvoir a feeling of mixed attraction and repulsion. In one half of her sensibility, she is greatly excited by the United States and precisely by its material side. She is fascinated by drugstore displays of soap and dentifrices, by the uniformly regulated traffic, by the "good citizenship" of Americans, by the anonymous camaraderie of the big cities, by jazz and expensive record players and huge collections of records, and above all—to speak frankly—by the orange juice, the martinis, and the whiskey. She speaks elatedly of "my" America, "my" New York; she has a child's greedy possessiveness toward this place which she is in the act of discovering.

Toward the end of the book, as she revises certain early judgments, she finds that she has become "an American." What she means is that she has become somewhat critical of the carnival aspects of American life which at first bewitched her; she is able to make discriminations between different kinds of jazz, different hotels, different night clubs. Very tentatively, she pushes beyond appearance and perceives that the American is not his possessions, that the American character is not fleshly but abstract. Yet at bottom she remains disturbed by what she has seen and felt, even marginally, of the American problem. This is not one of inequity, as she would prefer to believe, but of its opposite. The problem posed by the United States is, as Tocqueville saw, the problem of equality, its consequences, and what price shall be paid for it. How is wealth to be spread without the spread of uniformity? How create a cushion of plenty without stupefaction of the soul and the senses? It is a dilemma that glares from every picture window and whistles through every breezeway.

If Americans, as Mlle. de Beauvoir thinks, are apathetic politically, it is because they can take neither side with any great conviction—how can one be *against* the abolition of poverty? And how, on the other hand, can one champion a leveling of extremes? For Europeans of egalitarian sympathies, America *is* this dilemma, relentlessly marching toward them, a future which "works," and which for that very reason they have no wish to face. Hence the desire, so very evident in Mlle. de Beauvoir's impressions and in much journalism of the European left, not to know what America is really like, to identify it with "fascism" or "reaction," not to admit, in short, that it has realized, to a considerable extent, the economic and social goals of President Franklin D. Roosevelt and of progressive thought in general.

NORMAN PODHORETZ

6 The Know-Nothing Bohemians

Norman Podhoretz, who was to become a leading voice of the neoconservatives in the 1970s and 1980s, found little to celebrate in the intellectual leadership and philosophy of the Beat Generation. For him, the novels of Jack Kerouac glorified random experience and impulsiveness over career and social responsibility. A philosophy that regarded inhibition and conformity as obstacles to self-realization would, in Podhoretz's view, only release the contagion of self-centeredness. This attack on the Beats, written in 1958, was one of the first volleys foreshadowing a culture war that erupted in the late 1960s and continues today.

Allen Ginsberg's little volume of poems, *Howl*, which got the San Francisco renaissance off to a screaming start, was dedicated to Jack Kerouac ("new Buddha of American prose, who spit forth intelligence into eleven books written in half the number of years . . . creating a spontaneous bop prosody and original classic literature"), William Seward Burroughs ("author of *Naked Lunch*, an endless novel which will drive everybody mad"), and Neal Cassady ("author of *The First Third*, an autobiography . . . which enlightened Buddha"). So far, everybody's sanity has been spared by the inability of *Naked Lunch* to find a publisher,* and we may never

*It did, of course, find one a few years after this piece was written.

From *Doings and Undoings: The Fifties and After in American Writing* (New York: Farrar, Strauss and Co., 1964), 143–58. Reprinted by permission of Norman Podhoretz.

161

get the chance to discover what Buddha learned from Neal Cassady's autobiography, but thanks to the Viking and Grove Presses, two of Kerouac's original classics, *On the Road* and *The Subterraneans*, have now been revealed to the world. When *On the Road* appeared last year, Gilbert Millstein commemorated the event in the *New York Times* by declaring it to be "a historic occasion" comparable to the publication of *The Sun Also Rises* in the 1920's. But even before the novel was actually published, the word got around that Kerouac was the spokesman of a new group of rebels and Bohemians who called themselves the Beat Generation, and soon his photogenic countenance (unshaven, of course, and topped by an unruly crop of rich black hair falling over his forehead) was showing up in various mass-circulation magazines; he was being interviewed earnestly on television; and he was being featured in a Greenwich Village nightclub where, in San Francisco fashion, he read specimens of his spontaneous bop prosody against a background of jazz music.

Though the nightclub act reportedly flopped, *On the Road* sold well enough to hit the best-seller lists for several weeks, and it isn't hard to understand why. Americans love nothing so much as representative documents, and what could be more interesting in this Age of Sociology than a novel that speaks for the "young generation"? (The fact that Kerouac is thirty-five or thereabouts was generously not held against him.) Beyond that, however, I think that the unveiling of the Beat Generation was greeted with a certain relief by many people who had been disturbed by the notorious respectability and "maturity" of postwar writing. This was more like it—restless, rebellious, confused youth living it up, instead of thin, balding, buttoned-down instructors of English composing ironic verses with one hand while changing the baby's diapers with the other. Bohemianism is not particularly fashionable nowadays, but the image of Bohemia still exerts a powerful fascination—nowhere more so than in the suburbs, which are filled to overflowing with men and women who uneasily think of themselves as conformists and of Bohemianism as the heroic road. The whole point of *Marjorie Morningstar* was to assure the young marrieds of Mamaroneck that they were better off than the apparently glamorous *luftmenschen* of Greenwich Village, and the fact that Wouk had to work so hard at making this idea seem convincing is a good indication of the strength of prevailing doubt on the matter.

On the surface, at least, the Bohemianism of *On the Road* is very attractive. Here is a group of high-spirited young men running back and forth across the country (mostly hitchhiking, sometimes in their own secondhand cars), going to "wild" parties in New York and Denver and San Francisco, living on a shoestring (GI educational benefits, an occasional fifty bucks from a kindly aunt, an odd job as a typist, a fruit-picker, a parking-lot attendant), talking intensely about love and God and salvation, getting high on marijuana (but never heroin or cocaine), listening feverishly to jazz in crowded little joints, and sleeping freely with beautiful girls. Now and again there is a reference to gloom and melancholy, but the characteristic note struck by Kerouac is exuberance:

> We stopped along the road for a bite to eat. The cowboy went off to have a spare tire patched, and Eddie and I sat down in a kind of homemade diner. I heard a great laugh, the greatest laugh in the world, and here came this rawhide oldtimes Nebraska farmer with a bunch of other boys into the diner; you could hear his raspy cries clear across the plains, across the whole gray world of them that day. Everybody else laughed with him. He didn't have a care in the world and had the hugest regard for everybody. I said to myself, Wham, listen to that man laugh. That's the West, here I am in the West. He came booming into the diner, calling Maw's name, and she made the sweetest cherry pie in Nebraska, and I had some with a mountainous scoop of ice cream on top. "Maw, rustle me up some grub afore I have to start eating myself or some damn silly idee like that." And he threw himself on a stool and went hyaw hyaw hyaw hyaw. "And throw some beans in it." It was the spirit of the West sitting right next to me. I wished I knew his whole raw life and what the hell he'd been doing all these years beside laughing and yelling like that. Whooee, I told my soul, and the cowboy came back and off we went to Grand Island.

Kerouac's enthusiasm for the Nebraska farmer is part of his general readiness to find the source of all vitality and virtue in simple rural types and in the dispossessed urban groups (Negroes, bums, whores). His idea of life in New York is "millions and millions hustling forever for a buck among themselves . . . grabbing, taking, giving, sighing, dying, just so they could be buried in those awful cemetery cities beyond Long Island City," whereas the rest of America is populated almost exclusively by the true of heart. There are intimations here of a kind of know-nothing populist sentiment, but in other ways this attitude resembles Nelson Algren's belief that bums and whores and junkies are more interesting than white-collar workers or civil servants. The difference is that

Algren hates middle-class respectability for moral and political reasons—the middle class exploits and persecutes—while Kerouac, who is thoroughly unpolitical, seems to feel that respectability is a sign not of moral corruption but of spiritual death. "The only people for me," says Sal Paradise, the narrator of *On the Road*, "are the mad ones, the ones who are mad to live, mad to talk, mad to be saved, desirous of everything at the same time, the ones who never yawn or say a commonplace thing, but burn, burn, burn like fabulous yellow roman candles exploding like spiders across the stars. . . ." This tremendous emphasis on emotional intensity, this notion that to be hopped-up is the most desirable of all human conditions, lies at the heart of the Beat Generation ethos and distinguishes it radically from the Bohemianism of the past.

The Bohemianism of the 1920's represented a repudiation of the provinciality, philistinism, and moral hypocrisy of American life—a life, incidentally, which was still essentially small-town and rural in tone. Bohemia, in other words, was a movement created in the name of civilization: its ideals were intelligence, cultivation, spiritual refinement. The typical literary figure of the 1920's was a midwesterner (Hemingway, Fitzgerald, Sinclair Lewis, Eliot, Pound) who had fled from his home town to New York or Paris in search of a freer, more expansive, more enlightened way of life than was possible in Ohio or Minnesota or Michigan. The political radicalism that supplied the characteristic coloring of Bohemianism in the 1930's did nothing to alter the urban, cosmopolitan bias of the 1920's. At its best, the radicalism of the 1930's was marked by deep intellectual seriousness and aimed at a state of society in which the fruits of civilization would be more widely available—and ultimately available to all.

The Bohemianism of the 1950's is another kettle of fish altogether. It is hostile to civilization; it worships primitivism, instinct, energy, "blood." To the extent that it has intellectual interests at all, they run to mystical doctrines, irrationalist philosophies, and left-wing Reichianism. The only art the new Bohemians have any use for is jazz, mainly of the cool variety. Their predilection for bop language is a way of demonstrating solidarity with the primitive vitality and spontaneity they find in jazz and of expressing contempt for coherent, rational discourse which, being a product of the mind, is in their view a form of death. To be articulate is to admit that you have no feelings (for how can real feelings be expressed in syntactical language?), that you can't respond to anything (Kerouac responds to everything by saying "Wow!"), and that you are probably impotent.

At the one end of the spectrum, this ethos shades off into violence and criminality, main-line drug addiction and madness. Allen Ginsberg's poetry, with its lurid apocalyptic celebration of "angel-headed hipsters," speaks for the darker side of the new Bohemianism. Kerouac is milder. He shows little taste for violence, and the criminality he admires is the harmless kind. The hero of *On the Road*, Dean Moriarty, has a record: "From the age of eleven to seventeen he was usually in reform school. His specialty was stealing cars, gunning for girls coming out of high school in the afternoon, driving them out to the mountains, making them, and coming back to sleep in any available hotel bathtub in town." But Dean's criminality, we are told, "was not something that sulked and sneered; it was a wild yea-saying overburst of American joy; it was Western, the west wind, an ode from the Plains, something new, long prophesied, long a-coming (he only stole cars for joy rides)." And, in fact, the species of Bohemian that Kerouac writes about is on the whole rather law-abiding. In *The Subterraneans*, a bunch of drunken boys steal a pushcart in the middle of the night, and when they leave it in front of a friend's apartment building, he denounces them angrily for "screwing up the security of my pad." When Sal Paradise (in *On the Road*) steals some groceries from the canteen of an itinerant workers' camp in which he has taken a temporary job as a barracks guard, he comments, "I suddenly began to realize that everybody in America is a natural-born thief"—which, of course, is a way of turning his own stealing into a bit of boyish prankishness. Nevertheless, Kerouac is attracted to criminality, and that in itself is more significant than the fact that he personally feels constrained to put the brakes on his own destructive impulses.

Sex has always played a very important role in Bohemianism: sleeping around was the Bohemian's most dramatic demonstration of his freedom from conventional moral standards, and a defiant denial of the idea that sex was permissible only in marriage and then only for the sake of a family. At the same time, to be "promiscuous" was to assert the validity of sexual experience in and for itself. The "meaning" of Bohemian sex, then, was at once social and personal, a crucial element in the Bohemian's ideal of civilization. Here again the contrast with Beat Generation Bohemianism is sharp. On the one hand, there is a fair amount of sexual activity in *On the Road* and *The Subterraneans*. Dean Moriarty is a "new kind of American saint" at least partly because of his amazing sexual powers: he can keep three women satisfied simultaneously, and he can make love any time, anywhere (once he mounts a girl in the back seat of a car while poor Sal Paradise is trying to sleep in front). Sal, too, is always on the make, and though he isn't as successful as the great Dean, he does pretty well: offhand I can remember a girl in Denver, one on a bus, and another in New York, but a little research would certainly unearth a few more. The heroine of *The Subterraneans*, a Negro girl named Mardou Fox, seems to have switched from one to another member of the same gang and back again ("This has been an incestuous group in its time"), and we are given to understand that there is nothing unusual about such an arrangement. But the point of all this hustle and bustle is not freedom from ordinary social restrictions or defiance of convention (except in relation to homosexuality, which is Ginsberg's preserve: among "the best minds" of Ginsberg's generation who were destroyed by America are those "who let themselves be —— in the —— by saintly motorcyclists, and screamed with joy, / who blew and were blown by those human seraphim, the sailors, caresses of Atlantic and Caribbean love"). The sex in Kerouac's books goes hand in hand with a great deal of talk about forming permanent relationships ("although I have a hot feeling sexually and all that for her," says the poet Adam Moorad in *The Subterraneans*, "I really don't want to get any further into her not only for these reasons but finally, the big one, if I'm going to get involved with a girl now I want to be permanent like permanent and serious and long termed and I can't do that with her") and a habit of getting married and then duly divorced and remarried when another girl comes along. In fact, there are as many marriages and divorces in *On the Road* as in the Hollywood movie colony (must be that California climate): "All those years I was looking for the woman I wanted to marry," Sal Paradise tells us. "I couldn't meet a girl without saying to myself, What kind of wife would she make?" Even more revealing is Kerouac's refusal to admit that any of his characters ever makes love wantonly or lecherously—no matter how casual the encounter, it must always entail sweet feelings toward the girl. Sal, for example, is fixed up with Rita Bettencourt in Denver, whom he has never met before. "I got her in my bedroom after a long talk in the dark of the front room. She was a nice little girl, simple and true [naturally], and tremendously frightened of sex. I told her it was beautiful. I wanted to prove this to her. She let me prove it, but I was too impatient and proved nothing. She sighed in the dark. 'What do you want out of life?' I asked, and I used to ask that all the time of girls." This is rather touching, but only because the narrator is really just as frightened of sex as that nice little girl was. He is frightened of failure, and he worries about his performance. For *performance* is the point—performance and "good orgasms," which are the first duty of man and the only duty of woman. What seems to be involved here, in short, is sexual anxiety of enormous proportions—an anxiety that comes out very clearly in *The Subterraneans*, which is about a love affair between the young writer, Leo Percepied, and the Negro girl, Mardou Fox. Despite its protestations, the book is one long agony of fear and trembling over sex:

> I spend long nights and many hours making her, finally I have her, I pray for it to come, I can hear her breathing harder, I hope against hope it's time, a noise in the hall (or whoop of drunkards next door) takes her mind off and she can't make it and laughs— but when she does make it I hear her crying, whimpering, the shuddering electrical female orgasm makes her sound like a little girl crying, moaning in the night, it lasts a good twenty seconds and when it's over she moans, "O why can't it last longer," and "O when will I when you do?"—"Soon now I bet," I say, "you're getting closer and closer"—

Very primitive, very spontaneous, very elemental, very beat.

For the new Bohemians interracial friendships and love affairs apparently play the same role of social defiance that sex used to play in older Bohemian circles. Negroes and whites associate freely on a basis of complete equality and without a trace of racial hostility. But putting it that way understates the case, for not only is there no racial hostility; there is positive adulation for the "happy, true-hearted, ecstatic Negroes of America."

> At lilac evening I walked with every muscle aching among the lights of 27th and Welton in the Denver colored section, wishing I were a Negro, feeling that the best the white world had offered was not enough ecstasy for me, not enough life, joy, kicks, darkness, music, not enough night. . . . I wished I were a Denver Mexican, or even a poor overworked Jap, anything but what I was so drearily, a "white man" disillusioned. All my life I'd had white ambitions. . . . I passed the dark porches of Mexican and Negro homes; soft voices were there, occasionally the dusky knee of some mysterious sensuous gal; and dark faces of the men behind rose arbors. Little children sat like sages in ancient rocking chairs.

It will be news to the Negroes to learn that they are so happy and ecstatic; I doubt if a more idyllic picture of Negro life has been painted since certain Southern ideologues tried to convince the world that things were just as fine as fine could be for the slaves on the old plantation. Be that as it may, Kerouac's love for Negroes and other dark-skinned groups is tied up with his worship of primitivism, not with any radical social attitudes. Ironically enough, in fact, to see the Negro as more elemental than the white man, as Ned Polsky has acutely remarked, is "an inverted form of keeping the nigger in his place." But even if it were true that American Negroes, by virtue of their position in our culture, have been able to retain a degree of primitive spontaneity, the last place you would expect to find evidence of this is among Bohemian Negroes. Bohemianism, after all, is for the Negro a means of entry into the world of the whites, and no Negro Bohemian is going to cooperate in the attempt to identify him with Harlem or Dixieland. The only major Negro character in either of Kerouac's two novels is Mardou Fox, and she is about as primitive as Wilhelm Reich himself.

The plain truth is that the primitivism of the Beat Generation serves first of all as a cover for an anti-intellectualism so bitter that it makes the ordinary American's hatred of eggheads seem positively benign. Kerouac and his friends like to think of themselves as intellectuals ("they are intellectual as hell and know all about Pound without being pretentious or talking too much about it"), but this is only a form of newspeak. Here is an example of what Kerouac considers intelligent discourse—"formal and shining and complete, without the tedious intellectualness":

> We passed a little kid who was throwing stones at the cars in the road. "Think of it," said Dean. "One day he'll put a stone through a man's windshield and the man will crash and die—all on account of that little kid. You see what I mean? God exists without qualms. As we roll along this way I am positive beyond doubt that everything will be taken care of for us—that even you, as you drive, fearful of the wheel . . . the thing will go along of itself and you won't go off the road and I can sleep. Furthermore we know America, we're at home; I can go anywhere in America and get what I want because it's the same in every corner, I know the people, I know what they do. We give and take and go in the incredibly complicated sweetness zigzagging every side."

You see what he means? Formal and shining and complete. No tedious intellectualness. Completely unpretentious. "There was nothing clear about the things he said but what he meant to say was somehow made pure and clear." *Somehow.* Of course. If what he wanted to say had been carefully thought out and precisely articulated, that would have been tedious and pretentious and, no doubt, *somehow* unclear and clearly impure. But so long as he utters these banalities with his tongue tied and with no comprehension of their meaning, so long as he makes noises that come out of his soul (since they couldn't possibly have come out of his mind), he passes the test of true intellectuality.

Which brings us to Kerouac's spontaneous bop prosody. This "prosody" is not to be confused with bop language itself, which has such a limited vocabulary (Basic English is a verbal treasurehouse by comparison) that you couldn't write a note to the milkman in it, much less a novel. Kerouac, however, manages to remain true to the spirit of hipster slang while making forays into enemy territory (i.e., the English language) by his simple inability to express anything in words. The only method he has of describing an object is to summon up the same half-dozen adjectives over and over again: "greatest," "tremendous," "crazy," "mad," "wild," and perhaps one or two others. When it's more than just mad or crazy or wild, it becomes "really mad" or "really crazy" or "really wild." (All quantities in excess of three, incidentally, are subsumed under the rubric "innumerable," a word used innumerable times in *On the Road* but not so innumerably in *The Subterraneans*.) The same poverty of resources is apparent in those passages where Kerouac tries to handle a situation involving even slightly complicated feelings. His usual tactic is to run for cover behind cliché and vague signals to the reader. For instance: "I looked at him; my eyes were watering with embarrassment and tears. Still he stared at me. Now his eyes were blank and looking through me. . . . Something clicked in both of us. In me it was suddenly concern for a man who was years younger than I, five years, and whose fate was wound with mine across the passage of recent years; in him it was a matter that I can ascertain only from what he did afterward." If you can ascertain what this is all about, either beforehand, during, or afterward, you are surely no square.

In keeping with its populistic bias, the style of *On the Road* is folksy and lyrical. The prose of *The Subterraneans*, on the other hand, sounds like an inept parody of Faulkner at his worst, the main difference being that Faulkner usually produces bad writing out of an impulse to inflate the commonplace, while Kerouac gets into trouble by pursuing "spontaneity." Strictly speaking, spontaneity is a quality of feeling, not of writing: when we call a piece of writing spontaneous, we are registering our impression that the author hit upon the right words without sweating, that no "art" and no calculation entered into the picture, that his feelings seem to have spoken themselves, seem to have sprouted a tongue at the moment of composition. Kerouac apparently thinks that spontaneity is a matter of saying whatever comes into your head, in any order you happen to feel like saying it. It isn't the *right* words he wants (even if he knows what they might be) but the first words, or at any rate the words that most obviously announce themselves as deriving from emotion rather than cerebration, as coming from "life" rather than "literature," from the guts rather than the brain. (The brain, remember, is the angel of death.) But writing that springs easily and "spontaneously" out of strong feelings is *never* vague; it always has a quality of sharpness and precision because it is in the nature of strong feelings to be aroused by specific objects. The notion that a diffuse, generalized, and unrelenting enthusiasm is the mark of great sensitivity and responsiveness is utterly fantastic, an idea that comes from taking drunkenness or drug addiction as the state of perfect emotional vigor. The effect of such enthusiasm is actually to wipe out the world altogether, for if a filling station will serve as well as the Rocky Mountains to arouse a sense of awe and wonder, then both the filling station and the mountains are robbed of their reality. Kerouac's conception of feeling is one that only a solipsist could believe in—and a solipsist, be it noted, is a man who does not relate easily to anything outside himself.

Solipsism is precisely what characterizes Kerouac's fiction. *On the Road* and *The Subterraneans* are so patently autobiographical in content that they become almost impossible to discuss as novels; if spontaneity were indeed a matter of destroying the distinction between life and literature, these books would unquestionably be It. "As we were going out to the car Babe slipped and fell flat on her face. Poor girl was overwrought. Her brother Tim and I helped her up. We got in the car; Major and Betty joined us. The sad ride back to Denver began." Babe is a girl who is mentioned a few times in the course of *On the Road*; we don't know why she is overwrought on this occasion, and even if we did it wouldn't matter, since there is no reason for her presence in the book at all. But Kerouac tells us that she fell flat on her face while walking toward a car. It is impossible to believe that Kerouac made this detail up, that his imagination was creating a world real enough to include wholly gratuitous elements; if that were the case, Babe would have come alive as a human being. But she is only a name; Kerouac never even describes her. She is in the book because the sister of one of Kerouac's friends was there when he took a trip to Central City, Colorado, and she slips in *On the Road* because she slipped that day on the way to the car. What is true of Babe who fell flat on her face is true of virtually every incident in *On the Road* and *The Subterraneans*. Nothing that happens has any dramatic reason for happening. Sal Paradise meets such-and-such people on the road whom he likes or (rarely) dislikes; they exchange a few words, they have a few beers together, they part. It is all very unremarkable and commonplace, but for Kerouac it is always the greatest, the wildest, the most. What you get in these two books is a man proclaiming that he is *alive* and offering every trivial experience he has ever had in evidence. Once I did this, once I did that (he is saying), and by God, it *meant* something! Because I *responded*! But if it meant something, and you responded so powerfully, why can't you explain what it meant, and why do you have to insist so?

I think it is legitimate to say, then, that the Beat Generation's worship of primitivism and spontaneity is more than a cover for hostility to intelligence; it arises from a pathetic poverty of feeling as well. The hipsters and hipster-lovers of the Beat Generation are rebels, all right, but not against anything so sociological and historical as the middle class or capitalism or even respectability. This is the revolt of the spiritually underprivileged and the crippled of soul—young men who can't think straight and so hate anyone who can; young men who can't get outside the morass of self and so construct definitions of feeling that exclude all human beings who manage to live, even miserably, in a world of objects; young men who are burdened unto death with the specially poignant sexual anxiety that America—in its eternal promise of erotic glory and its spiteful withholding of actual erotic possibility—seems bent on breeding, and who therefore dream of the unattainable perfect orgasm, which excuses all sexual failures in the real world. Not long ago, Norman Mailer suggested that the rise of the hipster may represent "the first wind of a second revolution in this century, moving not forward toward action and more rational equitable distribution, but backward toward being and the secrets of human energy." To tell the truth, whenever I hear anyone talking about instinct and being and the secrets of human energy, I get nervous; next thing you know he'll be saying that violence is just fine, and then I begin wondering whether he really thinks that kicking someone in the teeth or sticking a knife between his ribs are deeds to be admired. History, after all—and especially the history of modern times—teaches that there is a close connection between ideologies of primitivistic vitalism and a willingness to look upon cruelty and bloodletting with complacency, if not down-right enthusiasm. The reason I bring this up is that the spirit of hip-sterism and the Beat Generation strikes me as the same spirit which animates the young savages in leather jackets who have been running amok in the last few years with their switchblades and zip guns. What does Mailer think of those wretched kids, I wonder? What does he think of the gang that stoned a nine-year-old boy to death in Central Park in broad daylight a few months ago, or the one that set fire to an old man drowsing on a bench near the Brooklyn waterfront one summer's day, or the one that pounced on a crippled child and orgiastically stabbed him over and over and over again even after he was good and dead? Is that what he means by the liberation of instinct and the mysteries of being? Maybe so. At least he says somewhere in his article that two eighteen-year-old hoodlums who bash in the brains of a candy-store keeper are murdering an institution, committing an act that "violates private property"—which is one of the most morally gruesome ideas I have ever come across, and which indicates where the ideology of hip-sterism can lead. I happen to believe that there is a direct connection between the flabbiness of American middle-class life and the spread of juvenile crime in the 1950's, but I also believe that juvenile crime can be explained partly in terms of the same resentment against nor-mal feeling and the attempt to cope with the world through intelligence that lies behind Kerouac and Ginsberg. Even the relatively mild ethos of Kerouac's books can spill over easily into brutality, for there is a sup-pressed cry in those books: Kill the intellectuals who can talk coher-ently, kill the people who can sit still for five minutes at a time, kill those incomprehensible characters who are capable of getting seriously involved with a woman, a job, a cause. How can anyone in his right mind pretend that this has anything to do with private property or the middle class? No. Being against what the Beat Generation stands for has to do with denying that incoherence is superior to precision, that ignorance is superior to knowledge, that the exercise of mind and discrimination is a form of death. It has to do with fighting the notion that sordid acts of violence are justifiable so long as they are commit-ted in the name of "instinct." It even has to do with fighting the poi-sonous glorification of the adolescent in American popular culture. It has to do, in other words, with one's attitude toward intelligence itself.

7 The Motion Picture Production Code

The Motion Picture Production Code had its origins in the early 1930s when Hollywood, plagued by drug and sex scandals, feared the possibility of government censorship. The Motion Picture Association was dominated by a handful of studios, as was the industry itself, and they controlled the production and distribution of films. The code was an effort at self-censorship based on the broadly accepted notions that no motion picture should lower the moral standards of the public and that almost all films were made for a family audience. Although many of the 1956 code's provisions (more liberal in some respects than those of earlier versions) may seem antediluvian by today's standards, they reflected a cultural consensus about the responsibilities of the arts and entertainment industry to the society. Explicit sexual scenes were forbidden, including open-mouth kissing and suggestive dancing. Films were not to ridicule religion or religious figures, nor were they to incite religious or racial hatred. Crime and lustful acts could be portrayed only in a negative light; violence could be shown only if it was not graphic; blasphemy and vulgarity were not permitted. As cultural tastes changed in the mid-1960s, the industry replaced the code with a rating system that designated films for a mature audience and those suitable for children and young adults. The concept of a common audience and a common culture would never quite be the same.

Excerpts from *The Production Code of the Motion Picture Producers and Directors of America, Inc., 1930–1934*, in *Political and Civil Rights in the United States,* ed. Thomas I. Emerson, David Haber, and Norman Dorsen (Boston: Little, Brown and Co., 1967), 700–704. Courtesy of the Motion Picture Association of America, Inc.

General Principles

1. No picture shall be produced which will lower the moral standards of those who see it. Hence the sympathy of the audience shall never be thrown to the side of crime, wrong-doing, evil, or sin.
2. Correct standards of life, subject only to the requirements of drama and entertainment, shall be presented.
3. Law—divine, natural, or human—shall not be ridiculed, nor shall sympathy be created for its violation.

Particular Applications

I. Crime:

1. Crime shall never be presented in such a way as to throw sympathy with the crime as against law and justice, or to inspire others with a desire for imitation.
2. Methods of crime shall not be explicitly presented or detailed in a manner calculated to glamorize crime or inspire imitation.
3. Action showing the taking of human life is to be held to the minimum. Its frequent presentation tends to lessen regard for the sacredness of life.
4. Suicide, as a solution of problems occurring in the development of screen drama, is to be discouraged unless absolutely necessary for the development of the plot, and shall never be justified, or glorified, or used specifically to defeat the ends of justice.
5. Excessive flaunting of weapons by criminals shall not be permitted.
6. There shall be no scenes of law-enforcing officers dying at the hands of criminals, unless such scenes are absolutely necessary to the plot.
7. Pictures dealing with criminal activities in which minors participate, or to which minors are related, shall not be approved if they tend to incite demoralizing imitation on the part of youth.
8. Murder:
    (a) The technique of murder must not be presented in a way that will inspire imitation.
    (b) Brutal killings are not to be presented in detail.
    (c) Revenge in modern times shall not be justified.
    (d) Mercy killing shall never be made to seem right or permissible.
9. Drug addiction or the illicit traffic in addiction-producing drugs shall not be shown if the portrayal:

(a) Tends in any manner to encourage, stimulate, or justify the use of such drugs; or

(b) Stresses, visually or by dialogue, their temporarily attractive effects; or

(c) Suggests that the drug habit may be quickly or easily broken; or

(d) Shows details of drug procurement or of the taking of drugs in any manner; or

(e) Emphasizes the profits of the drug traffic; or

(f) Involves children who are shown knowingly to use or traffic in drugs.

10. Stories on the kidnapping or illegal abduction of children are acceptable under the Code only when (1) the subject is handled with restraint and discretion and avoids details, gruesomeness, and undue horror, and (2) the child is returned unharmed.

II. Brutality:

Excessive and inhumane acts of cruelty and brutality shall not be presented. This includes all detailed and protracted presentation of physical violence, torture, and abuse.

III. Sex:

The sanctity of the institution of marriage and the home shall be upheld. No film shall infer that casual or promiscuous sex relationships are the accepted or common thing.

1. Adultery and illicit sex, sometimes necessary plot material, shall not be explicitly treated, nor shall they be justified or made to seem right and permissible.

2. Scenes of passion:
   (a) These should not be introduced except where they are definitely essential to the plot.
   (b) Lustful and open-mouth kissing, lustful embraces, suggestive posture and gestures are not to be shown.
   (c) In general, passion should be treated in such manner as not to stimulate the baser emotions.

3. Seduction or rape:
   (a) These should never be more than suggested, and then only when essential to the plot. They should never be shown explicitly.
   (b) They are never acceptable subject matter for comedy.
   (c) They should never be made to seem right and permissible.

4. The subject of abortion shall be discouraged, shall never be more than suggested, and when referred to shall be condemned. It must never be treated lightly or made the subject of comedy. Abortion shall never be shown explicitly or by inference, and a story must not indicate that an abortion has been performed. The word "abortion" shall not be used.

5. The methods and techniques of prostitution and white slavery shall never be presented in detail, nor shall the subjects be presented unless shown in contrast to right standards of behavior. Brothels in any clear identification as such may not be shown.

6. Sex perversion or any inference of it is forbidden.*

7. Sex hygiene and venereal diseases are not acceptable subject matter for theatrical motion pictures.

8. Children's sex organs are never to be exposed. This provision shall not apply to infants.

IV. Vulgarity:

Vulgar expressions and double meanings having the same effect are forbidden. This shall include but not be limited to such words and expressions as chippie, fairy, goose, nuts, pansy, S.O.B., son-of-a. The treatment of low, disgusting, unpleasant, though not necessarily evil, subjects should be guided always by the dictates of good taste and a proper regard for the sensibilities of the audience.

V. Obscenity:

1. Dances suggesting or representing sexual actions or emphasizing indecent movements are to be regarded as obscene.

2. Obscenity in words, gesture, reference, song, joke, or by suggestion, even when likely to be understood by only part of the audience, is forbidden.

VI. Blasphemy and Profanity:

1. Blasphemy is forbidden. Reference to the Deity, God, Lord, Jesus, Christ shall not be irreverent.

2. Profanity is forbidden. The words "hell" and "damn," while sometimes dramatically valid, will if used without moderation be considered offensive by many members of the audience. Their use shall

---

*Changed in 1961 to permit treatment of "sex aberration" when done with "care, discretion, and restraint."—Ed.

be governed by the discretion and prudent advice of the Code Administration.

VII. Costumes:

1. Complete nudity, in fact or in silhouette, is never permitted, nor shall there be any licentious notice by characters in the film of suggested nudity.
2. Indecent or undue exposure is forbidden.
   (a) The foregoing shall not be interpreted to exclude actual scenes photographed in a foreign land of the natives of that land, showing native life, provided:
      (1) Such scenes are included in a documentary film or travelogue depicting exclusively such land, its customs and civilization; and
      (2) Such scenes are not in themselves intrinsically objectionable.

VIII. Religion:

1. No film or episode shall throw ridicule on any religious faith.
2. Ministers of religion, or persons posing as such, shall not be portrayed as comic characters or as villains so as to cast disrespect on religion.
3. Ceremonies of any definite religion shall be carefully and respectfully handled.

IX. Special Subjects:

The following subjects must be treated with discretion and restraint and within the careful limits of good taste:

1. Bedroom scenes.
2. Hangings and electrocutions.
3. Liquor and drinking.
4. Surgical operations and childbirth.
5. Third-degree methods.

X. National Feelings:

1. The use of the flag shall be consistently respectful.
2. The history, institutions, prominent people, and citizenry of all nations shall be represented fairly.
3. No picture shall be produced that tends to incite bigotry or hatred among people of differing races, religions, or national origins. The use of such offensive words as Chink, Dago, Frog, Greaser, Hunkie, Kike, Nigger, Spick, Wop, Yid should be avoided.

XI. Titles:

The following titles shall not be used:

1. Titles which are salacious, indecent, obscene, profane, or vulgar.
2. Titles which violate any other clause of this Code.

XII. Cruelty to Animals:

In the production of motion pictures involving animals the producer shall consult with the authorized representative of the American Humane Association and invite him to be present during the staging of such animal action. There shall be no use of any contrivance or apparatus for tripping or otherwise treating animals in any unacceptably harsh manner.

DWIGHT D. EISENHOWER

8 | Farewell Address

In his farewell radio and television address of January 17, 1961, President Eisenhower, who had resisted pressure during his administration to increase military spending, warned Americans against "the unwarranted influence, whether sought or unsought, by the military-industry complex." The undertone of this remarkable speech reflects his concern over the tension between the responsibilities of a superpower and the necessities of democratic government. He stresses the need for "balance between our essential requirements as a nation and the duties imposed by the nation upon the individual." Yet as he left office, Eisenhower's quiet leadership, unappreciated by scholars and journalists at the time, seemed out of step with the new decade. It was his successor, John F. Kennedy, who claimed to speak for a younger generation eager for excitement and personal adventure.

My fellow Americans:

Three days from now, after half a century in the service of our country, I shall lay down the responsibilities of office as, in traditional and solemn ceremony, the authority of the Presidency is vested in my successor.

This evening I come to you with a message of leave-taking and farewell, and to share a few final thoughts with you, my countrymen.

Like every other citizen, I wish the new President, and all who will labor with him, Godspeed. I pray that the coming years will be blessed with peace and prosperity for all.

Our people expect their President and the Congress to find essential agreement on issues of great moment, the wise resolution of which will better shape the future of the Nation.

From *The Eisenhower Administration, 1953–1961: A Documentary History* (New York: Random House, 1971), 1373–77.

My own relations with the Congress, which began on a remote and tenuous basis when, long ago, a member of the Senate appointed me to West Point, have since ranged to the intimate during the war and immediate postwar period and, finally, to the mutually interdependent during these past eight years.

In this final relationship, the Congress and the Administration have, on most vital issues, cooperated well, to serve the national good rather than mere partisanship, and so have assured that the business of the Nation should go forward. So, my official relationship with the Congress ends in a feeling, on my part, of gratitude that we have been able to do so much together.

———

We now stand ten years past the midpoint of a century that has witnessed four major wars among great nations. Three of these involved our own country. Despite these holocausts America is today the strongest, the most influential, and most productive nation in the world. Understandably proud of this preeminence, we yet realize that America's leadership and prestige depend not merely upon our unmatched material progress, riches, and military strength but on how we use our power in the interests of world peace and human betterment.

———

Throughout America's adventure in free government, our basic purposes have been to keep the peace; to foster progress in human achievement, and to enhance liberty, dignity, and integrity among people and among nations. To strive for less would be unworthy of a free and religious people. Any failure traceable to arrogance or our lack of comprehension or readiness to sacrifice would inflict upon us grievous hurt both at home and abroad.

Progress toward these noble goals is persistently threatened by the conflict now engulfing the world. It commands our whole attention, absorbs our very beings. We face a hostile ideology—global in scope, atheistic in character, ruthless in purpose, and insidious in method. Unhappily, the danger it poses promises to be of indefinite duration. To meet it successfully, there is called for not so much the emotional and transitory sacrifices of crisis but rather those which enable us to carry forward steadily, surely, and without complaint the burdens of a prolonged and complex struggle—with liberty the stake. Only thus shall we remain, despite every provocation, on our charted course toward permanent peace and human betterment.

Crises there will continue to be. In meeting them, whether foreign or domestic, great or small, there is a recurring temptation to feel that some spectacular and costly action could become the miraculous solution to all current difficulties. A huge increase in newer elements of our defense, development of unrealistic programs to cure every ill in agriculture, a dramatic expansion in basic and applied research—these and many other possibilities, each possibly promising in itself, may be suggested as the only way to the road we wish to travel.

But each proposal must be weighed in the light of a broader consideration: the need to maintain balance in and among national programs—balance between the private and the public economy, balance between cost and hoped-for advantage—balance between the clearly necessary and the comfortably desirable; balance between our essential requirements as a nation and the duties imposed by the nation upon the individual; balance between actions of the moment and the national welfare of the future. Good judgment seeks balance and progress; lack of it eventually finds imbalance and frustration.

The record of many decades stands as proof that our people and their government have, in the main, understood these truths and have responded to them well, in the face of stress and threat. But threats, new in kind or degree, constantly arise. I mention two only.

———

A vital element in keeping the peace is our military establishment. Our arms must be mighty, ready for instant action, so that no potential aggressor may be tempted to risk his own destruction.

Our military organization today bears little relation to that known by any of my predecessors in peacetime, or indeed by the fighting men of World War II or Korea.

Until the latest of our world conflicts, the United States had no armaments industry. American makers of plowshares could, with time and as required, make swords as well. But now we can no longer risk emergency improvisation of national defense; we have been compelled to create a permanent armaments industry of vast proportions. Added to this, three and a half million men and women are directly engaged in the defense establishment. We annually spend on military security more than the net income of all United States corporations.

This conjunction of an immense military establishment and a large arms industry is new in the American experience. The total influence—economic, political, even spiritual—is felt in every city, every State house, every office of the Federal government. We recognize the imperative need for this development. Yet we must not fail to comprehend its grave implications. Our toil, resources, and livelihood are all involved; so is the very structure of our society.

In the councils of government we must guard against the acquisition of unwarranted influence, whether sought or unsought, by the military-industrial complex. The potential for the disastrous rise of misplaced power exists and will persist.

We must never let the weight of this combination endanger our liberties or democratic processes. We should take nothing for granted. Only an alert and knowledgeable citizenry can compel the proper meshing of the huge industrial and military machinery of defense with our peaceful methods and goals, so that security and liberty may prosper together.

Akin to and largely responsible for the sweeping changes in our industrial-military posture has been the technological revolution during recent decades.

In this revolution, research has become central; it also becomes more formalized, complex, and costly. A steadily increasing share is conducted for, by, or at the direction of the Federal government.

Today, the solitary inventor, tinkering in his shop, has been overshadowed by task forces of scientists in laboratories and testing fields. In the same fashion the free university, historically the fountainhead of free ideas and scientific discovery, has experienced a revolution in the conduct of research. Partly because of the huge costs involved, a government contract becomes virtually a substitute for intellectual curiosity. For every old blackboard there are now hundreds of new electronic computers.

The prospect of domination of the nation's scholars by Federal employment, project allocations, and the power of money is ever present—and is gravely to be regarded.

Yet, in holding scientific research and discovery in respect, as we should, we must also be alert to the equal and opposite danger that public policy could itself become the captive of a scientific-technological elite.

It is the task of statesmanship to mold, to balance, and to integrate these and other forces, new and old, within the principles of our democratic system—ever aiming toward the supreme goals of our free society.

———

Another factor in maintaining balance involves the element of time. As we peer into society's future, we—you and I, and our government—must avoid the impulse to live only for today, plundering for our own ease and convenience the precious resources of tomorrow. We cannot mortgage the material assets of our grandchildren without risking the loss also of their political and spiritual heritage. We want democracy to survive for all generations to come, not to become the insolvent phantom of tomorrow.

———

Down the long lane of the history yet to be written, America knows that this world of ours, ever growing smaller, must avoid becoming a community of dreadful fear and hate and be, instead, a proud confederation of mutual trust and respect.

Such a confederation must be one of equals. The weakest must come to the conference table with the same confidence as do we, protected as we are by our moral, economic, and military strength. That table, though scarred by many past frustrations, cannot be abandoned for the certain agony of the battlefield.

Disarmament, with mutual honor and confidence, is a continuing imperative. Together we must learn how to compose differences, not with arms but with intellect and decent purpose. Because this need is so sharp and apparent, I confess that I lay down my official responsibilities in this field with a definite sense of disappointment. As one who has witnessed the horror and the lingering sadness of war—as one who knows that another war could utterly destroy this civilization which has been so slowly and painfully built over thousands of years—I wish I could say tonight that a lasting peace is in sight.

Happily, I can say that war has been avoided. Steady progress toward our ultimate goal has been made. But so much remains to be done. As a private citizen I shall never cease to do what little I can to help the world advance along that road.

———

So—in this my last goodnight to you as your President—I thank you for the many opportunities you have given me for public service in war and peace. I trust that in that service you find some things worthy; as for the rest of it, I know you will find ways to improve performance in the future.

You and I—my fellow citizens—need to be strong in our faith that all nations, under God, will reach the goal of peace with justice. May we be ever unswerving in devotion to principle, confident but humble with power, diligent in pursuit of the Nation's great goals.

To all the peoples of the world, I once more give expression to America's prayerful and continuing aspiration:

We pray that peoples of all faiths, all races, all nations may have their great human needs satisfied; that those now denied opportunity shall come to enjoy it to the full; that all who yearn for freedom may experience its spiritual blessings; that those who have freedom will understand, also, its heavy responsibilities; that all who are insensitive to the needs of others will learn charity; that the scourges of poverty, disease, and ignorance will be made to disappear from the earth; and that in the goodness of time all peoples will come to live together in a peace guaranteed by the binding force of mutual respect and love.

DR. MARTIN LUTHER KING, JR.

9

Letter from Birmingham Jail

Jailed in Birmingham, Alabama, for disobeying a state court order barring demonstrations, Dr. Martin Luther King, Jr., penned a letter on April 16, 1963, to a group of local white clergymen. These men had been sympathetic to the cause of civil rights and had courageously condemned the militant segregationist politics of Governor George Wallace. Yet they criticized Dr. King's nonviolent demonstrations, fearing that his activities would "incite hatred and violence." King told them bluntly, "I have almost reached the regrettable conclusion that the Negro's great stumbling block is not the White Citizens' Counciler or the Ku Klux Klanner but the white moderate who is more devoted to 'order' than to justice; . . . who paternalistically believes that he can set the timetable for another man's freedom." King's letter was a clear message that the quiet consensus liberalism of the vital center was inadequate to the current crisis in black America. There was no longer a middle ground.

My Dear Fellow Clergymen:

While confined here in the Birmingham city jail, I came across your recent statement calling my present activities "unwise and untimely." Seldom do I pause to answer criticism of my work and ideas. If I sought to answer all the criticisms that cross my desk, my secretaries would have little time for anything other than such correspondence in the course of the day, and I would have no time for constructive work. But since I feel that you are men of genuine good will

From *Why We Can't Wait* (New York: Harper and Row, 1963, 1964), 77–100. © 1963 by Martin Luther King, Jr., and 1991 by Coretta Scott King. Reprinted by arrangement with The Heirs to the Estate of Martin Luther King, Jr., c/o Writers House, Inc., as agent for the proprietor.

and that your criticisms are sincerely set forth, I want to try to answer your statement in what I hope will be patient and reasonable terms.

I think I should indicate why I am here in Birmingham, since you have been influenced by the view which argues against "outsiders coming in." I have the honor of serving as president of the Southern Christian Leadership Conference, an organization operating in every southern state, with headquarters in Atlanta, Georgia. We have some eighty-five affiliated organizations across the South, and one of them is the Alabama Christian Movement for Human Rights. Frequently we share staff, educational, and financial resources with our affiliates. Several months ago the affiliate here in Birmingham asked us to be on call to engage in a nonviolent direct-action program if such were deemed necessary. We readily consented, and when the hour came we lived up to our promise. So I, along with several members of my staff, am here because I was invited here. I am here because I have organizational ties here.

But more basically, I am in Birmingham because injustice is here. Just as the prophets of the eighth century B.C. left their villages and carried their "thus saith the Lord" far beyond the boundaries of their home towns, and just as the Apostle Paul left his village of Tarsus and carried the gospel of Jesus Christ to the far corners of the Greco-Roman world, so am I compelled to carry the gospel of freedom beyond my own home town. Like Paul, I must constantly respond to the Macedonian call for aid.

Moreover, I am cognizant of the interrelatedness of all communities and states. I cannot sit idly by in Atlanta and not be concerned about what happens in Birmingham. Injustice anywhere is a threat to justice everywhere. We are caught in an inescapable network of mutuality, tied in a single garment of destiny. Whatever affects one directly, affects all indirectly. Never again can we afford to live with the narrow, provincial, "outside agitator" idea. Anyone who lives inside the United States can never be considered an outsider anywhere within its bounds.

You deplore the demonstrations taking place in Birmingham. But your statement, I am sorry to say, fails to express a similar concern for the conditions that brought about the demonstrations. I am sure that none of you would want to rest content with the superficial kind of social analysis that deals merely with effects and does not grapple with underlying causes. It is unfortunate that the city's white power structure left the Negro community with no alternative.

In any nonviolent campaign there are four basic steps: collection of the facts to determine whether injustices exist; negotiation; self-purification; and direct action. We have gone through all these steps in Birmingham. There can be no gainsaying the fact that racial injustice engulfs this community. Birmingham is probably the most thoroughly segregated city in the United States. Its ugly record of brutality is widely known. Negroes have experienced grossly unjust treatment in the courts. There have been more unsolved bombings of Negro homes and churches in Birmingham than in any other city in the nation. These are the hard, brutal facts of the case. On the basis of these conditions, Negro leaders sought to negotiate with the city fathers. But the latter consistently refused to engage in good-faith negotiation.

Then, last September, came the opportunity to talk with leaders of Birmingham's economic community. In the course of the negotiations, certain promises were made by the merchants—for example, to remove the stores' humiliating racial signs. On the basis of these promises, the Reverend Fred Shuttlesworth and the leaders of the Alabama Christian Movement for Human Rights agreed to a moratorium on all demonstrations. As the weeks and months went by, we realized that we were the victims of a broken promise. A few signs, briefly removed, returned; the others remained.

As in so many past experiences, our hopes had been blasted, and the shadow of deep disappointment settled upon us. We had no alternative except to prepare for direct action, whereby we would present our very bodies as a means of laying our case before the conscience of the local and the national community. Mindful of the difficulties involved, we decided to undertake a process of self-purification. We began a series of workshops on nonviolence, and we repeatedly asked ourselves: "Are you able to accept blows without retaliation?" "Are you able to endure the ordeal of jail?" We decided to schedule our direct-action program for the Easter season, realizing that except for Christmas, this is the main shopping period of the year. Knowing that a strong economic-withdrawal program would be the by-product of direct action, we felt that this would be the best time to bring pressure to bear on the merchants for the needed change.

Then it occurred to us that Birmingham's mayoral election was coming up in March, and we speedily decided to postpone action until after election day. When we discovered that the Commissioner of Public Safety, Eugene "Bull" Connor, had piled up enough votes to be in the runoff, we decided again to postpone action until the day after the runoff so that the demonstrations could not be used to cloud the issues. Like many others, we waited to see Mr. Connor defeated, and to this end we endured postponement after postponement. Having aided in this community need, we felt that our direct-action program could be delayed no longer.

You may well ask: "Why direct action? Why sit-ins, marches, and so forth? Isn't negotiation a better path?" You are quite right in calling for negotiation. Indeed, this is the very purpose of direct action. Nonviolent direct action seeks to create such a crisis and foster such a tension that a community which has constantly refused to negotiate is forced to confront the issue. It seeks so to dramatize the issue that it can no longer be ignored. My citing the creation of tension as part of the work of the nonviolent resister may sound rather shocking. But I must confess that I am not afraid of the word "tension." I have earnestly opposed violent tension, but there is a type of constructive, nonviolent tension which is necessary for growth. Just as Socrates felt that it was necessary to create a tension in the mind so that individuals could rise from the bondage of myths and half-truths to the unfettered realm of creative analysis and objective appraisal, so must we see the need for nonviolent gadflies to create the kind of tension in society that will help men rise from the dark depths of prejudice and racism to the majestic heights of understanding and brotherhood.

The purpose of our direct-action program is to create a situation so crisis-packed that it will inevitably open the door to negotiation. I therefore concur with you in your call for negotiation. Too long has our beloved Southland been bogged down in a tragic effort to live in monologue rather than dialogue.

One of the basic points in your statement is that the action that I and my associates have taken in Birmingham is untimely. Some have asked: "Why didn't you give the new city administration time to act?" The only answer that I can give to this query is that the new Birmingham administration must be prodded about as much as the outgoing one, before it will act. We are sadly mistaken if we feel that the election of Albert Boutwell as mayor will bring the millennium to Birmingham. While Mr. Boutwell is a much more gentle person than Mr. Connor, they are both segregationists, dedicated to maintenance of the status quo. I have hope that Mr. Boutwell will be reasonable enough to see the futility of massive resistance to desegregation. But he will not see this without pressure from devotees of civil rights. My friends, I must say to you that we have not made a single gain in civil rights without determined legal and nonviolent pressure. Lamentably, it is an historical fact that privileged groups seldom give up their privileges voluntarily.

Individuals may see the moral light and voluntarily give up their unjust posture; but, as Reinhold Niebuhr has reminded us, groups tend to be more immoral than individuals.

We know through painful experience that freedom is never voluntarily given by the oppressor; it must be demanded by the oppressed. Frankly, I have yet to engage in a direct-action campaign that was "well-timed" in the view of those who have not suffered unduly from the disease of segregation. For years now I have heard the word "Wait!" It rings in the ear of every Negro with piercing familiarity. This "Wait" has almost always meant "Never." We must come to see, with one of our distinguished jurists, that "justice too long delayed is justice denied."

We have waited for more than 340 years for our constitutional and God-given rights. The nations of Asia and Africa are moving with jet-like speed toward gaining political independence, but we still creep at horse-and-buggy pace toward gaining a cup of coffee at a lunch counter. Perhaps it is easy for those who have never felt the stinging darts of segregation to say, "Wait." But when you have seen vicious mobs lynch your mothers and fathers at will and drown your sisters and brothers at whim; when you have seen hate-filled policemen curse, kick, and even kill your black brothers and sisters; when you see the vast majority of your twenty million Negro brothers smothering in an airtight cage of poverty in the midst of an affluent society; when you suddenly find your tongue twisted and your speech stammering as you seek to explain to your six-year-old daughter why she can't go to the public amusement park that has just been advertised on television, and see tears welling up in her eyes when she is told that Funtown is closed to colored children, and see ominous clouds of inferiority beginning to form in her little mental sky, and see her beginning to distort her personality by developing an unconscious bitterness toward white people; when you have to concoct an answer for a five-year-old son who is asking: "Daddy, why do white people treat colored people so mean?"; when you take a cross-country drive and find it necessary to sleep night after night in the uncomfortable corners of your automobile because no motel will accept you; when you are humiliated day in and day out by nagging signs reading "white" and "colored"; when your first name becomes "nigger," your middle name becomes "John," and your wife and mother are never given the respected title "Mrs."; when you are harried by day and haunted by night by the fact that you are a Negro, living constantly at tiptoe stance, never quite knowing what to expect next, and are plagued with inner fears and outer resentments; when you are forever fighting a degenerating sense of "nobodiness"—then you will understand why we find it difficult to wait. There comes a time when the cup of endurance runs over, and men are no longer willing to be plunged into the abyss of despair. I hope, sirs, you can understand our legitimate and unavoidable impatience.

You express a great deal of anxiety over our willingness to break laws. This is certainly a legitimate concern. Since we so diligently urge people to obey the Supreme Court's decision of 1954 outlawing segregation in the public schools, at first glance it may seem rather paradoxical for us consciously to break laws. One may well ask: "How can you advocate breaking some laws and obeying others?" The answer lies in the fact that there are two types of laws: just and unjust. I would be the first to advocate obeying just laws. One has not only a legal but a moral responsibility to obey just laws. Conversely, one has a moral responsibility to disobey unjust laws. I would agree with St. Augustine that "an unjust law is no law at all."

Now, what is the difference between the two? How does one determine whether a law is just or unjust? A just law is a man-made code that squares with the moral law or the law of God. An unjust law is a code that is out of harmony with the moral law. To put it in the terms of St. Thomas Aquinas: An unjust law is a human law that is not rooted in eternal law and natural law. Any law that uplifts human personality is just. Any law that degrades human personality is unjust. All segregation statutes are unjust because segregation distorts the soul and damages the personality. It gives the segregator a false sense of superiority and the segregated a false sense of inferiority. Segregation, to use the terminology of the Jewish philosopher Martin Buber, substitutes an "I—it" relationship for an "I—thou" relationship and ends up relegating persons to the status of things. Hence segregation is not only politically, economically, and sociologically unsound; it is morally wrong and sinful. Paul Tillich has said that sin is separation. Is not segregation an existential expression of man's tragic separation, his awful estrangement, his terrible sinfulness? Thus it is that I can urge men to obey the 1954 decision of the Supreme Court, for it is morally right; and I can urge them to disobey segregation ordinances, for they are morally wrong.

Let us consider a more concrete example of just and unjust laws. An unjust law is a code that a numerical or power majority group compels a minority group to obey but does not make binding on itself. This is *difference* made legal. By the same token, a just law is a code that a majority compels a minority to follow and that it is willing to follow itself. This is *sameness* made legal.

Let me give another explanation. A law is unjust if it is inflicted on a minority that, as a result of being denied the right to vote, had no part in enacting or devising the law. Who can say that the legislature of Alabama, which set up that state's segregation laws, was democratically elected? Throughout Alabama all sorts of devious methods are used to prevent Negroes from becoming registered voters, and there are some counties in which, even though Negroes constitute a majority of the population, not a single Negro is registered. Can any law enacted under such circumstances be considered democratically structured?

Sometimes a law is just on its face and unjust in its application. For instance, I have been arrested on a charge of parading without a permit. Now, there is nothing wrong in having an ordinance which requires a permit for a parade. But such an ordinance becomes unjust when it is used to maintain segregation and to deny citizens the First Amendment privilege of peaceful assembly and protest.

I hope you are able to see the distinction I am trying to point out. In no sense do I advocate evading or defying the law, as would the rabid segregationist. That would lead to anarchy. One who breaks an unjust law must do so openly, lovingly, and with a willingness to accept the penalty. I submit that an individual who breaks a law that conscience tells him is unjust, and who willingly accepts the penalty of imprisonment in order to arouse the conscience of the community over its injustice, is in reality expressing the highest respect for law.

Of course, there is nothing new about this kind of civil disobedience. It was evidenced sublimely in the refusal of Shadrach, Meshach, and Abednego to obey the laws of Nebuchadnezzar, on the ground that a higher moral law was at stake. It was practiced superbly by the early Christians, who were willing to face hungry lions and the excruciating pain of chopping blocks rather than submit to certain unjust laws of the Roman Empire. To a degree, academic freedom is a reality today because Socrates practiced civil disobedience. In our own nation, the Boston Tea Party represented a massive act of civil disobedience.

We should never forget that everything Adolf Hitler did in Germany was "legal" and everything the Hungarian freedom fighters did in Hungary was "illegal." It was "illegal" to aid and comfort a Jew in Hitler's Germany. Even so, I am sure that, had I lived in Germany at the time, I would have aided and comforted my Jewish brothers. If today I lived in a Communist country where certain principles dear to the Christian faith are suppressed, I would openly advocate disobeying that country's antireligious laws.

I must make two honest confessions to you, my Christian and Jewish brothers. First, I must confess that over the past few years I have been gravely disappointed with the white moderate. I have almost reached the regrettable conclusion that the Negro's great stumbling block in his stride toward freedom is not the White Citizens' Counciler or the Ku Klux Klanner but the white moderate who is more devoted to "order" than to justice; who prefers a negative peace which is the absence of tension to a positive peace which is the presence of justice; who constantly says: "I agree with you in the goal you seek, but I cannot agree with your methods of direct action"; who paternalistically believes he can set the timetable for another man's freedom; who lives by a mythical concept of time and who constantly advises the Negro to wait for a "more convenient season." Shallow understanding from people of good will is more frustrating than absolute misunderstanding from people of ill will. Lukewarm acceptance is much more bewildering than outright rejection.

I had hoped that the white moderate would understand that law and order exist for the purpose of establishing justice and that when they fail in this purpose they become the dangerously structured dams that block the flow of social progress. I had hoped that the white moderate would understand that the present tension in the South is a necessary phase of the transition from an obnoxious negative peace, in which the Negro passively accepted his unjust plight, to a substantive and positive peace, in which all men will respect the dignity and worth of human personality. Actually, we who engage in nonviolent direct action are not the creators of tension. We merely bring to the surface the hidden tension that is already alive. We bring it out in the open, where it can be seen and dealt with. Like a boil that can never be cured so long as it is covered up but must be opened with all its ugliness to the natural medicines of air and light, injustice must be exposed, with all the tension its exposure creates, to the light of human conscience and the air of national opinion before it can be cured.

In your statement you assert that our actions, even though peaceful, must be condemned because they precipitate violence. But is this a logical assertion? Isn't this like condemning a robbed man because his possession of money precipitated the evil act of robbery? Isn't this like condemning Socrates because his unswerving commitment to truth and his philosophical inquiries precipitated the act by the misguided populace in which they made him drink hemlock? Isn't this like condemning Jesus because his unique God-consciousness and never-ceasing devotion to God's will precipitated the evil act of crucifixion? We must come to see that, as the Federal courts have consistently affirmed, it is wrong to urge an individual to cease his efforts to gain his basic constitutional rights because the quest may precipitate violence. Society must protect the robbed and punish the robber.

I had also hoped that the white moderate would reject the myth concerning time in relation to the struggle for freedom. I have just received a letter from a white brother in Texas. He writes: "All Christians know that the colored people will receive equal rights eventually, but it is possible that you are in too great a religious hurry. It has taken Christianity almost two thousand years to accomplish what it has. The teachings of Christ take time to come to earth." Such an attitude stems from a tragic misconception of time, from the strangely irrational notion that there is something in the very flow of time that will inevitably cure all ills. Actually, time itself is neutral; it can be used either destructively or constructively. More and more I feel that the people of ill will have used time much more effectively than have the people of good will. We will have to repent in this generation not merely for the hateful words and actions of the bad people but for the appalling silence of the good people. Human progress never rolls in on wheels of inevitability; it comes through the tireless efforts of men willing to be coworkers with God, and without this hard work, time itself becomes an ally of the forces of social stagnation. We must use time creatively, in the knowledge that the time is always ripe to do right. Now is the time to make real the promise of democracy and transform our pending national elegy into a creative psalm of brotherhood. Now is the time to lift our national policy from the quicksand of racial injustice to the solid rock of human dignity.

You speak of our activity in Birmingham as extreme. At first I was rather disappointed that fellow clergymen would see my nonviolent efforts as those of an extremist. I began thinking about the fact that I stand in the middle of two opposing forces in the Negro community. One is a force of complacency, made up in part of Negroes who, as a result of long years of oppression, are so drained of self-respect and a sense of "somebodiness" that they have adjusted to segregation; and in part of the few middle-class Negroes who, because of a degree of academic and economic security and because in some ways they profit by segregation, have become insensitive to the problems of the masses. The other force is one of bitterness and hatred, and it comes perilously close to advocating violence. It is expressed in the various black nationalist groups that are springing up across the nation, the largest and best-known being Elijah Muhammad's Muslim movement. Nourished by the Negro's frustration over the continued existence of racial discrimination, this movement is made up of people who have lost faith in America, who have absolutely repudiated Christianity, and who have concluded that the white man is an incorrigible "devil."

I have tried to stand between these two forces, saying that we need emulate neither the "do-nothingism" of the complacent nor the hatred and despair of the black nationalist. For there is the more excellent way of love and nonviolent protest. I am grateful to God that through the influence of the Negro church the way of nonviolence became an integral part of our struggle.

If this philosophy had not emerged, by now many streets of the South would, I am convinced, be flowing with blood. And I am further convinced that if our white brothers dismiss as "rabble-rousers" and "outside agitators" those of us who employ nonviolent direct action, and if they refuse to support our nonviolent efforts, millions of Negroes will, out of frustration and despair, seek solace and security in black-nationalist ideologies—a development that would inevitably lead to a frightening racial nightmare.

Oppressed people cannot remain oppressed forever. The yearning for freedom eventually manifests itself, and that is what has happened to the American Negro. Something within has reminded him of his birthright of freedom, and something without has reminded him that it can be gained. Consciously or unconsciously, he has been caught up by the *Zeitgeist*, and with his black brothers of Africa and his brown and yellow brothers of Asia, South America, and the Caribbean, the United States Negro is moving with a sense of great urgency toward the promised land of racial justice. If one recognizes this vital urge that has engulfed the Negro community, one should readily understand why public demonstrations are taking place. The Negro has many pent-up resentments and latent frustrations, and he must release them. So let him march; let him make prayer pilgrimages to the city hall; let him go on freedom rides—and try to understand why he must do so. If his repressed emotions are not released in nonviolent ways, they will seek expression through violence; this is not a threat but a fact of history. So I have not said to my people: "Get rid of your discontent." Rather, I have tried to say that this normal and healthy discontent can be chaneled into the creative outlet of nonviolent direct action. And now this approach is being termed extremist.

But though I was initially disappointed at being categorized as an extremist, as I continued to think about the matter I gradually gained a measure of satisfaction from the label. Was not Jesus an extremist for love: "Love your enemies, bless them that curse you, do good to them that hate you, and pray for them which despitefully use you, and persecute you." Was not Amos an extremist for justice: "Let justice roll down like waters and righteousness like an ever-flowing stream." Was not Paul an extremist for the Christian gospel: "I bear in my body the marks of the Lord Jesus." Was not Martin Luther an extremist: "Here I stand; I cannot do otherwise, so help me God." And John Bunyan: "I will stay in jail to the end of my days before I make a butchery of my conscience." And Abraham Lincoln: "This nation cannot survive half slave and half free." And Thomas Jefferson: "We hold these truths to be self-evident, that all men are created equal . . ." So the question is not whether we will be extremists but what kind of extremists we will be. Will we be extremists for hate or for love? Will we be extremists for the preservation of injustice or for the extension of justice? In that dramatic scene on Calvary's hill three men were crucified. We must never forget that all three were crucified for the same crime—the crime of extremism. Two were extremists for immorality, and thus fell below their environment. The other, Jesus Christ, was an extremist for love, truth, and goodness, and thereby rose above his environment. Perhaps the South, the nation, and the world are in dire need of creative extremists.

I had hoped that the white moderate would see this need. Perhaps I was too optimistic; perhaps I expected too much. I suppose I should have realized that few members of the oppressor race can understand the deep groans and passionate yearnings of the oppressed race, and still fewer have the vision to see that injustice must be rooted out by strong, persistent, and determined action. I am thankful, however, that some of our white brothers in the South have grasped the meaning of this social revolution and committed themselves to it. They are still all too few in quantity, but they are big in quality. Some—such as Ralph McGill, Lillian Smith, Harry Golden, James McBride Dabbs, Ann Braden, and Sarah Patton Boyle—have written about our struggle in eloquent and prophetic terms. Others have marched with us down nameless streets of the South. They have languished in filthy, roach-infested jails, suffering the abuse and brutality of policemen who view them as "dirty nigger-lovers." Unlike so many of their moderate brothers and sisters, they have recognized the urgency of the moment and sensed the need for powerful "action" antidotes to combat the disease of segregation.

Let me take note of my other major disappointment. I have been so greatly disappointed with the white church and its leadership. Of course, there are some notable exceptions. I am not unmindful of the fact that each of you has taken some significant stands on this issue. I commend you, Reverend Stallings, for your Christian stand on this past Sunday, in welcoming Negroes to your worship service on a non-segregated basis. I commend the Catholic leaders of this state for integrating Spring Hill College several years ago.

But despite these notable exceptions, I must honestly reiterate that I have been disappointed with the church. I do not say this as one of those negative critics who can always find something wrong with the church. I say this as a minister of the gospel who loves the church, who was nurtured in its bosom, who has been sustained by its spiritual blessings, and who will remain true to it as long as the cord of life shall lengthen.

When I was suddenly catapulted into the leadership of the bus protest in Montgomery, Alabama, a few years ago, I felt we would be supported by the white church. I felt that the white ministers, priests, and rabbis of the South would be among our strongest allies. Instead, some have been outright opponents, refusing to understand the freedom movement and misrepresenting its leaders; all too many others have been more cautious than courageous and have remained silent behind the anesthetizing security of stained-glass windows.

In spite of my shattered dreams, I came to Birmingham with the hope that the white religious leadership of this community would see the justice of our cause and, with deep moral concern, would serve as the channel through which our just grievances could reach the power structure. I had hoped that each of you would understand. But again I have been disappointed.

I have heard numerous southern religious leaders admonish their worshipers to comply with a desegregation decision because it is the law, but I have longed to hear white ministers declare: "Follow this decree because integration is morally right and because the Negro is your brother." In the midst of blatant injustices inflicted upon the Negro, I have watched white churchmen stand on the sideline and mouth pious irrelevancies and sanctimonious trivialities. In the midst of a mighty struggle to rid our nation of racial and economic injustice, I have heard many ministers say: "Those are social issues, with which the gospel has no real concern." And I have watched many churches commit themselves to a completely otherworldly religion which makes a strange, un-Biblical distinction between body and soul, between the sacred and the secular.

I have traveled the length and breadth of Alabama, Mississippi, and all the other southern states. On sweltering summer days and crisp autumn mornings I have looked at the South's beautiful churches with their lofty spires pointing heavenward. I have beheld the impressive outlines of her massive religious education buildings. Over and over I have found myself asking: "What kind of people worship here? Who is their God? Where were their voices when the lips of Governor Barnett dripped with words of interposition and nullification? Where were they when Governor Wallace gave a clarion call for defiance and hatred? Where were their voices of support when bruised and weary Negro men and women decided to rise from the dark dungeons of complacency to the bright hills of creative protest?"

Yes, these questions are still in my mind. In deep disappointment I have wept over the laxity of the church. But be assured that my tears have been tears of love. There can be no deep disappointment where there is not deep love. Yes, I love the church. How could I do otherwise? I am in the rather unique position of being the son, the grandson, and the great-grandson of preachers. Yes, I see the church as the body of Christ. But, oh! How we have blemished and scarred that body through social neglect and through fear of being nonconformists.

There was a time when the church was very powerful—in the time when the early Christians rejoiced at being deemed worthy to suffer for what they believed. In those days the church was not merely a thermometer that recorded the ideas and principles of popular opinion; it was a thermostat that transformed the mores of society. Whenever the early Christians entered a town, the people in power became disturbed and immediately sought to convict the Christians for being "disturbers of the peace" and "outside agitators." But the Christians pressed on, in the conviction that they were "a colony of heaven," called to obey God rather than man. Small in number, they were big in commitment. They were too God-intoxicated to be "astronomically intimidated." By their effort and example they brought an end to such ancient evils as infanticide and gladiatorial contests.

Things are different now. So often the contemporary church is a weak, ineffectual voice with an uncertain sound. So often it is an archdefender of the status quo. Far from being disturbed by the presence of the church, the power structure of the average community is consoled by the church's silent—and often even vocal—sanction of things as they are.

But the judgment of God is upon the church as never before. If today's church does not recapture the sacrificial spirit of the early church, it will lose its authenticity, forfeit the loyalty of millions, and be dismissed as an irrelevant social club with no meaning for the twentieth century. Every day I meet young people whose disappointment with the church has turned into outright disgust.

Perhaps I have once again been too optimistic. Is organized religion too inextricably bound to the status quo to save our nation and the world? Perhaps I must turn my faith to the inner spiritual church, the church within the church, as the true *ekklesia* and the hope of the world. But again I am thankful to God that some noble souls from the ranks of organized religion have broken loose from the paralyzing chains of conformity and joined us as active partners in the struggle for freedom. They have left their secure congregations and walked the streets of Albany, Georgia, with us. They have gone down the highways of the South on tortuous rides for freedom. Yes, they have gone to jail with us. Some have been dismissed from their churches, have lost the support of their bishops and fellow ministers. But they have acted in the faith that right defeated is stronger than evil triumphant. Their witness has been the spiritual salt that has preserved the true meaning of the gospel in these troubled times. They have carved a tunnel of hope through the dark mountain of disappointment.

I hope the church as a whole will meet the challenge of this decisive hour. But even if the church does not come to the aid of justice, I have no despair about the future. I have no fear about the outcome of our struggle in Birmingham, even if our motives are at present misunderstood. We will reach the goal of freedom in Birmingham and all over the nation, because the goal of America is freedom. Abused and scorned though we may be, our destiny is tied up with America's destiny. Before the Pilgrims landed at Plymouth, we were here. Before the pen of Jefferson etched the majestic words of the Declaration of Independence across the pages of history, we were here. For more than two centuries our forebears labored in this country without wages; they made cotton king; they built the homes of their masters while suffering gross injustice and shameful humiliation—and yet out of a bottomless vitality they continued to thrive and develop. If the inexpressible cruelties of slavery could not stop us, the opposition we now face will surely fail. We will win our freedom because the sacred heritage of our nation and the eternal will of God are embodied in our echoing demands.

Before closing I feel impelled to mention one other point in your statement that has troubled me profoundly. You warmly commended the Birmingham police force for keeping "order" and "preventing violence." I doubt that you would have so warmly commended the police force if you had seen its dogs sinking their teeth into unarmed, non-violent Negroes. I doubt that you would so quickly commend the policemen if you were to observe their ugly and inhumane treatment of Negroes here in the city jail; if you were to watch them push and curse old Negro women and young Negro girls; if you were to see them slap and kick old Negro men and young boys; if you were to observe them, as they did on two occasions, refuse to give us food because we wanted to sing our grace together. I cannot join you in your praise of the Birmingham police department.

It is true that the police have exercised a degree of discipline in handling the demonstrators. In this sense they have conducted themselves rather "nonviolently" in public. But for what purpose? To preserve the evil system of segregation. Over the past few years I have consistently preached that nonviolence demands that the means we use must be as pure as the ends we seek. I have tried to make clear that it is wrong to use immoral means to attain moral ends. But now I must affirm that it is just as wrong, or perhaps even more so, to use moral means to preserve immoral ends. Perhaps Mr. Connor and his policemen have been rather nonviolent in public, as was Chief Pritchett in Albany, Georgia, but they have used the moral means of nonviolence to maintain the immoral end of racial injustice. As T. S. Eliot has said: "The last temptation is the greatest treason: To do the right deed for the wrong reason."

I wish you had commended the Negro sit-inners and demonstrators of Birmingham for their sublime courage, their willingness to suffer, and their amazing discipline in the midst of great provocation. One day the South will recognize its real heroes. They will be the James Merediths, with the noble sense of purpose that enables them to face jeering and hostile mobs, and with the agonizing loneliness that characterizes the life of the pioneer. They will be old, oppressed, battered Negro women, symbolized in a seventy-two-year-old woman in Montgomery, Alabama, who rose up with a sense of dignity and with her people decided not to ride segregated buses, and who responded with ungrammatical profundity to one who inquired about her weariness: "My feet is tired, but my soul is at rest." They will be the young high school and college students, the young ministers of the gospel and a host of their elders, courageously and nonviolently sitting-in at lunch counters and willingly going to jail for conscience's sake. One day the South will know that when these disinherited children of God sat down at lunch counters, they were in reality standing up for what is best in the American dream and for the most sacred values in our Judaeo-Christian heritage, thereby bringing our nation back to those great wells of democracy which were dug deep by the founding fathers in their formulation of the Constitution and the Declaration of Independence.

Never before have I written so long a letter. I'm afraid it is much too long to take your precious time. I can assure you that it would have been much shorter if I had been writing from a comfortable desk, but what else can one do when he is alone in a narrow jail cell, other than write long letters, think long thoughts, and pray long prayers?

If I have said anything in this letter that overstates the truth and indicates an unreasonable impatience, I beg you to forgive me. If I have said anything that understates the truth and indicates my having a patience that allows me to settle for anything less than brotherhood, I beg God to forgive me.

I hope this letter finds you strong in the faith. I also hope that circumstances will soon make it possible for me to meet each of you, not as an integrationist or a civil rights leader but as a fellow clergyman and a Christian brother. Let us all hope that the dark clouds of racial prejudice will soon pass away and the deep fog of misunderstanding will be lifted from our fear-drenched communities, and in some not too distant tomorrow the radiant stars of love and brotherhood will shine over our great nation with all their scintillating beauty.

> Yours for the cause
> of Peace and Brotherhood,
> Martin Luther King, Jr.

JOHN F. KENNEDY

10 Commencement Address at American University

In this speech of June 10, 1963, considered one of his finest, President John F. Kennedy offered to change the tone of Soviet-American relations. In its most memorable passage he claimed, "If we cannot end now our differences, at least we can help make the world safe for diversity. For, in the final analysis, our most basic common link is that we all inhabit this small planet. We all breathe the same air. We all cherish our children's future. And we are all mortal." After steering the country through the harrowing Cuban missile crisis, he had become increasingly serious about finding common ground with the Soviet Union on the issue of nuclear arms. Kennedy had no expectation of ever achieving a grand global disarmament scheme. Rather, he thought peace would come in small steps, and he was eager to begin by negotiating a nuclear test ban treaty. As a testimony of good faith, he promised that "the United States does not propose to conduct nuclear tests in the atmosphere so long as other states do not do so." By the end of that summer the United States, Great Britain, and the Soviet Union had concluded a treaty banning all nuclear tests in the atmosphere—the first major arms control treaty of the Cold War.

From *Public Papers of the Presidents: John F. Kennedy* (Washington, DC: Government Printing Office, 1964), 459–64.

It is with great pride that I participate in this ceremony of the American University, sponsored by the Methodist Church, founded by Bishop John Fletcher Hurst, and first opened by President Woodrow Wilson in 1914. This is a young and growing university, but it has already fulfilled Bishop Hurst's enlightened hope for the study of history and public affairs in a city devoted to the making of history and to the conduct of the public's business. By sponsoring this institution of higher learning for all who wish to learn, whatever their color or their creed, the Methodists of this area and the Nation deserve the Nation's thanks, and I commend all those who are today graduating.

Professor Woodrow Wilson once said that every man sent out from a university should be a man of his nation as well as a man of his time, and I am confident that the men and women who carry the honor of graduating from this institution will continue to give from their lives, from their talents, a high measure of public service and public support.

"There are few earthly things more beautiful than a university," wrote John Masefield, in his tribute to English universities—and his words are equally true today. He did not refer to spires and towers, to campus greens and ivied walls. He admired the splendid beauty of the university, he said, because it was "a place where those who hate ignorance may strive to know, where those who perceive truth may strive to make others see."

I have, therefore, chosen this time and this place to discuss a topic on which ignorance too often abounds and the truth is too rarely perceived—yet it is the most important topic on earth: world peace.

What kind of peace do I mean? What kind of peace do we seek? Not a Pax Americana enforced on the world by American weapons of war. Not the peace of the grave or the security of the slave. I am talking about genuine peace, the kind of peace that makes life on earth worth living, the kind that enables men and nations to grow and to hope and to build a better life for their children—not merely peace for Americans but peace for all men and women, not merely peace in our time but peace for all time.

I speak of peace because of the new face of war. Total war makes no sense in an age when great powers can maintain large and relatively invulnerable nuclear forces and refuse to surrender without resort to those forces. It makes no sense in an age when a single nuclear weapon contains almost ten times the explosive force delivered by all of the allied air forces in the Second World War. It makes no sense in an age when the deadly poisons produced by a nuclear exchange would be carried by wind and water and soil and seed to the far corners of the globe and to generations yet unborn.

Today the expenditure of billions of dollars every year on weapons acquired for the purpose of making sure we never need to use them is essential to keeping the peace. But surely the acquisition of such idle stockpiles—which can only destroy and never create—is not the only, much less the most efficient, means of assuring peace.

I speak of peace, therefore, as the necessary rational end of rational men. I realize that the pursuit of peace is not as dramatic as the pursuit of war—and frequently the words of the pursuer fall on deaf ears. But we have no more urgent task.

Some say that it is useless to speak of world peace or world law or world disarmament—and that it will be useless until the leaders of the Soviet Union adopt a more enlightened attitude. I hope they do. I believe we can help them do it. But I also believe that we must reexamine our own attitude—as individuals and as a Nation—for our attitude is as essential as theirs. And every graduate of this school, every thoughtful citizen who despairs of war and wishes to bring peace, should begin by looking inward—by examining his own attitude toward the possibilities of peace, toward the Soviet Union, toward the course of the cold war, and toward freedom and peace here at home.

First: Let us examine our attitude toward peace itself. Too many of us think it is impossible. Too many think it unreal. But that is a dangerous, defeatist belief. It leads to the conclusion that war is inevitable, that mankind is doomed, that we are gripped by forces we cannot control.

We need not accept that view. Our problems are manmade—therefore, they can be solved by man. And man can be as big as he wants. No problem of human destiny is beyond human beings. Man's reason and spirit have often solved the seemingly unsolvable—and we believe they can do it again.

I am not referring to the absolute, infinite concept of universal peace and good will of which some fantasies and fanatics dream. I do not deny the value of hopes and dreams, but we merely invite discouragement and incredulity by making that our only and immediate goal.

Let us focus instead on a more practical, more attainable peace— based not on a sudden revolution in human nature but on a gradual evolution in human institutions—on a series of concrete actions and effective agreements which are in the interest of all concerned. There is no single, simple key to this peace—no grand or magic formula to be adopted by one or two powers. Genuine peace must be the product of many nations, the sum of many acts. It must be dynamic, not static, changing to meet the challenge of each new generation. For peace is a process—a way of solving problems.

With such a peace, there will still be quarrels and conflicting interests, as there are within families and nations. World peace, like community peace, does not require that each man love his neighbor—it requires only that they live together in mutual tolerance, submitting their disputes to a just and peaceful settlement. And history teaches us that enmities between nations, as between individuals, do not last forever. However fixed our likes and dislikes may seem, the tide of time and events will often bring surprising changes in the relations between nations and neighbors.

So let us persevere. Peace need not be impracticable, and war need not be inevitable. By defining our goal more clearly, by making it seem more manageable and less remote, we can help all peoples to see it, to draw hope from it, and to move irresistibly toward it.

Second: Let us reexamine our attitude toward the Soviet Union. It is discouraging to think that their leaders may actually believe what their propagandists write. It is discouraging to read a recent authoritative Soviet text on *Military Strategy* and find, on page after page, wholly baseless and incredible claims—such as the allegation that "American imperialist circles are preparing to unleash different types of wars, . . . that there is a very real threat of a preventive war being unleashed by American imperialists against the Soviet Union, . . . [and that] the political aims of the American imperialists are to enslave economically and politically the European and other capitalist countries . . . [and] to achieve world domination . . . by means of aggressive wars."

Truly, as it was written long ago: "The wicked flee when no man pursueth." Yet it is sad to read these Soviet statements—to realize the extent of the gulf between us. But it is also a warning—a warning to the American people not to fall into the same trap as the Soviets, not to see only a distorted and desperate view of the other side, not to see conflict as inevitable, accommodation as impossible, and communication as nothing more than an exchange of threats.

No government or social system is so evil that its people must be considered as lacking in virtue. As Americans, we find communism profoundly repugnant as a negation of personal freedom and dignity.

But we can still hail the Russian people for their many achievements—in science and space, in economic and industrial growth, in culture and in acts of courage.

Among the many traits the peoples of our two countries have in common, none is stronger than our mutual abhorrence of war. Almost unique, among the major world powers, we have never been at war with each other. And no nation in the history of battle ever suffered more than the Soviet Union suffered in the course of the Second World War. At least 20 million lost their lives. Countless millions of homes and farms were burned or sacked. A third of the nation's territory, including nearly two thirds of its industrial base, was turned into a wasteland—a loss equivalent to the devastation of this country east of Chicago.

Today, should total war ever break out again—no matter how—our two countries would become the primary targets. It is an ironic but accurate fact that the two strongest powers are the two in the most danger of devastation. All we have built, all we have worked for, would be destroyed in the first 24 hours. And even in the cold war, which brings burdens and dangers to so many countries, including this Nation's closest allies—our two countries bear the heaviest burdens. For we are both devoting massive sums of money to weapons that could be better devoted to combatting ignorance, poverty, and disease. We are both caught up in a vicious and dangerous cycle in which suspicion on one side breeds suspicion on the other, and new weapons beget counterweapons.

In short, both the United States and its allies, and the Soviet Union and its allies, have a mutually deep interest in a just and genuine peace and in halting the arms race. Agreements to this end are in the interests of the Soviet Union as well as ours—and even the most hostile nations can be relied upon to accept and keep those treaty obligations, and only those treaty obligations, which are in their own interest.

So, let us not be blind to our differences—but let us also direct attention to our common interests and to the means by which those differences can be resolved. And if we cannot end now our differences, at least we can help make the world safe for diversity. For, in the final analysis, our most basic common link is that we all inhabit this small planet. We all breathe the same air. We all cherish our children's future. And we are all mortal.

Third: Let us reexamine our attitude toward the cold war, remembering that we are not engaged in a debate, seeking to pile up debating points. We are not here distributing blame or pointing the finger of judgment.

We must deal with the world as it is, and not as it might have been had the history of the last 18 years been different.

We must, therefore, persevere in the search for peace in the hope that constructive changes within the Communist bloc might bring within reach solutions which now seem beyond us. We must conduct our affairs in such a way that it becomes in the Communists' interest to agree on a genuine peace. Above all, while defending our own vital interests, nuclear powers must avert those confrontations which bring an adversary to a choice of either a humiliating retreat or a nuclear war. To adopt that kind of course in the nuclear age would be evidence only of the bankruptcy of our policy—or of a collective death wish for the world.

To secure these ends, America's weapons are nonprovocative, carefully controlled, designed to deter, and capable of selective use. Our military forces are committed to peace and disciplined in self-restraint. Our diplomats are instructed to avoid unnecessary irritants and purely rhetorical hostility.

For we can seek a relaxation of tensions without relaxing our guard. And, for our part, we do not need to use threats to prove that we are resolute. We do not need to jam foreign broadcasts out of fear our faith will be eroded. We are unwilling to impose our system on any unwilling people—but we are willing and able to engage in peaceful competition with any people on earth.

Meanwhile, we seek to strengthen the United Nations, to help solve its financial problems, to make it a more effective instrument for peace, to develop it into a genuine world security system—a system capable of resolving disputes on the basis of law, of insuring the security of the large and the small, and of creating conditions under which arms can finally be abolished.

At the same time we seek to keep peace inside the non-Communist world, where many nations, all of them our friends, are divided over issues which weaken Western unity, which invite Communist intervention, or which threaten to erupt into war. Our efforts in West New Guinea, in the Congo, in the Middle East, and in the Indian subcontinent have been persistent and patient despite criticism from both sides. We have also tried to set an example for others—by seeking to adjust small but significant differences with our own closest neighbors in Mexico and in Canada.

Speaking of other nations, I wish to make one point clear. We are bound to many nations by alliances. Those alliances exist because our concern and theirs substantially overlap. Our commitment to defend Western Europe and West Berlin, for example, stands undiminished because of the identity of our vital interests. The United States will make no deal with the Soviet Union at the expense of other nations and other peoples, not merely because they are our partners but also because their interests and ours converge.

Our interests converge, however, not only in defending the frontiers of freedom but in pursuing the paths of peace. It is our hope—and the purpose of allied policies—to convince the Soviet Union that she, too, should let each nation choose its own future, so long as that choice does not interfere with the choices of others. The Communist drive to impose their political and economic system on others is the primary cause of world tension today. For there can be no doubt that if all nations could refrain from interfering in the self-determination of others, the peace would be much more assured.

This will require a new effort to achieve world law—a new context for world discussions. It will require increased understanding between the Soviets and ourselves. And increased understanding will require increased contact and communication. One step in this direction is the proposed arrangement for a direct line between Moscow and Washington, to avoid on each side the dangerous delays, misunderstandings, and misreadings of the other's actions which might occur at a time of crisis.

We have also been talking in Geneva about other first-step measures of arms control, designed to limit the intensity of the arms race and to reduce the risks of accidental war. Our primary long-range interest in Geneva, however, is general and complete disarmament—designed to take place by stages, permitting parallel political developments to build the new institutions of peace which would take the place of arms. The pursuit of disarmament has been an effort of this Government since the 1920's. It has been urgently sought by the past three administrations. And however dim the prospects may be today, we intend to continue this effort—to continue it in order that all countries, including our own, can better grasp what the problems and possibilities of disarmament are.

The one major area of these negotiations where the end is in sight, yet where a fresh start is badly needed, is in a treaty to outlaw nuclear tests. The conclusion of such a treaty, so near and yet so far, would check the spiraling arms race in one of its most dangerous areas. It would place the nuclear powers in a position to deal more effectively with one of the greatest hazards which man faces in 1963, the further spread of nuclear arms. It would increase our security—it would decrease the prospects of war. Surely this goal is sufficiently important to require our steady pursuit, yielding neither to the temptation to give up the whole effort nor the temptation to give up our insistence on vital and responsible safeguards.

I am taking this opportunity, therefore, to announce two important decisions in this regard.

First: Chairman Khrushchev, Prime Minister Macmillan, and I have agreed that high-level discussions will shortly begin in Moscow, looking toward early agreement on a comprehensive test ban treaty. Our hopes must be tempered with the caution of history—but with our hopes go the hopes of all mankind.

Second: To make clear our good faith and solemn convictions on the matter, I now declare that the United States does not propose to conduct nuclear tests in the atmosphere so long as other states do not do so. We will not be the first to resume. Such a declaration is no substitute for a formal binding treaty, but I hope it will help us achieve one. Nor would such a treaty be a substitute for disarmament, but I hope it will help us achieve it.

Finally, my fellow Americans, let us examine our attitude toward peace and freedom here at home. The quality and spirit of our own society must justify and support our efforts abroad. We must show it in the dedication of our own lives—as many of you who are graduating today will have a unique opportunity to do, by serving without pay in the Peace Corps abroad or in the proposed National Service Corps here at home.

But wherever we are, we must all, in our daily lives, live up to the age-old faith that peace and freedom walk together. In too many of our cities today, the peace is not secure because freedom is incomplete.

It is the responsibility of the executive branch at all levels of government—local, State, and National—to provide and protect that freedom for all of our citizens by all means within their authority. It is the responsibility of the legislative branch at all levels, wherever that authority is not now adequate, to make it adequate. And it is the responsibility of all citizens in all sections of this country to respect the rights of all others and to respect the law of the land.

All this is not unrelated to world peace. "When a man's ways please the Lord," the Scriptures tell us, "he maketh even his enemies to be at peace with him." And is not peace, in the last analysis, basically a matter of human rights—the right to live out our lives without fear of devastation, the right to breathe air as nature provided it, the right of future generations to a healthy existence?

While we proceed to safeguard our national interests, let us also safeguard human interests. And the elimination of war and arms is clearly in the interest of both. No treaty, however much it may be to the advantage of all, however tightly it may be worded, can provide absolute security against the risks of deception and evasion. But it can— if it is sufficiently effective in its enforcement and if it is sufficiently in the interests of its signers—offer far more security and far fewer risks than an unabated, uncontrolled, unpredictable arms race.

The United States, as the world knows, will never start a war. We do not want a war. We do not now expect a war. This generation of Americans has already had enough—more than enough—of war and hate and oppression. We shall be prepared if others wish it. We shall be alert to try to stop it. But we shall also do our part to build a world of peace where the weak are safe and the strong are just. We are not helpless before that task or hopeless of its success. Confident and unafraid, we labor on—not toward a strategy of annihilation but toward a strategy of peace.

11 | The Sharon Statement

Although it gained much less attention than the Port Huron Statement, this brief document—adopted at a conference hosted by William F. Buckley, Jr., in Sharon, Connecticut, September 9–11, 1960—may have had a greater impact. Written by young conservatives who were alienated by the Modern Republicanism of Eisenhower and Nixon, it stated two central themes of a newly strident conservatism: antistatism and anticommunism. In contrast to those who sought détente with the Soviet Union, the Young Americans for Freedom asserted that "the United States should stress victory over, rather than coexistence with, this menace." In many respects these conservatives were more effective activists than their left-wing Students for a Democratic Society counterparts. Most of the SDSers were eventually consigned to the political fringes, whereas many of the YAFers played a central role in the conservative takeover of the Republican Party in the 1970s.

In this time of moral and political crisis, it is the responsibility of the youth of America to affirm certain eternal truths.

We, as young conservatives, believe:

That foremost among the transcendent values is the individual's use of his God-given free will, whence derives his right to be free from the restrictions of arbitrary force;

That liberty is indivisible, and that political freedom cannot long exist without economic freedom;

From *The Other Side of the Sixties: Young Americans for Freedom and the Rise of Conservative Politics,* ed. John A. Andrew (New Brunswick, NJ: Rutgers University Press, 1997), 221–22.

211

That the purposes of government are to protect these freedoms through the preservation of internal order, the provision of national defense, and the administration of justice;

That when government ventures beyond these rightful functions, it accumulates power which tends to diminish order and liberty;

That the Constitution of the United States is the best arrangement yet devised for empowering government to fulfill its proper role, while restraining it from the concentration and abuse of power;

That the genius of the Constitution—the division of powers—is summed up in the clause which reserves primacy to the several states, or to the people, in those spheres not specifically delegated to the Federal Government;

That the market economy, allocating resources by the free play of supply and demand, is the single economic system compatible with the requirements of personal freedom and constitutional government, and that it is at the same time the most productive supplier of human needs;

That when government interferes with the work of the market economy, it tends to reduce the moral and physical strength of the nation; that when it takes from one man to bestow on another, it diminishes the incentive of the first, the integrity of the second, and the moral autonomy of both;

That we will be free only so long as the national sovereignty of the United States is secure: that history shows periods of freedom are rare and can exist only when free citizens concertedly defend their rights against all enemies;

That the forces of international Communism are, at present, the greatest single threat to these liberties;

That the United States should stress victory over, rather than coexistence with, this menace; and

That American foreign policy must be judged by this criterion: does it serve the just interests of the United States?

STUDENTS FOR A
DEMOCRATIC SOCIETY

12

The Port Huron Statement

"We are people of this generation, . . . looking uncomfortably to the world we inherit," reads the opening sentence of the founding manifesto of Students for a Democratic Society, written at Port Huron, Michigan, in August 1962. The students gathered there rebelled against the dominant consensus that had narrowed most issues into technical problems. It was their intent to create a New Left that, unlike the Old Left, was not lured by doctrinaire socialism or communism. In standing against their time and the legacy of the left, they declared, "It has been said that our liberal and socialist predecessors were plagued by vision without program, while our own generation is plagued by program without vision." To fill that void, these students articulated their vision of a participatory democracy that would merge the Jeffersonian ideal of citizen democracy with the socialist ideal of an economy largely under political control. The Port Huron Statement and the Sharon Statement were clear signs that many in the silent generation were finding their voices.

Introduction: Agenda for a Generation

We are people of this generation, bred in at least modest comfort, housed now in universities, looking uncomfortably to the world we inherit.

When we were kids the United States was the wealthiest and strongest country in the world: the only one with the atom bomb, the least scarred by modern war, an initiator of the United Nations that we thought would distribute Western influence throughout the world. Freedom and equality for each individual, government of, by, and for

From the founding statement of Students for a Democratic Society, 1966, 46–63.

the people—these American values we found good, principles by which we could live as men. Many of us began maturing in complacency.

As we grew, however, our comfort was penetrated by events too troubling to dismiss. First, the permeating and victimizing fact of human degradation, symbolized by the Southern struggle against racial bigotry, compelled most of us from silence to activism. Second, the enclosing fact of the Cold War, symbolized by the presence of the Bomb, brought awareness that we ourselves, and our friends, and millions of abstract "others" we knew more directly because of our common peril, might die at any time. We might deliberately ignore, or avoid, or fail to feel all other human problems but not these two, for these were too immediate and crushing in their impact, too challenging in the demand that we as individuals take the responsibility for encounter and resolution.

While these and other problems either directly oppressed us or rankled our consciences and became our own subjective concerns, we began to see complicated and disturbing paradoxes in our surrounding America. The declaration "all men are created equal . . ." rang hollow before the facts of Negro life in the South and the big cities of the North. The proclaimed peaceful intentions of the United States contradicted its economic and military investments in the Cold War status quo.

We witnessed, and continue to witness, other paradoxes. With nuclear energy whole cities can easily be powered, yet the dominant nation-states seem more likely to unleash destruction greater than that incurred in all wars of human history. Although our own technology is destroying old and creating new forms of social organization, men still tolerate meaningless work and idleness. While two-thirds of mankind suffers undernourishment, our own upper classes revel amidst superfluous abundance. Although world population is expected to double in forty years, the nations still tolerate anarchy as a major principle of international conduct, and uncontrolled exploitation governs the sapping of the earth's physical resources. Although mankind desperately needs revolutionary leadership, America rests in national stalemate, its goals ambiguous and tradition-bound instead of informed and clear, its democratic system apathetic and manipulated rather than "of, by, and for the people."

Not only did tarnish appear on our image of American virtue, not only did disillusion occur when the hypocrisy of American ideals was discovered, but we began to sense that what we had originally seen as the American Golden Age was actually the decline of an era. The worldwide outbreak of revolution against colonialism and imperialism, the entrenchment of totalitarian states, the menace of war, overpopulation, international disorder, supertechnology—these trends were testing the tenacity of our own commitment to democracy and freedom and our abilities to visualize their application to a world in upheaval.

Our work is guided by the sense that we may be the last generation in the experiment with living. But we are a minority—the vast majority of our people regard the temporary equilibriums of our society and world as eternally functional parts. In this is perhaps the outstanding paradox: we ourselves are imbued with urgency, yet the message of our society is that there is no viable alternative to the present. Beneath the reassuring tones of the politicians, beneath the common opinion that America will "muddle through," beneath the stagnation of those who have closed their minds to the future is the pervading feeling that there simply are no alternatives, that our times have witnessed the exhaustion not only of Utopias but of any new departures as well. Feeling the press of complexity upon the emptiness of life, people are fearful of the thought that at any moment things might be thrust out of control. They fear change itself, since change might smash whatever invisible framework seems to hold back chaos for them now. For most Americans, all crusades are suspect, threatening. The fact that each individual sees apathy in his fellows perpetuates the common reluctance to organize for change. The dominant institutions are complex enough to blunt the minds of their potential critics and entrenched enough to swiftly dissipate or entirely repel the energies of protest and reform, thus limiting human expectancies. Then, too, we are a materially improved society, and by our own improvements we seem to have weakened the case for further change.

Some would have us believe that Americans feel contentment amidst prosperity—but might it not be better called a glaze above deeply felt anxieties about their role in the new world? And if these anxieties produce a developed indifference to human affairs, do they not as well produce a yearning to believe there *is* an alternative to the present, that something *can* be done to change circumstances in the school, the workplaces, the bureaucracies, the government? It is to this latter yearning, at once the spark and engine of change, that we direct our present appeal. The search for truly democratic alternatives to the present, and a commitment to social experimentation with them, is a worthy and fulfilling human enterprise, one which moves us and, we hope, others today. On such a basis do we offer this document of our convictions and analysis: as an effort in understanding and changing the conditions of humanity in the late twentieth century, an effort rooted in the ancient, still unfulfilled conception of man attaining determining influence over his circumstances of life.

Values

Making values explicit—an initial task in establishing alternatives—is an activity that has been devalued and corrupted. The conventional moral terms of the age, the politician's moralities—"free world," "people's democracies"—reflect realities poorly, if at all, and seem to function more as ruling myths than as descriptive principles. But neither has our experience in the universities brought us moral enlightenment. Our professors and administrators sacrifice controversy to public relations; their curriculums change more slowly than the living events of the world; their skills and silence are purchased by investors in the arms race; passion is called unscholastic. The questions we might want raised—what is really important? can we live in a different and better way? if we wanted to change society, how would we do it?—are not thought to be questions of a "fruitful, empirical nature" and thus are brushed aside.

Unlike youth in other countries we are used to moral leadership being exercised and moral dimensions being clarified by our elders. But today, for us, not even the liberal and socialist preachments of the past seem adequate to the forms of the present. Consider the old slogans: Capitalism Cannot Reform Itself, United Front against Fascism, General Strike, All Out on May Day. Or, more recently, No Cooperation with Commies and Fellow Travellers, Ideologies Are Exhausted, Bipartisanship, No Utopias. These are incomplete, and there are few new prophets. It has been said that our liberal and socialist predecessors were plagued by vision without program, while our own generation is plagued by program without vision. All around us there is astute grasp of method, technique—the committee, the ad hoc group, the lobbyist, the hard and soft sell, the make, the projected image—but, if pressed critically, such expertise is incompetent to explain its implicit ideals. It is highly fashionable to identify oneself by old categories, or by naming a respected political figure, or by explaining "how we would vote" on various issues.

Theoretic chaos has replaced the idealistic thinking of old—and, unable to reconstitute theoretic order, men have condemned idealism itself. Doubt has replaced hopefulness—and men act out a defeatism that is labelled realistic. The decline of utopia and hope is in fact one of the defining features of social life today. The reasons are various: the dreams of the older left were perverted by Stalinism and never recreated; the congressional stalemate makes men narrow their view of the possible; the specialization of human activity leaves little room for sweeping thought; the horrors of the twentieth century, symbolized in the gas ovens and concentration camps and atom bombs, have blasted hopefulness. To be idealistic is to be considered apocalyptic, deluded. To have no serious aspirations, on the contrary, is to be "tough-minded."

In suggesting social goals and values, therefore, we are aware of entering a sphere of some disrepute. Perhaps matured by the past, we have no sure formulas, no closed theories—but that does not mean values are beyond discussion and tentative determination. A first task of any social movement is to convince people that the search for orienting theories and the creation of human values is complex but worthwhile. We are aware that to avoid platitudes we must analyze the concrete conditions of social order. But to direct such an analysis we must use the guideposts of basic principles. Our own social values involve conceptions of human beings, human relationships, and social systems.

We regard *men* as infinitely precious and possessed of unfulfilled capacities for reason, freedom, and love. In affirming these principles we are aware of countering perhaps the dominant conceptions of man in the twentieth century: that he is a thing to be manipulated, and that he is inherently incapable of directing his own affairs. We oppose the depersonalization that reduces human beings to the status of things— if anything, the brutalities of the twentieth century teach that means and ends are intimately related, that vague appeals to "posterity" cannot justify the mutilations of the present. We oppose, too, the doctrine of human incompetence because it rests essentially on the modern fact that men have been "competently" manipulated into incompetence— we see little reason why men cannot meet with increasing skill the complexities and responsibilities of their situation, if society is organized not for minority but for majority participation in decision-making.

Men have unrealized potential for self-cultivation, self-direction, self-understanding, and creativity. It is this potential that we regard as crucial and to which we appeal, not to the human potentiality for violence, unreason, and submission to authority. The goal of man and society should be human independence: a concern not with an image of popularity but with finding a meaning in life that is personally authentic; a quality of mind not compulsively driven by a sense of powerlessness, nor one which unthinkingly adopts status values, nor one which represses all threats to its habits but one which has full, spontaneous access to present and past experiences, one which easily unites the fragmented parts of personal history, one which openly faces problems which are troubling and unresolved, one with an intuitive awareness of possibilities, an active sense of curiosity, an ability and willingness to learn.

This kind of independence does not mean egotistic individualism—the object is not to have one's way so much as it is to have a way that is one's own. Nor do we deify man—we merely have faith in his potential.

Human relationships should involve fraternity and honesty. Human interdependence is contemporary fact; human brotherhood must be willed, however, as a condition of future survival and as the most appropriate form of social relations. Personal links between man and man are needed, especially to go beyond the partial and fragmentary bonds of function that bind men only as worker to worker, employer to employee, teacher to student, American to Russian.

Loneliness, estrangement, isolation describe the vast distance between man and man today. These dominant tendencies cannot be overcome by better personnel management, nor by improved gadgets, but only when a love of man overcomes the idolatrous worship of things by man. As the individualism we affirm is not egoism, the selflessness we affirm is not self-elimination. On the contrary, we believe in generosity of a kind that imprints one's unique individual qualities in the relation to other men, and to all human activity. Further, to dislike isolation is not to favor the abolition of privacy; the latter differs from isolation in that [it] occurs or is abolished according to individual will.

We would replace power rooted in possession, privilege, or circumstance by power and uniqueness rooted in love, reflectiveness, reason, and creativity. As a *social system* we seek the establishment of a democracy of individual participation, governed by two central aims: that the individual share in those social decisions determining the quality and direction of his life; that society be organized to encourage independence in men and provide the media for their common participation.

In a participatory democracy, the political life would be based in several root principles:

>that decision-making of basic social consequence be carried on by public groupings;
>that politics be seen positively, as the art of collectively creating an acceptable pattern of social relations;

that politics have the function of bringing people out of isolation and into community, thus being a necessary, though not sufficient, means of finding meaning in personal life;

that the political order serve to clarify problems in a way instrumental to their solution: it should provide outlets for the expression of personal grievance and aspiration; opposing views should be organized so as to illuminate choices and facilitate the attainment of goals; channels should be commonly available to relate men to knowledge and to power so that private problems—from bad recreation facilities to personal alienation—are formulated as general issues.

The economic sphere would have as its basis the principles:

that work should involve incentives worthier than money or survival: it should be educative, not stultifying; creative, not mechanical; self-directed, not manipulated; encouraging independence, a respect for others, a sense of dignity and a willingness to accept social responsibility, since it is this experience that has crucial influence on habits, perceptions, and individual ethics;

that the economic experience is so personally decisive that the individual must share in its full determination;

that the economy itself is of such social importance that its major resources and means of production should be open to democratic participation and subject to democratic social regulation.

Like the political and economic ones, major social institutions—cultural, educational, rehabilitative, and others—should be generally organized with the well-being and dignity of man as the essential measure of success.

In social change or interchange, we find violence to be abhorrent because it requires generally the transformation of the target, be it a human being or a community of people, into a depersonalized object of hate. It is imperative that the means of violence be abolished and the institutions—local, national, international—that encourage nonviolence as a condition of conflict be developed.

These are our central values, in skeletal form. It remains vital to understand their denial or attainment in the context of the modern world.

The Students

In the last few years, thousands of American students demonstrated that they at least felt the urgency of the times. They moved actively and directly against racial injustices, the threat of war, violations of individual rights of conscience, and, less frequently, against economic manipulation. They succeeded in restoring a small measure of controversy to the campuses after the stillness of the McCarthy period. They succeeded, too, in gaining some concessions from the people and institutions they opposed, especially in the fight against racial bigotry.

The significance of these scattered movements lies not in their success or failure in gaining objectives—at least not yet. Nor does the significance lie in the intellectual "competence" or "maturity" of the students involved—as some pedantic elders allege. The significance is in the fact that the students are breaking the crust of apathy and overcoming the inner alienation that remain the defining characteristics of American college life.

If student movements for change are still rarities on the campus scene, what is commonplace there? The real campus, the familiar campus, is a place of private people, engaged in their notorious "inner emigration." It is a place of commitment to business-as-usual, getting ahead, playing it cool. It is a place of mass affirmation of the Twist but mass reluctance toward the controversial public stance. Rules are accepted as "inevitable," bureaucracy as "just circumstances," irrelevance as "scholarship," selflessness as "martyrdom." . . .

Almost no students value activity as citizens. Passive in public, they are hardly more idealistic in arranging their private lives: Gallup concludes they will settle for "low success, and won't risk high failure." There is not much willingness to take risks (not even in business), no settling of dangerous goals, no real conception of personal identity except one manufactured in the image of others, no real urge for personal fulfillment except to be almost as successful as the very successful people. Attention is being paid to social status (the quality of shirt collars, meeting people, getting wives or husbands, making solid contacts for later on); much, too, is paid to academic status (grades, honors, the med school rat race). But neglected generally is real intellectual status, the personal cultivation of the mind.

"Students don't even give a damn about the apathy," one has said. Apathy toward apathy begets a privately constructed universe, a place of systematic study schedules, two nights each week for beer, a girl or two, and early marriage; a framework infused with personality, warmth, and under control, no matter how unsatisfying otherwise.

Under these conditions university life loses all relevance to some. Four hundred thousand of our classmates leave college every year.

But apathy is not simply an attitude; it is a product of social institutions, and of the structure and organization of higher education itself. The extracurricular life is ordered according to *in loco parentis* theory, which ratifies the Administration as the moral guardian of the young.

The accompanying "let's pretend" theory of student extracurricular affairs validates student government as a training center for those who want to spend their lives in political pretense and discourages initiative from the more articulate, honest, and sensitive students. The bounds and style of controversy are delimited before controversy begins. The university "prepares" the student for "citizenship" through perpetual rehearsals and, usually, through emasculation of what creative spirit there is in the individual.

The academic life contains reinforcing counterparts to the way in which extracurricular life is organized. The academic world is founded on a teacher-student relation analogous to the parent-child relation which characterizes *in loco parentis*. Further, academia includes a radical separation of the student from the material of study. That which is studied, the social reality, is "objectified" to sterility, dividing the student from life—just as he is restrained in active involvement by the deans controlling student government. The specialization of function and knowledge, admittedly necessary to our complex technological and social structure, has produced an exaggerated compartmentalization of study and understanding. This has contributed to an overly parochial view, by faculty, of the role of its research and scholarship; to a discontinuous and truncated understanding, by students, of the surrounding social order; and to a loss of personal attachment, by nearly all, to the worth of study as a humanistic enterprise.

There is, finally, the cumbersome academic bureaucracy extending throughout the academic as well as the extracurricular structures, contributing to the sense of outer complexity and inner powerlessness that transforms the honest searching of many students to a ratification of convention and, worse, to a numbness to present and future catastrophes. The size and financing systems of the university enhance the permanent trusteeship of the administrative bureaucracy, their power leading to a shift within the university toward the value standards of business and the administrative mentality. Huge foundations and other private financial interests shape the underfinanced colleges and universities, not only making them more commercial but less disposed to diagnose society critically, less open to dissent. Many social and physical scientists, neglecting the liberating heritage of higher learning, develop "human relations" or "morale-producing" techniques for the corporate economy, while others exercise their intellectual skills to accelerate the arms race.

Tragically, the university could serve as a significant source of social criticism and an initiator of new modes and molders of attitudes. But the actual intellectual effect of the college experience is hardly distinguishable from that of any other communications channel—say, a television set—passing on the stock truths of the day. Students leave college somewhat more "tolerant" than when they arrived but basically unchallenged in their values and political orientations. With administrators ordering the institution, and faculty the curriculum, the student learns by his isolation to accept elite rule within the university, which prepares him to accept later forms of minority control. The real function of the educational system—as opposed to its more rhetorical function of "searching for truth"—is to impart the key information and styles that will help the student get by, modestly but comfortably, in the big society beyond.

The Society Beyond

Look beyond the campus, to America itself. That student life is more intellectual, and perhaps more comfortable, does not obscure the fact that the fundamental qualities of life on the campus reflect the habits of society at large. The fraternity president is seen at the junior manager levels; the sorority queen has gone to Grosse Pointe; the serious poet burns for a place, any place, to work; the once-serious and never-serious poets work at the advertising agencies. The desperation of people threatened by forces about which they know little and of which they can say less; the cheerful emptiness of people "giving up" all hope of changing things; the faceless ones polled by Gallup who listed "international affairs" fourteenth on their list of "problems" but who also expected thermonuclear war in the next few years—in these and other forms, Americans are in withdrawal from public life, from any collective effort at directing their own affairs.

Some regard these national doldrums as a sign of healthy approval of the established order—but is it approval by consent or manipulated acquiescence? Others declare that the people are withdrawn because compelling issues are fast disappearing—perhaps there are fewer bread-lines in America, but is Jim Crow gone, is there enough work and work more fulfilling, is world war a diminishing threat, and what of the rev-olutionary new peoples? Still others think the national quietude is a necessary consequence of the need for elites to resolve complex and specialized problems of modern industrial society—but, then, why should *business* elites help decide foreign policy, and who controls the elites anyway, and are they solving mankind's problems? Others, finally, shrug knowingly and announce that full democracy never worked anywhere in the past—but why lump qualitatively different civ-ilizations together, and how can a social order work well if its best thinkers are skeptics, and is man really doomed forever to the domi-nation of today?

There are no convincing apologies for the contemporary malaise. While the world tumbles toward the final war, while men in other nations are trying desperately to alter events, while the very future qua future is uncertain—America is without community, impulse, without the inner momentum necessary for an age when societies cannot suc-cessfully perpetuate themselves by their military weapons, when democracy must be viable because of the quality of life, not its quan-tity of rockets.

The apathy here is, first *subjective*—the felt powerlessness of ordinary people, the resignation before the enormity of events. But sub-jective apathy is encouraged by the *objective* American situation—the actual structural separation of people from power, from relevant knowledge, from pinnacles of decision-making. Just as the university influences the student way of life, so do major social institutions cre-ate the circumstances in which the isolated citizen will try hope-lessly to understand his world and himself.

The very isolation of the individual—from power and community and ability to aspire—means the rise of a democracy without publics. With the great mass of people structurally remote and psychologically hesitant with respect to democratic institutions, those institutions themselves attenuate and become, in the fashion of the vicious circle, progressively less accessible to those few who aspire to serious par-ticipation in social affairs. The vital democratic connection between community and leadership, between the mass and the several elites, has been so wrenched and perverted that disastrous policies go unchal-lenged time and again.

LYNDON B. JOHNSON

13 | Commencement Address at the University of Michigan

In the brief period before Lyndon Johnson's presidency was consumed by the Vietnam War, the president attempted to place his own stamp on twentieth-century American liberalism and make domestic reform the hallmark of his administration. In this speech of May 22, 1964, Johnson unveiled his dream of the Great Society. He called for revitalization of America's decaying cities, a superior educational system for all, an end to poverty and racial injustice, and the restoration of the environment. At the heart of his vision was a belief that government could mobilize the talents, energies, and resources of the people toward broad common goals. Although privately cynical about other politicians, Johnson remained optimistic about the capacity of government and political leadership to solve deep-rooted social problems. Conservatives grumbled on the sidelines, but overt objections to overtaxation, overregulation, and bureaucratization of the economy would come in the 1970s, a time of disillusionment with this liberal vision.

President [Harlan H.] Hatcher, Governor [George] Romney, Senators [Pat] McNamara and [Philip A.] Hart, Congressmen [George] Meader and [Neil] Staebler, and other members of the fine Michigan delegation, members of the graduating class, my fellow Americans:

From *Public Papers of the Presidents: Lyndon B. Johnson, 1963–1964* (Washington, DC: Government Printing Office, 1965), 704–7.

It is a great pleasure to be here today. This university has been coeducational since 1870, but I do not believe it was on the basis of your accomplishments that a Detroit high school girl said, "In choosing a college, you first have to decide whether you want a coeducational school or an educational school."

Well, we can find both here at Michigan, although perhaps at different hours.

I came out here today very anxious to meet the Michigan student whose father told a friend of mine that his son's education had been a real value. It stopped his mother from bragging about him.

I have come today from the turmoil of your Capital to the tranquility of your campus to speak about the future of your country.

The purpose of protecting the life of our Nation and preserving the liberty of our citizens is to pursue the happiness of our people. Our success in that pursuit is the test of our success as a Nation.

For a century we labored to settle and to subdue a continent. For half a century we called upon unbounded invention and untiring industry to create an order of plenty for all of our people.

The challenge of the next half-century is whether we have the wisdom to use that wealth to enrich and elevate our national life, and to advance the quality of our American civilization.

Your imagination, your initiative, and your indignation will determine whether we build a society where progress is the servant of our needs, or a society where old values and new visions are buried under unbridled growth. For in your time we have the opportunity to move not only toward the rich society and the powerful society but upward to the Great Society.

The Great Society rests on abundance and liberty for all. It demands an end to poverty and racial injustice, to which we are totally committed in our time. But that is just the beginning.

The Great Society is a place where every child can find knowledge to enrich his mind and to enlarge his talents. It is a place where leisure is a welcome chance to build and reflect, not a feared cause of boredom and restlessness. It is a place where the city of man serves not only the needs of the body and the demands of commerce but the desire for beauty and the hunger for community.

It is a place where man can renew contact with nature. It is a place which honors creation for its own sake and for what it adds to the understanding of the race. It is a place where men are more concerned with the quality of their goals than the quantity of their goods.

But most of all, the Great Society is not a safe harbor, a resting place, a final objective, a finished work. It is a challenge constantly renewed, beckoning us toward a destiny where the meaning of our lives matches the marvelous products of our labor.

So I want to talk to you today about three places where we begin to build the Great Society—in our cities, in our countryside, and in our classrooms.

Many of you will live to see the day, perhaps 50 years from now, when there will be 400 million Americans—four-fifths of them in urban areas. In the remainder of this century urban population will double; city land will double; and we will have to build homes, highways, and facilities equal to all those built since this country was first settled. So in the next 40 years we must rebuild the entire urban United States.

Aristotle said: "Men come together in cities in order to live, but they remain together in order to live the good life." It is harder and harder to live the good life in American cities today.

The catalog of ills is long: there is the decay of the centers and the despoiling of the suburbs. There is not enough housing for our people or transportation for our traffic. Open land is vanishing, and old landmarks are violated.

Worst of all, expansion is eroding the precious and time-honored values of community with neighbors and communion with nature. The loss of these values breeds loneliness and boredom and indifference.

Our society will never be great until our cities are great. Today the frontier of imagination and innovation is inside those cities and not beyond their borders.

New experiments are already going on. It will be the task of your generation to make the American city a place where future generations will come not only to live but to live the good life.

I understand that if I stayed here tonight I would see that Michigan students are really doing their best to live the good life.

This is the place where the Peace Corps was started. It is inspiring to see how all of you, while you are in this country, are trying so hard to live at the level of the people.

A second place where we begin to build the Great Society is in our countryside. We have always prided ourselves on being not only America the strong and America the free but America the beautiful. Today that beauty is in danger. The water we drink, the food we eat, the very air that we breathe are threatened with pollution. Our parks are overcrowded, our seashores overburdened. Green fields and dense forests are disappearing.

A few years ago we were greatly concerned about the "Ugly American." Today we must act to prevent an ugly America.

For once the battle is lost, once our natural splendor is destroyed, it can never be recaptured. And once man can no longer walk with beauty or wonder at nature, his spirit will wither and his sustenance be wasted.

A third place to build the Great Society is in the classrooms of America. There your children's lives will be shaped. Our society will not be great until every young mind is set free to scan the farthest reaches of thought and imagination. We are still far from that goal.

Today, 8 million adult Americans, more than the entire population of Michigan, have not finished 5 years of school. Nearly 20 million have not finished 8 years of school. Nearly 54 million—more than one-quarter of all America—have not even finished high school.

Each year more than 100,000 high school graduates, with proved ability, do not enter college because they cannot afford it. And if we cannot educate today's youth, what will we do in 1970 when elementary school enrollment will be 5 million greater than 1960? And high school enrollment will rise by 5 million. College enrollment will increase by more than 3 million.

In many places, classrooms are overcrowded and curricula are outdated. Most of our qualified teachers are underpaid, and many of our paid teachers are unqualified. So we must give every child a place to sit and a teacher to learn from. Poverty must not be a bar to learning, and learning must offer an escape from poverty.

But more classrooms and more teachers are not enough. We must seek an educational system which grows in excellence as it grows in size. This means better training for our teachers. It means preparing youth to enjoy their hours of leisure as well as their hours of labor. It means exploring new techniques of teaching to find new ways to stimulate the love of learning and the capacity for creation.

These are three of the central issues of the Great Society. While our Government has many programs directed at those issues, I do not pretend that we have the full answer to those problems.

But I do promise this: we are going to assemble the best thought and the broadest knowledge from all over the world to find those answers for America. I intend to establish working groups to prepare a series of White House conferences and meetings—on the cities, on natural beauty, on the quality of education, and on other emerging challenges. And from these meetings and from this inspiration and from these studies we will begin to set our course toward the Great Society.

The solution to these problems does not rest on a massive program in Washington, nor can it rely solely on the strained resources of local authority. They require us to create new concepts of cooperation, a creative federalism, between the National Capital and the leaders of local communities.

Woodrow Wilson once wrote: "Every man sent out from his university should be a man of his Nation as well as a man of his time."

Within your lifetime powerful forces, already loosed, will take us toward a way of life beyond the realm of our experience, almost beyond the bounds of our imagination.

For better or for worse, your generation has been appointed by history to deal with those problems and to lead America toward a new age. You have the chance never before afforded to any people in any age. You can help build a society where the demands of morality, and the needs of the spirit, can be realized in the life of the Nation.

So, will you join in the battle to give every citizen the full equality which God enjoins and the law requires, whatever his belief, or race, or the color of his skin?

Will you join in the battle to give every citizen an escape from the crushing weight of poverty?

Will you join in the battle to make it possible for all nations to live in enduring peace—as neighbors and not as mortal enemies?

Will you join in the battle to build the Great Society, to prove that our material progress is only the foundation on which we will build a richer life of mind and spirit?

There are those timid souls who say this battle cannot be won, that we are condemned to a soulless wealth. I do not agree. We have the power to shape the civilization that we want. But we need your will, your labor, your hearts, if we are to build that kind of society.

Those who came to this land sought to build more than just a new country. They sought a new world. So I have come here today to your campus to say that you can make their vision our reality. So let us from this moment begin our work so that in the future men will look back and say: It was then, after a long and weary way, that man turned the exploits of his genius to the full enrichment of his life.

Thank you. Goodby.

CARL OGLESBY

14 Trapped in a System

In October 1965, at an antiwar demonstration in
Washington, DC, the president of Students for a
Democratic Society delivered a passionate attack on
vital center American liberalism and its strong commitment to anticommunism. Carl Oglesby accused
"corporate liberalism" of placing profits over people.
He wanted a more radical liberalism that would put
America on the side of third-world revolutions in
Cuba, Vietnam, and South Africa. This speech represented a turn of the student movement away from an
alliance with anti-Communist liberalism and toward
a more radical stance and more militant tactics.

Seven months ago at the April March on Washington, Paul Potter, then President of Students for a
Democratic Society, stood in approximately this spot and said that we
must name the system that creates and sustains the war in Vietnam—
name it, describe it, analyze it, understand it, and change it.

Today I will try to name it—to suggest an analysis which, to be quite
frank, may disturb some of you—and to suggest what changing it may
require of us.

We are here again to protest again a growing war. Since it is a very
bad war, we acquire the habit of thinking that it must be caused by very
bad men. But we only conceal reality, I think, by denouncing on such
grounds the menacing coalition of industrial and military power, or the
brutality of the blitzkrieg we are waging against Vietnam, or the ominous signs around us that heresy may soon no longer be permitted. We

From "Trapped in a System" in *The New Radicals,* ed. Paul Jacobs and Saul Landau
(New York: Random House, 1966), 257–66. © 1966 by Paul Jacobs and Saul Landau. Reprinted by permission of Carl Oglesby.

must simply observe and quite plainly say that this coalition, this blitzkrieg, and this demand for acquiescence are creatures, all of them, of a Government that since 1932 has considered itself to be fundamentally *liberal*.

The original commitment in Vietnam was made by President Truman, a mainstream liberal. It was seconded by President Eisenhower, a moderate liberal: It was intensified by the late President Kennedy, a flaming liberal. Think of the men who now engineer that war—those who study the maps, give the commands, push the buttons, and tally the dead: Bundy, McNamara, Rusk, Lodge, Goldberg, the President himself.

They are not moral monsters.

They are all honorable men.

They are all liberals.

But so, I'm sure, are many of us who are here today in protest. To understand the war, then, it seems necessary to take a closer look at this American liberalism. Maybe we are in for some surprises. Maybe we have here two quite different liberalisms: one authentically humanist; the other not so human at all.

Not long ago, I considered myself a liberal. And if someone had asked me what I meant by that, I'd perhaps have quoted Thomas Jefferson or Thomas Paine, who first made plain our nation's unprovisional commitment to human rights. But what do you think would happen if these two heroes could sit down now for a chat with President Johnson and McGeorge Bundy?

They would surely talk of the Vietnam war. Our dead revolutionaries would soon wonder why their country was fighting against what appeared to be a revolution. The living liberals would hotly deny that it is one: there are troops coming in from outside; the rebels get arms from other countries; most of the people are not on their side; and they practice terror against their own. Therefore, *not* a revolution.

What would our dead revolutionaries answer? They might say: "What fools and bandits, sirs, you make then of us. Outside help? Do you remember Lafayette? Or the 3,000 British freighters the French navy sank for our side? Or the arms and men we got from France and Spain? And what's this about terror? Did you never hear what we did to our own loyalists? Or about the thousands of rich American Tories who fled for their lives to Canada? And as for popular support, do you not know that we had less than one-third of our people with us? That, in fact, the colony of New York recruited more troops for the British than for the revolution? Should we give it all back?"

Revolutions do not take place in velvet boxes. They never have. It is only the poets who make them lovely. What the National Liberation Front is fighting in Vietnam is a complex and vicious war. This war is also a revolution, as honest a revolution as you can find anywhere in history. And this is a fact which all our intricate official denials will never change.

But it doesn't make any difference to our leaders anyway. Their aim in Vietnam is really much simpler than this implies. It is to safeguard what they take to be American interests around the world against revolution or revolutionary change, which they always call Communism—as if that were that. In the case of Vietnam, this interest is, first, the principle that revolution shall not be tolerated anywhere, and second, that South Vietnam shall never sell its rice to China—or even to North Vietnam.

There is simply no such thing now, for us, as a just revolution— never mind that for two-thirds of the world's people the 20th Century might as well be the Stone Age; never mind the melting poverty and hopelessness that are the basic facts of life for most modern men; and never mind that for these millions there is now an increasingly perceptible relationship between their sorrow and our contentment.

Can we understand why the Negroes of Watts rebelled? Then why do we need a devil theory to explain the rebellion of the South Vietnamese? Can we understand the oppression in Mississippi, or the anguish that our Northern ghettos make epidemic? Then why can't we see that our proper human struggle is not with Communism or revolutionaries but with the social desperation that drives good men to violence, both here and abroad?

To be sure, we have been most generous with our aid, and in Western Europe, a mature industrial society, that aid worked. But there are always political and financial strings. And we have never shown ourselves capable of allowing others to make those traumatic institutional changes that are often the prerequisites of progress in colonial societies. For all our official feeling for the millions who are enslaved to what we so self-righteously call the yoke of Communist tyranny, we make no real effort at all to crack through the much more vicious right-wing tyrannies that our businessmen traffic with and our nation profits from every day. And for all our cries about the international Red conspiracy to take over the world, we take only pride in the fact of our 6,000 military bases on foreign soil.

We gave Rhodesia a grave look just now—but we keep on buying her chromium, which is cheap because black slave labor mines it.

We deplore the racism of Verwoerd's fascist South Africa—but our banks make big loans to that country, and our private technology makes it a nuclear power.

We are saddened and puzzled by random back-page stories of revolt in this or that Latin American state—but are convinced by a few pretty photos in the Sunday supplement that things are getting better, that the world is coming our way, that change from disorder can be orderly, that our benevolence will pacify the distressed, that our might will intimidate the angry.

Optimists, may I suggest that these are quite unlikely fantasies. They are fantasies because we have lost that mysterious social desire for human equity that from time to time has given us genuine moral drive. We have become a nation of young, bright-eyed, hard-hearted, slim-waisted, bullet-headed make-out artists. A nation—may I say it?—of beardless liberals.

You say I am being hard? Only think.

This country, with its thirty-some years of liberalism, can send 200,000 young men to Vietnam to kill and die in the most dubious of wars, but it cannot get 100 voter registrars to go into Mississippi.

What do you make of it?

The financial burden of the war obliges us to cut millions from an already pathetic War on Poverty budget. But in almost the same breath, Congress appropriates $140 million for the Lockheed and Boeing companies to compete with each other on the supersonic transport project—that Disneyland creation that will cost us all about $2 billion before it's done.

What do you make of it?

Many of us have been earnestly resisting for some years now the idea of putting atomic weapons into West German hands, an action that would perpetuate the division of Europe and thus the Cold War. Now just this week we find out that, with the meagerest of security systems, West Germany has had nuclear weapons in her hands for the past six years.

What do you make of it?

Some will make of it that I overdraw the matter. Many will ask: What about the other side? To be sure, there is the bitter ugliness of Czechoslovakia, Poland, those infamous Russian tanks in the streets of Budapest. But my anger only rises to hear some say that sorrow cancels sorrow, or that *this one's* shame deposits in *that one's* account the right to shamefulness.

And others will make of it that I sound mighty anti-American. To these, I say: Don't blame *me* for *that!* Blame those who mouthed my liberal values and broke my American heart.

Just who might they be, by the way? Let's take a brief factual inventory of the latter-day Cold War.

In 1953 our Central Intelligence Agency managed to overthrow Mossadegh in Iran, the complaint being his neutralism in the Cold War and his plans to nationalize the country's oil resources to improve his people's lives. Most evil aims, most evil man. In his place we put in General Zahedi, a World War II Nazi collaborator. New arrangements on Iran's oil gave 25-year leases on 40% of it to three U.S. firms, one of which was Gulf Oil. The CIA's leader for this coup was Kermit Roosevelt. In 1960 Kermit Roosevelt became a vice president of Gulf Oil.

In 1954, the democratically elected Arbenz of Guatemala wanted to nationalize a portion of United Fruit Company's plantations in his country, land he needed badly for a modest program of agrarian reform. His government was overthrown in a CIA-supported right-wing coup. The following year, Gen. Walter Bedell Smith, director of the CIA when the Guatemala venture was being planned, joined the board of directors of the United Fruit Company.

Comes 1960 and Castro cries we are about to invade Cuba. The Administration sneers, "poppycock," and we Americans believe it. Comes 1961 and the invasion. Comes with it the awful realization that the United States Government had lied.

Comes 1962 and the missile crisis, and our Administration stands prepared to fight global atomic war on the curious principle that another state does not have the right to its own foreign policy.

Comes 1963 and British Guiana, where Cheddi Jagan wants independence from England and a labor law modelled on the Wagner Act. And Jay Lovestone, the AFL-CIO foreign policy chief, acting, as always, quite independently of labor's rank and file, arranges with our Government to finance an eleven-week dock strike that brings Jagan down, ensuring that the state will remain *British* Guiana, and that any workingman who wants a wage better than 50¢ a day is a dupe of Communism.

Comes 1964. Two weeks after Undersecretary Thomas Mann announces that we have abandoned the *Alianza's* principle of no aid to tyrants, Brazil's Goulart is overthrown by the vicious right-winger Ademar Barros, supported by a show of American gunboats at Rio de Janeiro. Within 24 hours the new head of state, Mazzilli, receives a congratulatory wire from our President.

Comes 1965. The Dominican Republic. Rebellion in the streets. We scurry to the spot with 20,000 neutral Marines and our neutral peacemakers—like Ellsworth Bunker, Jr., ambassador to the Organization of American States. Most of us know that our neutral Marines fought openly on the side of the junta, a fact that the Administration still denies. But how many also know that what was at stake was our new Caribbean Sugar Bowl? That this same neutral peacemaking Bunker is a board member and stock owner of the National Sugar Refining Company, a firm his father founded in the good old days, and one which has a major interest in maintaining the status quo in the Dominican Republic? Or that the President's close personal friend and advisor, our new Supreme Court Justice Abe Fortas, has sat for the past 19 years on the board of the Sucrest Company, which imports black-strap molasses from the Dominican Republic? Or that the rhetorician of corporate liberalism and the late President Kennedy's close friend, Adolf Berle, was chairman of that same board? Or that our roving ambassador Averell Harriman's brother Roland is on the board of National Sugar? Or that our former ambassador to the Dominican Republic, Joseph Farland, is a board member of the South Puerto Rico Sugar Co., which owns 275,000 acres of rich land in the Dominican Republic and is the largest employer on the island—at about one dollar a day?

Neutralists! God save the hungry people of the world from such neutralists!

We do not say these men are evil. We say, rather, that good men can be divided from their compassion by the institutional system that inherits us all. Generation in and out, we are put to use. People become instruments. Generals do not hear the screams of the bombed; sugar executives do not see the misery of the cane cutters—for to do so is to be that much *less* the general, that much *less* the executive.

The foregoing facts of recent history describe one main aspect of the estate of Western liberalism. Where is our American humanism here? What went wrong?

Let's stare our situation coldly in the face. All of us are born to the colossus of history, our American corporate system—in many ways, an awesome organism. There is one fact that describes it: with about 5% of the world's people, we consume about half the world's goods. We take a richness that is in good part not our own, and we put it in our pockets, our garages, our split-levels, our bellies, and our futures.

On the *face* of it, it is a crime that so few should have so much at the expense of so many. Where is the moral imagination so abused as to call this just? Perhaps many of us feel a bit uneasy in our sleep. We are not, after all, a cruel people. And perhaps we don't really need this super-dominance that deforms others. But what can we do? The investments are made. The financial ties are established. The plants abroad are built. Our system *exists*. One is swept up into it. How intolerable—to be born moral but addicted to a stolen and maybe surplus luxury. Our goodness threatens to become counterfeit before our eyes—unless we change. But change threatens us with uncertainty—at least.

Our problem, then, is to justify this system and give its theft another name—to make kind and moral what is neither, to perform some alchemy with language that will make this injustice seem to be a most magnanimous gift.

A hard problem. But the Western democracies, in the heyday of their colonial expansionism, produced a hero worthy of the task.

Its name was free enterprise, and its partner was an *illiberal liberalism* that said to the poor and the dispossessed: What we acquire of your resources we repay in civilization. The white man's burden. But this was too poetic. So a much more hardheaded theory was produced. This theory said that colonial status is in fact a *boon* to the colonized. We give them technology and bring them into modern times.

But this deceived no one but ourselves. We were delighted with this new theory. The poor saw in it merely an admission that their claims were irrefutable. They stood up to us, without gratitude. We were shocked—but also confused, for the poor seemed again to be right. How long is it going to be the case, we wondered, that the poor will be right and the rich will be wrong?

Liberalism faced a crisis. In the face of the collapse of the European empires, how could it continue to hold together our twin need for richness and righteousness? How can we continue to sack the ports of Asia and still dream of Jesus?

The challenge was met with a most ingenious solution: the ideology of anti-Communism. This was the bind: we cannot call revolution bad, because we started that way ourselves, and because it is all too easy to see why the dispossessed should rebel. So we will call revolution *Communism*. And we will reserve for ourselves the right to say what Communism means. We take note of revolution's enormities, wrenching them where necessary from their historical context and often exaggerating them, and say: Behold, Communism is a bloodbath. We take note of those reactionaries who stole the revolution, and say: Behold, Communism is a betrayal of the people. We take note of the revolution's need to consolidate itself, and say: Behold, Communism is a tyranny.

It has been all these things, and it will be these things again, and we will never be at a loss for those tales of atrocity that comfort us so in our self-righteousness. Nuns will be raped and bureaucrats will be disembowelled. Indeed, revolution is a fury. For it is a letting loose of outrages pent up sometimes over centuries. But the more brutal and longer-lasting the suppression of this energy, all the more ferocious will be its explosive release.

Far from helping Americans deal with this truth, the anti-Communist ideology merely tries to disguise it so that things may stay the way they are. Thus, it depicts our presence in other lands not as a coercion but a protection. It allows us even to say that the napalm in Vietnam is only another aspect of our humanitarian love—like those exorcisms in the Middle Ages that so often killed the patient. So we say to the Vietnamese peasant, the Cuban intellectual, the Peruvian worker: "You are better dead than Red. If it hurts or if you don't understand why—sorry about that."

This is the action of *corporate liberalism*. It performs for the corporate state a function quite like what the Church once performed for the feudal state. It seeks to justify its burdens and protect it from change. As the Church exaggerated this office in the Inquisition, so with liberalism in the McCarthy time—which, if it was a reactionary phenomenon, was still made possible by our anti-Communist corporate liberalism.

Let me then speak directly to humanist liberals. If my facts are wrong, I will soon be corrected. But if they are right, then you may face a crisis of conscience. Corporatism or humanism: which? For it has come to that. Will you let your dreams be used? Will you be a grudging apologist for the corporate state? Or will you help try to change it—not in the name of this or that blueprint or "ism" but in the name of simple human decency and democracy and the vision that wise and brave men saw in the time of our own Revolution?

And if your commitment to human value is unconditional, then disabuse yourselves of the notion that statements will bring change if only the right statements can be written, or that interviews with the mighty will bring change if only the mighty can be reached, or that marches will bring change if only we can make them massive enough, or that policy proposals will bring change if only we can make them responsible enough.

We are dealing now with a colossus that does not want to be changed. It will not change itself. It will not cooperate with those who want to change it. Those allies of ours in the Government—are they really our allies? If they *are*, then they don't need advice, they need *constituencies*; they don't need study groups, they need a *movement*. And if they are *not*, then all the more reason for building that movement with a most relentless conviction.

There are people in this country today who are trying to build that movement, who aim at nothing less than a humanist reformation. And the humanist liberals must understand that it is this movement with which their own best hopes are most in tune. We radicals know the same history that you liberals know, and we can understand your occasional cynicism, exasperation, and even distrust. But we ask you to put these aside and help us risk a leap. Help us find enough time for the enormous work that needs doing here. Help us build. Help us shake the future in the name of plain human hope.

LESLIE FIEDLER

15 The New Mutants

This essay, written in 1965 by the literary critic Leslie Fiedler, expresses the bafflement of many older intellectuals with the cultural and sexual revolution being trumpeted by the young radicals. Fiedler saw the longhaired young as involved in a "revolt against masculinity" in which they derogated responsibility in favor of "the pursuit of loveliness" and the unfolding cultural rebellion as a protest against the "bourgeois-Protestant version of Humanism with its view of man as justified by rationality, work, duty, vocation, maturity, success; and its concomitant understanding of childhood and adolescence as a temporarily privileged time of preparation for assuming these burdens." Even former Marxists such as Fiedler were alarmed by the counterculture's apparent flight from the rational.

The young to whom I have been referring, the mythologically representative minority (who, by a process that infuriates the mythologically inert majority out of which they come, "stand for" their times), live in a community in which what used to be called the "Sexual Revolution," the Freudian-Laurentian revolt of their grandparents and parents, has triumphed as imperfectly and unsatisfactorily as all revolutions always triumph. They confront, therefore, the necessity of determining not only what meanings "love" can have in their new world, but—even more disturbingly—what significance, if any, "male" and "female" now possess. For a while, they (or at least their literary spokesmen recruited from the generation just before them) seemed content to celebrate a kind of *reductio* or *exaltatio ad absurdum* of their parents' once revolutionary sexual goals: the Reichian-inspired Cult of the Orgasm.

From *The Collected Essays of Leslie Fiedler*, 2 vols. (New York: Stein and Day, 1971), 2:392–400. Reprinted by permission of Leslie Fiedler.

Young men and women eager to be delivered of traditional ideologies of love find especially congenial the belief that not union or relationship (much less offspring) but physical release is the end of the sexual act; and that, therefore, it is a matter of indifference with whom or by what method ones pursues the therapeutic climax, so long as that climax is total and repeated frequently. And Wilhelm Reich happily detaches this belief from the vestiges of Freudian rationalism, setting it instead in a context of Science Fiction and witchcraft; but his emphasis upon "full genitality," upon growing up and away from infantile pleasures, strikes the young as a disguised plea for the "maturity" they have learned to despise. In a time when the duties associated with adulthood promise to become irrelevant, there seems little reason for denying oneself the joys of babyhood—even if these are associated with such repressive fantasies as escaping it all in the arms of little sister (in the Gospel according to J. D. Salinger) or flirting with the possibility of getting into bed with Papa (in the Gospel according to Norman Mailer).

Only Norman O. Brown in *Life Against Death* has come to terms on the level of theory with the aspiration to take the final evolutionary leap and cast off adulthood completely, at least in the area of sex. His post-Freudian program for pansexual, nonorgasmic love rejects "full genitality" in favor of a species of indiscriminate bundling, a dream of unlimited subcoital intimacy which Brown calls (in his vocabulary the term is an honorific) "polymorphous perverse." And here finally is an essential clue to the nature of the second sexual revolution, the postsexual revolution, first evoked in literature by Brother Antoninus more than a decade ago, in a verse prayer addressed somewhat improbably to the Christian God:

> Annul in me my manhood, Lord, and make
> Me woman sexed and weak . . .
> Make me then
> Girl-hearted, virgin-souled, woman-docile, maiden-meek . . .

Despite the accents of this invocation, however, what is at work is not essentially a homosexual revolt or even a rebellion against women, though its advocates seek to wrest from women their ancient privileges of receiving the Holy Ghost and pleasuring men, and though the attitudes of the movement can be adapted to the antifemale bias of, say, Edward Albee. If in *Who's Afraid of Virginia Woolf* Albee can portray the relationship of two homosexuals (one in drag) as the model of contemporary marriage, this must be because contemporary marriage has in fact turned into something much like that parody. And it is true that what survives of bourgeois marriage and the bourgeois family is a target which the new barbarians join the old homosexuals in reviling, seeking to replace Mom, Pop, and the kids with a neo-Whitmanian gaggle of giggling *camerados*. Such groups are, in fact, whether gathered in coffee houses, university cafeterias, or around the literature tables on campuses, the peacetime equivalents, as it were, to the demonstrating crowd. But even their program of displacing Dick-Jane-Spot-Baby, etc., the WASP family of grade school primers, is not the fundamental motive of the postsexual revolution.

What is at stake from Burroughs to Bellow, Ginsberg to Albee, Salinger to Gregory Corso is a more personal transformation: a radical metamorphosis of the Western male—utterly unforeseen in the decades before us but visible now in every high school and college classroom, as well as on the paperback racks in airports and supermarkets. All around us, young males are beginning to retrieve for themselves the cavalier role once piously and class-consciously surrendered to women: *that of being beautiful and being loved.* Here once more the example of the Negro—the feckless and adorned Negro male with the blood of Cavaliers in his veins—has served as a model. And what else is left to young men, in any case, after the devaluation of the grim duties they had arrogated to themselves in place of the pursuit of loveliness?

All of us who are middle-aged and were Marxists, which is to say, who once numbered ourselves among the last assured Puritans, have surely noticed in ourselves a vestigial roundhead rage at the new hair styles of the advanced or—if you please—delinquent young. Watching young men titivate their locks (the comb, the pocket mirror, and the bobby pin having replaced the jackknife, catcher's mitt, and brass knuckles), we feel the same baffled resentment that stirs in us when we realize that they have rejected work. A job and unequivocal maleness—these are two sides of the same Calvinist coin, which in the future buys nothing.

Few of us, however, have really understood how the Beatle hairdo is part of a syndrome of which high heels, jeans tight over the buttocks, etc., are other aspects, symptomatic of a larger retreat from masculine aggressiveness to female allure—in literature and the arts to the style called "camp." And fewer still have realized how that style, though the invention of homosexuals, is now the possession of basically heterosexual males as well, a strategy in their campaign to establish a new relationship not only with women but with their own masculinity. In the course of that campaign, they have embraced certain kinds of gesture and garb, certain accents and tones traditionally associated with females or female impersonators—which is why we have been observing recently (in life as well as fiction and verse) young boys, quite unequivocally male, playing all the traditional roles of women: the vamp, the coquette, the whore, the icy tease, the pure young virgin.

Not only oldsters, who had envisioned and despaired of quite another future, are bewildered by this turn of events, but young girls, too, seem scarcely to know what is happening—looking on with that new, schizoid stare which itself has become a hallmark of our times. And the crop-headed jocks, those crew-cut athletes who represent an obsolescent masculine style based on quite other values, have tended to strike back blindly, beating the hell out of some poor kid whose hair is too long or whose pants are too tight—quite as they once beat up young communists for revealing that their politics had become obsolete. Even heterosexual writers, however, have been slow to catch up, the revolution in sensibility running ahead of that in expression; and they have perforce permitted homosexuals to speak for them (Burroughs and Genet and Baldwin and Ginsberg and Albee and a score of others), even to invent the forms in which the future will have to speak.

The revolt against masculinity is not limited, however, to simple matters of coiffure and costume, visible even to athletes, or to the adaptation of certain campy styles and modes to new uses. There is also a sense in which two large social movements that have set the young in motion and furnished images of action for their books—movements as important in their own right as porno-politics and the pursuit of the polymorphous perverse—are connected analogically to the abdication from traditional maleness. The first of these is nonviolent or passive resistance, so oddly come back to the land of its inventor, that icy Thoreau who dreamed a love which ". . . has not much human blood in it, but consists with a certain disregard for men and their erections. . . ."

The civil rights movement, however, in which nonviolence has found a home, has been hospitable not only to the sort of post-humanist I have been describing; so that at a demonstration (Selma, Alabama, will do as an example) the true hippie will be found side by side with backwoods Baptists, nuns on a spiritual spree, boy bureaucrats practicing to take power, resurrected socialists, Unitarians in search of a God, and just plain tourists, gathered, as once at the Battle of Bull Run, to see the fun. For each of these, nonviolence will have a different sort of fundamental meaning—as a tactic, a camouflage, a passing fad, a pious gesture—but for each in part, and for the post-humanist especially, it will signify the possibility of heroism without aggression, effective action without guilt.

There have always been two contradictory American ideals: to be the occasion of maximum violence, and to remain absolutely innocent. Once, however, these were thought hopelessly incompatible for males (except, perhaps, as embodied in works of art), reserved strictly for women: the spouse of the wife beater, for instance, or the victim of rape. But males have now assumed these classic roles; and just as a particularly beleaguered wife occasionally slipped over the dividing line into violence, so do the new passive protesters—leaving us to confront (or resign to the courts) such homey female questions as: *Did Mario Savio really bite that cop in the leg as he sagged limply toward the ground?*

The second social movement is the drug cult, more widespread among youth, from its squarest limits to its most beat, than anyone seems prepared to admit in public; and at its beat limit at least inextricably involved with the civil rights movement, as the recent arrests of Peter DeLissovoy and Susan Ryerson revealed even to the ordinary newspaper reader. "Police said that most of the recipients [of marijuana] were college students," the U.P. story runs. "They quoted Miss Ryerson and DeLissovoy as saying that many of the letter packets were sent to civil rights workers." Only fiction and verse, however, have dealt with the conjunction of homosexuality, drugs, and civil rights, eschewing the general piety of the press, which has been unwilling to compromise "good works" on behalf of the Negro by associating them with the deep radicalism of a way of life based on the ritual consumption of "pot."

The widespread use of such hallucinogens as peyote, marijuana, the "Mexican mushroom," LSD, etc., as well as pep pills, goof balls, airplane glue, certain kinds of cough syrups, and even, though in many fewer cases, heroin, is not merely a matter of a changing taste in stimulants but of the programmatic espousal of an antipuritanical mode of existence—hedonistic and detached—one more strategy in the war on time and work. But it is also (to pursue my analogy once more) an attempt to arrogate to the male certain traditional privileges of the female. What could be more womanly, as Elémire Zolla was already pointing out some years ago, than permitting the penetration of the body by a foreign object which not only stirs delight but even (possibly) creates new life?

In any case, with drugs we have come to the crux of the futurist revolt, the hinge of everything else, as the young tell us over and over in their writing. When the movement was first finding a voice, Allen Ginsberg set this aspect of it in proper context in an immensely comic, utterly serious poem called "America," in which "pot" is associated with earlier forms of rebellion, a commitment to catatonia, and a rejection of conventional male potency:

> America I used to be a communist when I was a kid I'm not
> sorry.
> I smoke marijuana every chance I get.
> I sit in my house for days on end and stare at the roses in the
> closet.
> When I go to Chinatown I . . . never get laid . . .

Similarly, Michael McClure reveals in his essay "*Phi Upsilon Kappa*" that before penetrating the "cavern of Anglo-Saxon," whence he emerged with the slogan of the ultimate Berkeley demonstrators, he had been on mescalin. "I have emerged from a dark night of the soul; I entered it by Peyote." And by now, drug-taking has become as standard a feature of the literature of the young as oral-genital love-making. I flip open the first issue of yet another ephemeral San Francisco little magazine quite at random and read: "I tie up and the main pipe [the ante-cobital vein, for the clinically inclined] swells like a prideful beggar beneath the skin. Just before I get on it is always the worst." Worse than the experience, however, is its literary rendering; and the badness of such confessional fiction, flawed by the sentimentality of those who desire to live "like a cunning vegetable," is a badness we older readers find it only too easy to perceive, as our sons and daughters find it only too easy to overlook. Yet precisely here the age and the mode define themselves, for not in the master but in the hacks new forms are established, new lines drawn.

Here, at any rate, is where the young lose us in literature as well as life, since here they pass over into real revolt, i.e., what we really cannot abide, hard as we try. The mother who has sent her son to private schools and on to Harvard, to keep him out of classrooms overcrowded with poor Negroes, rejoices when he sets out for Mississippi with his comrades in SNCC but shudders when he turns on with LSD; just as the ex-Marxist father, who has earlier proved radicalism impossible, rejoices to see his son stand up, piously and pompously, for CORE or SDS but trembles to hear him quote Alpert and Leary or praise Burroughs. Just as certainly as liberalism is the LSD of the aging, LSD is the radicalism of the young.

If whiskey long served as an appropriate symbolic excess for those who chafed against Puritan restraint without finally challenging it—temporarily releasing them to socially harmful aggression and (hopefully) sexual self-indulgence—the new popular drugs provide an excess quite as satisfactorily symbolic to the post-Puritans, releasing them from sanity to madness by destroying in them the inner restrictive order which has somehow survived the dissolution of the outer. It is finally insanity, then, that the futurists learn to admire and emulate, quite as they learn to pursue vision instead of learning, hallucination rather than logic. The schizophrenic replaces the sage as their ideal, their new culture hero, figured forth as a giant schizoid Indian (his madness modeled in part on the author's own experiences with LSD) in Ken Kesey's *One Flew Over the Cuckoo's Nest*.

The hippier young are not alone, however, in their taste for the insane; we live in a time when readers in general respond sympathetically to madness in literature wherever it is found, in established writers as well as in those trying to establish new modes. Surely it is not the lucidity and logic of Robert Lowell or Theodore Roethke or John Berryman which we admire but their flirtation with incoherence and disorder. And certainly it is Mailer at his most nearly psychotic, Mailer the creature rather than the master of his fantasies, who moves us to admiration; while in the case of Saul Bellow, we endure the theoretical optimism and acceptance for the sake of the delightful melancholia, the fertile paranoia which he cannot disavow any more than the talent at whose root they lie. Even essayists and analysts recommend themselves to us these days by a certain redemptive nuttiness; at any rate, we do not love, say, Marshall McLuhan less because he continually risks sounding like the body-fluids man in *Dr. Strangelove*.

We have, moreover, recently been witnessing the development of a new form of social psychiatry* (a psychiatry of the future already anticipated by the literature of the future) which considers some varieties of "schizophrenia" not diseases to be cured but forays into an unknown psychic world: random penetrations by bewildered internal cosmonauts of a realm that it will be the task of the next generations to explore. And if the accounts which the returning schizophrenics give (the argument

*Described in an article in the *New Left Review* of November-December 1964 by R. D. Laing, who advocates "ex-patients helping future patients go mad."

of the apologists runs) of the "places" they have been are fantastic and garbled, surely they are no more so than, for example, Columbus' reports of the world he had claimed for Spain, a world bounded—according to his newly drawn maps—by Cathay on the north and Paradise on the south.

In any case, poets and junkies have been suggesting to us that the new world appropriate to the new men of the latter twentieth century is to be discovered only by the conquest of inner space: by an adventure of the spirit, an extension of psychic possibility, of which the flights into outer space—moonshots and expeditions to Mars—are precisely such unwitting metaphors and analogues as the voyages of exploration were of the earlier breakthrough into the Renaissance, from whose consequences the young seek now so desperately to escape. The laureate of that new conquest is William Burroughs, and it is fitting that the final word be his:

> "This war will be won in the air. In the Silent Air with Image Rays. You were a pilot remember? Tracer bullets cutting the right wing you were free in space a few seconds before in blue space between eyes. Go back to Silence. Keep Silence. Keep Silence. K.S. K.S. . . . From Silence re-write the message that is you. You are the message I send to The Enemy. My Silent Message." The Naked Astronauts were free in space. . . .

CASEY HAYDEN AND MARY KING

16 Sex and Caste

In the fall of 1965 the women's movement had yet to coalesce, but it was beginning to find its voice. In retrospect, it seems inevitable that the rhetoric of empowerment that characterized the civil rights movement and the new left in the early 1960s would resonate to other constituent groups. As this manifesto to a number of other women in the peace and freedom movements indicates, women active in these movements were beginning to make important connections between their condition and that of African Americans and the poor. By the end of the twentieth century, gender issues along with those of race and class were to demarcate some of the most important ideological fault lines in American politics.

November 18, 1965

We've talked a lot, to each other and to some of you, about our own and other women's problems in trying to live in our personal lives and in our work as independent and creative people. In these conversations we've found what seem to be recurrent ideas or themes. Maybe we can look at these things many of us perceive, often as a result of insights learned from the movement:

Sex and caste: There seem to be many parallels that can be drawn between treatment of Negroes and treatment of women in our society as a whole. But in particular, women we've talked to who work in the movement seem to be caught up in a common-law caste system that operates, sometimes subtly, forcing them to work around or outside hierarchical structures of power which may exclude them. Women seem to be placed in the same position of assumed subordination in personal

From *Personal Politics: The Roots of Women's Liberation in the Civil Rights Movement and the New Left,* ed. Sara Evans (New York: Vintage Books, 1979), 235–38.

situations too. It is a caste system which, at its worst, uses and exploits women.

This is complicated by several facts, among them: 1) The caste system is not institutionalized by law (women have the right to vote, to sue for divorce, etc.); 2) Women can't withdraw from the situation (à la nationalism) or overthrow it; 3) There are biological differences (even though those biological differences are usually discussed or accepted without taking present and future technology into account so we probably can't be sure what these differences mean). Many people who are very hip to the implications of the racial caste system, even people in the movement, don't seem to be able to see the sexual caste system and if the question is raised they respond with: "That's the way it's supposed to be. There are biological differences." Or with other statements which recall a white segregationist confronted with integration.

Women and problems of work: The caste system perspective dictates the roles assigned to women in the movement, and certainly even more to women outside the movement. Within the movement, questions arise in situations ranging from relationships of women organizers to men in the community, to who cleans the freedom house, to who holds leadership positions, to who does secretarial work, and who acts as spokesman for groups. Other problems arise between women with varying degrees of awareness of themselves as being as capable as men but held back from full participation, or between women who see themselves as needing more control of their work than other women demand. And there are problems with relationships between white women and black women.

Women and personal relations with men: Having learned from the movement to think radically about the personal worth and abilities of people whose role in society had gone unchallenged before, a lot of women in the movement have begun trying to apply those lessons to their own relations with men. Each of us probably has her own story of the various results, and of the internal struggle occasioned by trying to break out of very deeply learned fears, needs, and self-perceptions, and of what happens when we try to replace them with concepts of people and freedom learned from the movement and organizing.

Institutions: Nearly everyone has real questions about those institutions which shape perspectives on men and women: marriage, child rearing patterns, women's (and men's) magazines, etc. People are beginning to think about and even to experiment with new forms in these areas.

Men's reactions to the questions raised here: A very few men seem to feel, when they hear conversations involving these problems, that they have a right to be present and participate in them, since they are so deeply involved. At the same time, very few men can respond non-defensively since the whole idea is either beyond their comprehension or threatens and exposes them. The usual response is laughter. That inability to see the whole issue as serious, as the strait-jacketing of both sexes, and as societally determined often shapes our own response so that we learn to think in their terms about ourselves and to feel silly rather than trust our inner feelings. The problems we're listing here, and what others have said about them, are therefore largely drawn from conversations among women only—and that difficulty in establishing dialogue with men is a recurring theme among people we've talked to.

Lack of community for discussion: Nobody is writing, or organizing or talking publicly about women, in any way that reflects the problems that various women in the movement come across and which we've tried to touch on above. Consider this quote from an article in the centennial issue of *The Nation*:

> However equally we consider men and women, the work plans for husbands and wives cannot be given equal weight. A woman should not aim for "a second-level career" because she is a *woman*; from girlhood on she should recognize that, if she is also going to be a wife and mother, she will not be able to give as much to her work as she would if single. That is, she should not feel that she cannot aspire to directing the laboratory simply because she is a woman, but rather because she is also a wife and mother; as such, her work as a lab technician (or the equivalent in another field) should bring both satisfaction and the knowledge that, through it, she is fulfilling an additional role, making an additional contribution.

And that's about as deep as the analysis goes publicly, which is not nearly so deep as we've heard many of you go in chance conversations.

The reason we want to try to open up dialogue is mostly subjective. Working in the movement often intensifies personal problems, especially if we start trying to apply things we're learning there to our personal lives. Perhaps we can start to talk with each other more openly than in the past and create a community of support for each other so we can deal with ourselves and others with integrity and can therefore keep working.

Objectively, the chances seem nil that we could start a movement based on anything as distant to general American thought as a sex-caste system. Therefore, most of us will probably want to work full time on problems such as war, poverty, race. The very fact that the country can't face, much less deal with, the questions we're raising means that the movement is one place to look for some relief. Real efforts at dialogue within the movement and with whatever liberal groups, community women, or students might listen are justified. That is, all the problems between men and women and all the problems of women functioning in society as equal human beings are among the most basic that people face. We've talked in the movement about trying to build a society which would see basic human problems (which are now seen as private troubles) as public problems and would try to shape institutions to meet human needs rather than shaping people to meet the needs of those with power. To raise questions like those above illustrates very directly that society hasn't dealt with some of its deepest problems and opens discussion of why that is so. (In one sense, it is a radicalizing question that can take people beyond legalistic solutions into areas of personal and institutional change.) The second objective reason we'd like to see discussion begin is that we've learned a great deal in the movement and perhaps this is one area where a determined attempt to apply ideas we've learned there can produce some new alternatives.

RICHARD M. NIXON

17

The Watergate Charges

Protecting the National Security

In his first formal speech on the Watergate charges, delivered in a television broadcast on August 15, 1973, President Richard M. Nixon steadfastly denied what the public eventually found to be true: Despite the protestation that he "had no knowledge of the so-called cover-up," the disclosure of his tapes and papers revealed his personal direction of the cover-up. In a moment of unabashed hypocrisy, Nixon criticized the rebels of the 1960s for asserting "the right to take the law into their own hands." As if Vietnam had not done enough to undermine the credibility of those in power, Watergate only added another layer of cynicism.

Now that most of the major witnesses in the Watergate phase of the Senate committee hearings on campaign practices have been heard, the time has come for me to speak out about the charges made and to provide a perspective on the issue for the American people.

For over four months Watergate has dominated the news media. During the past three months the three major networks have devoted an average of over 22 hours of television time each week to this subject. The Senate committee has heard over two million words of testimony.

From *Richard M. Nixon, 1913–: Chronology, Documents, Bibliographical Aids,* ed. Howard F. Bremer (Dobbs Ferry, NY: Oceana Publications, 1975), 203–10.

This investigation began as an effort to discover the facts about the break-in and bugging at the Democratic national headquarters and other campaign abuses.

But [as] the weeks have gone by, it has become clear that both the hearings themselves and some of the commentaries on them have become increasingly absorbed in an effort to implicate the President personally in the illegal activities that took place.

Because the abuses occurred during my Administration, and in the campaign for my re-election, I accept full responsibility for them. I regret that these events took place. And I do not question the right of a Senate committee to investigate charges made against the President to the extent that this is relevant to legislative duties.

However, it is my constitutional responsibility to defend the integrity of this great office against false charges. I also believe that it is important to address the overriding question of what we as a nation can learn from this experience, and what we should now do. I intend to discuss both of these subjects tonight.

The record of the Senate hearings is lengthy. The facts are complicated, the evidence conflicting. It would not be right for me to try to sort out the evidence, to rebut specific witnesses, or to pronounce my own judgments about their credibility. That is for the committee and for the courts.

I shall not attempt to deal tonight with the various charges in detail. Rather, I shall attempt to put the events in perspective from the standpoint of the Presidency.

On May 22d, before the major witnesses had testified. I issued a detailed statement addressing the charges that had been made against the President.

I have today issued another written statement, which addresses the charges that have been made since then as they relate to my own conduct, and which describes the efforts that I made to discover the facts about the matter.

On May 22, I stated in very specific terms—and I state again to every one of you listening tonight—these facts: I had no prior knowledge of the Watergate break-in; I neither took part in nor knew about any of the subsequent cover-up activities; I neither authorized nor encouraged subordinates to engage in illegal or improper campaign tactics.

That was and that is the simple truth. In all of the millions of words of testimony, there is not the slightest suggestion that I had any knowledge of the planning for the Watergate break-in. As for the cover-up, my statement has been challenged by only one of the 35 witnesses who appeared—a witness who offered no evidence beyond his own impressions, and whose testimony has been contradicted by every other witness in a position to know the facts.

Tonight, let me explain to you what I did about Watergate after the break-in occurred, so that you can better understand the fact that I also had no knowledge of the so-called cover-up.

From the time when the break-in occurred, I pressed repeatedly to know the facts, and particularly whether there was any involvement of anyone at the White House. I considered two things essential:

First, that the investigation should be thorough and above-board: and second, that if there were any higher involvement, we should get the facts out first. As I said at my August 29 press conference last year, "What really hurts in matters of this sort is not the fact that they occur, because overzealous people in campaigns do things that are wrong. What really hurts is if you try to cover it up." I believed that then, and certainly the experience of this last year has proved that to be true.

I knew that the Justice Department and the F.B.I. were conducting intensive investigations—as I had insisted that they should. The White House counsel, John Dean, was assigned to monitor these investigations, and particularly to check into any possible White House involvement. Throughout the summer of 1972, I continued to press the question, and I continued to get the same answer: I was told again and again that there was no indication that any persons were involved other than the seven who were known to have planned and carried out the operation, and who were subsequently indicted and convicted.

On Sept. 12 at a meeting that I held with the Cabinet, the senior White House staff, and a number of legislative leaders, Attorney General Kleindienst reported on the investigation. He told us it had been the most extensive investigation since the assassination of President Kennedy, and that it has established that only those seven were involved.

On Sept. 15, the day the seven were indicted, I met with John Dean, the White House counsel. He gave me no reason whatever to believe that any others were guilty; I assumed that the indictments of only the seven by the grand jury confirmed the reports he had been giving to that effect throughout the summer.

On Feb. 16, I met with Acting Director [L. Patrick] Gray prior to submitting his name to the Senate for confirmation as permanent director of the F.B.I. I stressed to him that he would be questioned closely about the F.B.I.'s conduct of the Watergate investigation. I asked him if he still had full confidence in it. He replied that he did; that he was proud of its thoroughness and that he could defend it with enthusiasm before the committee.

Because I trusted the agencies conducting the investigations, because I believed the reports I was getting, I did not believe the newspaper accounts that suggested a cover-up. I was convinced there was no cover-up, because I was convinced that no one had anything to cover up.

It was not until March 21 of this year that I received new information from the White House counsel that led me to conclude that the reports I had been getting for over nine months were not true. On that day, I launched an intensive effort of my own to get the facts and to get the facts out. Whatever the facts might be, I wanted the White House to be the first to make them public.

At first I entrusted the task of getting me the facts to Mr. Dean. When, after spending a week at Camp David, he failed to produce the written report I had asked for, I turned to John Ehrlichman and to the Attorney General—while also making independent inquiries of my own. By mid-April I had received Mr. Ehrlichman's report, and also one from the Attorney General based on new information uncovered by the Justice Department.

These reports made it clear to me that the situation was far more serious than I had imagined. It at once became evident to me that the responsibility for the investigation in the case should be given to the Criminal Division of the Justice Department. I turned over all the information I had to the head of that department, Assistant Attorney General Henry Petersen, a career Government employee with an impeccable nonpartisan record, and I instructed him to pursue the matter thoroughly. I ordered all members of the Administration to testify fully before the grand jury.

And with my concurrence, on May 18 Attorney General [Elliot] Richardson appointed a special prosecutor to handle the matter, and the case is now before the grand jury.

Far from trying to hide the facts, my effort throughout has been to discover the facts—and to lay those facts before the appropriate law-enforcement authorities so that justice could be done and the guilty dealt with.

I relied on the best law-enforcement agencies in the country to find and report the truth. I believed they had done so—just as they believed they had done so.

Many have urged that in order to help prove the truth of what I have said, I should turn over to the special prosecutor and the Senate committee recordings of conversations that I held in my office or on my telephone.

However, a much more important principle is involved in this question than what the tapes might prove about Watergate.

Each day a President of the United States is required to make difficult decisions on grave issues. It is absolutely necessary, if the President is to be able to do his job as the country expects, that he be able to talk openly and candidly with his advisers about issues and individuals. This kind of frank discussion is only possible when those who take part in it know that what they say is in strictest confidence.

The Presidency is not the only office that requires confidentiality. A member of Congress must be able to talk in confidence with his assistants. Judges must be able to confer in confidence with their law clerks and with each other. For very good reasons, no branch of government has ever compelled disclosure of confidential conversations between officers of other branches of government and their advisers about government business.

This need for confidence is not confined to Government officials. The law has long recognized that there are kinds of conversations that are entitled to be kept confidential, even at the cost of doing without critical evidence in a legal proceeding. This rule applies, for example, to conversations between a lawyer and a client, between a priest and a penitent, and between a husband and a wife. In each case it is thought so important that the parties be able to talk freely to each other that for hundreds of years the law has said that these conversations are "privileged" and that their disclosure cannot be compelled in a court.

It is even more important that the confidentiality of conversations between a President and his advisers be protected. This is no mere luxury, to be dispensed with whenever a particular issue raises sufficient uproar. It is absolutely essential to the conduct of the Presidency. in this and in all future Administrations.

If I were to make public these tapes, containing as they do blunt and candid remarks on many different subjects, the confidentiality of the Office of the President would always be suspect from now on. It would make no difference whether it was to serve the interests of a court, of a Senate committee, or the President himself—the same damage would be done to the principle, and that damage would be irreparable. Persons talking with the President would never again be sure that recordings or notes of what they said would not suddenly be made public. No one would want to advance tentative ideas that might later seem unsound. No diplomat would want to speak candidly in those sensitive negotiations which could bring peace or avoid war. No Senator or Congressman would want to talk frankly about the Congressional horse-trading that might get a vital bill passed. No one would want to speak bluntly about public figures, here and abroad.

That is why I shall continue to oppose efforts which would set a precedent that would cripple all future Presidents by inhibiting conversations between them and those they look to for advice. This principle of confidentiality of Presidential conversations is at stake in the question of these tapes. I must, and I shall, oppose any efforts to destroy this principle, which is so vital to the conduct of this great office.

Turning now to the basic issues which have been raised by Watergate, I recognize that merely answering the charges that have been made against the President is not enough. The word "Watergate" has come to represent a much broader set of concerns.

To most of us, "Watergate" has come to mean not just a burglary and bugging of party headquarters, but a whole series of acts that either represent or appear to represent an abuse of trust. It has come to stand for excessive partisanship, for "enemy lists," for efforts to use the great institutions of Government for partisan political purposes.

For many Americans, the term "Watergate" also has come to include a number of national security matters that have been brought into the investigation, such as those involved in my efforts to stop massive leaks of vital diplomatic and military secrets, and to counter the wave of bombings and burnings and other violent assaults of just a few years ago.

Let me speak first of the political abuses.

I know from long experience, that a political campaign is always a hard and a tough contest. A candidate for high office has an obligation to his party, to his supporters, and to the cause he represents. He must always put forth his best efforts to win. But he also has an obligation to the country to conduct that contest within the law and within the limits of decency.

No political campaign ever justifies obstructing justice, or harassing individuals. or compromising those great agencies of government that should and must be above politics. To the extent that these things were done in the 1972 campaign, they were serious abuses. And I deplore them.

Practices of that kind do not represent what I believe Government should be, or what I believe politics should be. In a free society, the institutions of government belong to the people. They must never he used against the people.

And in the future, my Administration will be more vigilant in ensuring that such abuses do not take place, and that officials at every level understand that they are not to take place.

And I reject the cynical view that politics is inevitably or even usually a dirty business. Let us not allow what a few overzealous people did in Watergate to tar the reputation of the millions of dedicated Americans of both parties who fought hard but clean for the candidates of their choice in 1972. By their unselfish efforts, these people make our system work and they keep America free.

I pledge to you tonight that I will do all that I can to ensure that one of the results of Watergate is a new level of political decency and integrity in America—in which what has been wrong in our politics no longer corrupts or demeans what is right in our politics.

Let me turn now to the difficult questions that arise in protecting the national security.

It is important to recognize that these are difficult questions and that reasonable and patriotic men and women may differ on how they should be answered.

Only last year, the Supreme Court said that implicit in the President's constitutional duty is "the power to protect our Government against those who would subvert or overthrow it by unlawful means." How to carry out this duty is often a delicate question to which there is no easy answer.

For example, every President since World War II has believed that in internal security matters the President has the power to authorize wiretaps without first obtaining a search warrant.

An act of Congress in 1968 had seemed to recognize such power. Last year the Supreme Court held to the contrary. And my Administration is of course now complying with that Supreme Court decision. But until the Supreme Court spoke, I had been acting, as did my predecessors—President Truman, President Eisenhower, President Kennedy, President Johnson—in a reasonable belief that in certain circumstances the Constitution permitted and sometimes even required such measures to protect the national security in the public interest.

Although it is the President's duty to protect the security of the country, we of course must be extremely careful in the way we go about this—for if we lose our liberties we will have little use for security. Instances have now come to light in which a zeal for security did go too far and did interfere impermissibly with individual liberty.

It is essential that such mistakes not be repeated. But it is also essential that we do not overreact to particular mistakes by tying the President's hands in a way that would risk sacrificing our security, and with it our liberties.

I shall continue to meet my constitutional responsibility to protect the security of this nation so that Americans may enjoy their freedom. But I shall and can do so by constitutional means, in ways that will not threaten that freedom.

As we look at Watergate in a longer perspective, we can see that its abuses resulted from the assumption by those involved that their case placed them beyond the reach of those rules that apply to other persons and that hold a free society together.

That attitude can never be tolerated in our country. However, it did not suddenly develop in the year 1972. It became fashionable in the nineteen-sixties, as individuals and groups increasingly asserted the right to take the law into their own hands, insisting that their purposes represented a higher morality. Then, their attitude was praised in the press and even from some of our pulpits as evidence of a new idealism. Those of us who insisted on the old restraints, who warned of the overriding importance of operating within the law and by the rules, were accused of being reactionaries.

That same attitude brought a rising spiral of violence and fear of riots and arson and bombings, all in the name of peace and in the name of justice. Political discussion turned into savage debate. Free speech was brutally suppressed as hecklers shouted down or even physically assaulted those with whom they disagreed. Serious people raised serious questions about whether we could survive as a free democracy.

The notion that the end justifies the means proved contagious. Thus it is not surprising, even though it is deplorable, that some persons in

1972 adopted the morality that they themselves had rightly condemned and committed acts that have no place in our political system.

Those acts cannot be defended. Those who were guilty of abuses must be punished. But ultimately the answer does not lie merely in the jailing of a few overzealous persons who mistakenly thought their cause justified their violations of the law.

Rather, it lies in a commitment by all of us to show a renewed respect for the mutual restraints that are the mark of a free and civilized society. It requires that we learn once again to work together, if not united in all of our purposes, then at least united in respect for the system by which our conflicts are peacefully resolved and our liberties maintained.

If there are laws we disagree with, let us work to change them—but let us obey them until they are changed. If we have disagreements over Government policies, let us work those out in a decent and civilized way, within the law, and with respect for our differences.

We must recognize that one excess begets another, and that the extremes of violence and discord in the 1960s contributed to the extremes of Watergate.

Both are wrong. Both should be condemned. No individual, no group, and no political party has a corner on the market on morality in America.

If we learn the important lessons of Watergate, if we do what is necessary to prevent such abuses in the future—on both sides—we can emerge from this experience a better and a stronger nation.

Let me turn now to an issue that is important above all else, and that is critically affecting your life today and will affect your life and your children's in the years to come.

After 12 weeks and 2 million words of televised testimony, we have reached a point at which a continued, backward-looking obsession with Watergate is causing this nation to neglect matters of far greater importance to all of the American people.

We must not stay so mired in Watergate that we fail to respond to challenges of surpassing importance to America and the world. We cannot let an obsession with the past destroy our hopes for the future.

Legislation vital to your health and well-being sits unattended on the Congressional calendar. Confidence at home and abroad in our economy, our currency, and our foreign policy is being sapped by uncertainty. Critical negotiations are taking place on strategic weapons, on troop levels in Europe that can affect the security of this nation and the peace of the world long after Watergate is forgotten. Vital events are taking place in Southeast Asia which could lead to a tragedy for the cause of peace.

These are matters that cannot wait. They cry out for action now. And either we, your elected representatives here in Washington, ought to get on with the jobs that need to be done—for you—or every one of you ought to be demanding to know why.

The time has come to turn Watergate over to the courts, where the questions of guilt or innocence belong. The time has come for the rest of us to get on with the urgent business of our nation.

Last November, the American people were given the clearest choice of this century. Your votes were a mandate, which I accepted, to complete the initiatives we began in my first term and to fulfill the promises I made for my second term.

This Administration was elected to control inflation, to reduce the power and size of government, to cut the cost of government so that you can cut the cost of living, to preserve and defend those fundamental values that have made America great, to keep the nation's military strength second to none, to achieve peace with honor in Southeast Asia and to bring home our prisoners of war, and to build a new prosperity, without inflation and without war, to create a structure of peace in the world that would endure long after we are gone.

These are great goals. They are worthy of a great people. And I would not be true to your trust if I let myself be turned aside from achieving those goals.

If you share my belief in these goals—if you want the mandate you gave this Administration to be carried out—then I ask for your help to insure that those who would exploit Watergate in order to keep us from doing what we were elected to do will not succeed.

I ask tonight for your understanding, so that as a nation we can learn the lessons of Watergate, and gain from that experience.

I ask for your help in reaffirming our dedication to the principles of decency, honor, and respect for the institutions that have sustained our progress through these past two centuries.

And I ask for your support, in getting on once again with meeting your problems, improving your life, and building your future.

With your help. with God's help, we will achieve these great goals for America.